AN

ELEMENTARY GRAMMAR

OF THE

COORG LANGUAGE

AN

ELEMENTARY GRAMMAR

OF THE

COORG LANGUAGE.

BY

CAPTAIN R. A. COLE,
SUPERINTENDENT OF COORG.

GYAN

Published by

GYAN

Gyan Publishing House
5, Ansari Road
Daryaganj, New Delhi-110002
Phone: 011-47034999, 9811692060
E-mail: books@gyanbooks.com

Distribution Network
gyanbooks.com
India, USA, Canada, UK, Australia, France

ISBN: 978-81-212-7324-4 (PB)
First Published, 1867

2nd Impression 2023

Printed at: Gyan Press, Delhi.

AN ELEMENTARY GRAMMAR OF THE COORG LANGUAGE
Author: CAPTAIN R. A. COLE

AN

ELEMENTARY GRAMMAR

OF THE

COORG LANGUAGE.

BY

CAPTAIN R. A. COLE,

SUPERINTENDENT OF COORG.

BANGALORE:

PRINTED AT THE WESLEYAN MISSION PRESS,

1867.

DEDICATED

By Permission

TO

LEWIN BENTHAM BOWRING, Esq.

COMMISSIONER

OF

MYSORE AND COORG,

TO WHOM I AM SO MUCH INDEBTED FOR THE OPPORTUNITIES AFFORDED ME TO TRACE OUT THE ORIGIN OF THE GALLANT RACE OF COORGS.

CONTENTS.

PREFACE.

In the early part of 1865 I was appointed to the acting charge of the Province of Coorg, in the room of Mr. W. H. Kerr, of the Madras Civil service, who had to leave on account of ill-health; and my first duty was to proceed on Jummabundy, or the Annual Revenue Settlement, to the picturesque Talook of Paddy Nalkanadu, which lies along the verge of the Western Ghauts, from the lofty summits of which the whole of the Canara country is visible and the blue waters of the Indian Ocean beyond.

This Talook is the very stronghold of the Coorgs, and I found that many of them could not speak Canarese, the official language, but only a dialect, which I could not understand. The officials also, when desirous of making remarks to each other, used to employ this dialect; and I determined on trying to acquire it too. I was, however, much taken aback on learning that it was a mere spoken patois, and that Dr. Moegling, the celebrated German missionary, to whom the cause of Education in Coorg is so much indebted, had given up the attempt to learn the language, owing to the difficulty of conveying the exact pronunciation of the words. I have, however, made an attempt by giving the Canarese letters for the written portion of this hitherto unknown dialect, and the Roman alphabet for the conveyance of the several peculiarities in the pronunciation. The attempt, poor as it is, has been persevered in and is offered to the philologist, better acquainted with the cognate languages of India, to decide as to what language or languages it has been derived from; and thereby ascertain, if possible, the origin if this peculiar and most interesting race of warlike Mountaineers.

Before, however, proceeding to offer a few remarks on the philological part of the subject, it may be of use and interest to give some account of the Province itself, to many a terra incognita, even in India. No acconnt could be better given than in the language of the eminent Missionary, to whom I have already alluded. The following account, taken from his "*Memories of Coorg*," will be found most graphic and interesting.

" Coorg has shared the common fate of Indian names. As the Badaga people on the Nilagiri [Neilgherries] have been named Burghers, so Kodagu has been anglicized into Coorg ; when and by whom I am unable to tell.

The Western ghatts gradually rise to the Southward, till they attain their greatest elevation in the Dodda betta near Otte. The mountainous country between the river Hemávati on the North and the Tambàchéri pass on the South, South-Canara and North-Malabar on the West, and Mysore on the East, has for ages borne the name of Kodagu. It is situated between the twelfth and thirteenth degrees of North latitude, its greatest length from North to South is about 60 miles, its breadth from East to West about forty miles ; these dimensions however, continue but for a short space. The low-parts of Coorg are not less than 3000 feet above thesea, its highest peaks, the Pushpagiri near Subrahmanya, and the Tadiandamòl near Nàlkanadu, have a full view of the Indian Ocean, though at a distance of 40 or 50 miles, rising as they do to a height of 5,682 and 5,781 feet. The aspect of the Coorg mountains from the low West is extremely grand and picturesque. Eastward they descend gradually to the high table land of Mysore. Mercara [properly Madikeri] is 4,506 feet above the sea, Nalkanadu palace (where a Coorg princess, a wife of Tippu,* now upwards of eighty years of age, is residing) 3797, Virarajendrapett Bungalow 3,399, Fraserpett 3,200, Kolur Betta 4,500.

Coorg is the great treasury from which South Canara and North Malabar, from one monsoon to the other, draw their supply of water. From the Kumaradhare, which springs from the foot of the Pushpagiri and joins the Netravati near Uppinangadi, on the North, to the Barpolle which disembogues into the Western Sea near Cannanore, a dozen streams, issuing from the sides of the Coorg mountains intersect the country, and having watered it, return to the ocean from which their waters were carried into the hills and forests of Coorg by the clouds of the past season.

Throughout the year the great waterworks in the humid valleys, the forest-clad hills and Alpine atmosphere of Coorg are in motion. From the end of December to the end of March, rain, indeed, is scarce, but the valleys are seldom without their fogs, more or less dense, in the mornings and evenings, and heavy dews are frequent.

---

* Since deceased.

During these months the dry East wind prevails, which has long ceased to carry remains of North-east monsoon-clouds to the Western water-shed. Towards the end of March the sky beings to collect clouds, the winds are regular, the air grows moister. In April and May the sun increases in power, the sea-breeze dies away, thunder-storms and frequent showers, indicating the approach of the monsoon, cool the atmosphere from time to time. The temperature, generally warm and moist, reminds one of summer-days and nights in Europe

I cannot refrain here, though it be at the risk of tiring the patience of the kind reader, from attempting a description of a natural phenomenon, peculiar in this degree of beauty to the April and May-nights of Coorg. I advert to the yearly appearance of the fire-fly. These beautiful insects are, I know, not peculiar to Coorg. They have their periods of nocturnal revelry all over India, I believe. But nowhere have I seen them in such astonishing abundance and brilliancy as in Coorg. A thunder-storm, succeeded by a rich shower, has closed a sultry day. The sun has set unobserved. The Western sky is overhung which clouds. In the cloudless East, the full moon rises slowly. The air perfectly pellucid; the stars glittering in fresh glory; not a breath of wind; all still. You turn from the broad red orb of the rising moon to the host of golden stars on the deep azure, from them to the retreating clouds, lit up here by faint lightnings, there by the pale beams of the moon, their bold edges fringed with silver, and wonder at the beauties of the world above, where on the dark blue depths of heaven light seems to vie with light in the illumination of the vast dome, built by the unseen Master. But a scene of strange beauty is spread below. Shrub and bush and tree, as far as the eye can reach, burn with magic light. The ground, the air, teem with lustre, every leaf seems to have its own fairy lamp. The valley at your feet, the wooded hills to your right and left, the dark distant forest, all lit up and gleam in-ever-varying splendour, as if every star had sent a representative to bear his part in this nightly illumination of the poor dark Earth. Whence all at once these innumerable lights? No sound is heard, silently all these shining throngs pass before you in fantastic confusion. Look at this bush, that tree! Myriads of fiery sparks brighten up with red glare through the labyrinth of leaves and branches: a moment and they vanish. Now they flash up brighter than ever, as if this world of phosphoric lustre was animated by pulsations keeping regular time. You sit and think you could sit all night beholding the fairy scene. I have seen nothing to be compared with these dissolving views, except perhaps the phosphoric splendour of our tropical seas, when under a soft breeze your boat glides through the placid waters in a starlight night, throwing out large furrows to the right and left sparkling with myriads of blue lights, which spread strange brightness around the dark vessel, and gather again in its wake, forming as long line of radiancy to mark its course over the deep.

The thunderstorms during this season are often magnificent. The war of the elements is carried on here in grander style than in the low country. Banks and mountains of clouds move against each other with the order of armies. The sound of heavy cannon is heard from a distance, solitary discharges of the electric fluid shoot through the gloom. Now whole batteries are brought into action, deafening thunders roll over your head, and your eye shuts involuntarily against the dazzling brilliancy of the fire bolts. At last both hosts engage in close combat. The roar of artillery is heard at greater intervals, the lightnings lose their intense and fearful glare, and the rain pours down in torrents.

Towards the end of May the clouds take up a firm position in the Western sky and grow in strength. In June the rapport between the Western Sea and the atmosphere of Coorg is fully established. Rain prevails, descending at times softly, but more frequently with great violence under heavy gusts of wind. In the beginning of July the great atmospheric rain-battery seems to be in perfect working order. As fast as the sea can raise its steam, and the strong West wind carry the thick masses over the narrow strip of intervening low country to the heights of Coorg, the rain pours down in floods, day and night, in heavy monsoons, with few intervals, all July and August. The clouds seem to be inexhaustible, the rain eternal. A greater quantity of water descends upon Coorg in one week of these two months, than upon many countries of Europe during a whole year. A flat country would be deluged. But the Coorg Hills after being throughly bathed from head to foot, send the ministering floods, controlled by the steep banks of the rivers, to the East and West, and stand forth in their ancient strength and beauty, when the curtain of the monsoon is withdrawn. The yearly fall of rain in Coorg often exceeds 160 inches. In September the sun breaks through the dense atmosphere. In October the North-east wind, strong and cold, gains the ascendency and clears the sky ; in November however it often carries heavy clouds from the Eastern coasts which discharge themselves in showers upon Coorg. The greater part of December is foggy, but towards the end of the month the weather becomes delightful, clear and fresh, in the mornings and evenings often too cold to be pleasant."

As may be excepted from the preceding account, the temperature of Coorg is moderate and equable. The daily variation of the thermometer within doors does not exceed 6° or 8°, often not more than 2°. It seldom rises higher than 74° or falls below 60°, in the open air. During the dry season the range is a little higher ; the daily extremes are from 62° or 63° to 68° or 70°. The annual extremes are probably 80° and 82°. The maximum height of the barometer occurs during the dry weather, when the mercury stands at 26.220 and the lowest in July, when it falls to 25.912 The mean daily range is .050. The diurnal maximum occurs at 10 A. M. the minimum at 5 P. M. The climate of Coorg, accordingly, especially in the more elevated and open situations, is pleasant and salubrious, not much inferior, some think, to that of the Neilgherries. The average temperature is about 60°, the most favourable to health. The nights are cool throughout the year. You are able to take exercise in the open air at all hours almost all the year round, European children in particular enjoy excellent health, and their rosy cheeks contrast most favourably with the pale faces of those of the low country. Though the atmosphere is for a great part of the year loaded with moisture, yet on account of the equability of temperature rheumatic affections, coughs, colds, etc., are comparatively rare. With asthmatic affections, chronic disorders of the liver, and dysentéric complaints, the rarified, often cold and damp air of Mercara, the European head-quarters, does not, of course agree ; but Fraserpett, on the eastern frontier of Coorg, situated at a distance of only twenty miles, and 1,300 feet lower than Mercara, affords a considerable and salutary change.

The climate of the valleys, however, particularly during the hot months preceding the monsoon, when as the natives say, the old and the new waters are mixed, is far from healthy. Fevers, agues and bowel complaints are then very frequent. For the rest of the year, the natives of the country pronounce the cilmate to be excellent. [It is worthy of note, that the time succeeding the rains, which in many parts of India is the most unhealthy season of the year, has no danger to health in Coorg.] The account which natives of Mysore or from the Western Coast give of the climate of Coorg is much more unfavourable. They have experience on their side. Of the large numbers of people, whom Tippu sent from Mysore to replace the ancient inhabitants, or who, during the various wars, forcibly carried off by the Coorg Rajahs from Mysore, to cultivative their lands in Coorg, not many survived the change. Nor do the natives of the Western Coast, who immigrate into Coorg, ever become completely inured to the climate of their new home.

The entire country consists of a succession of lofty narrow ridges, having valleys of various extent between them. The ridges lie parallel to each other, commencing in general with a steep abutment to the westward, and running in the general direction of the western ghatts and of the North-western monsoon, *i e* from North-west to South-east, until they terminate in the plains of Mysore and Wynad. Of these numerous ridges the following are the most remarkable:—

The first to the Northward rises above the Bisli ghatt, and terminates at the Kaveri, near Ramasawamy Kanawe, and is of no great elevation. It separates the districts of Yelusavira Shime to the North from the rest of Coorg.

Next to this, with the table-land of Somavarapett intervening, is a ridge, the western extremity of which commences by a remarkably bluff peak of great elevation, called Pushpagiri or Subrhmanya as a landmark, and which is considered a most holy place, the abode of gods and rishis, too holy indeed for a common mortal to set his foot upon it. The Hindus are consequenly afraid of ascending the peak. The scenery round its base is bold, rocky and grand, and towards Somavarapett, it becomes exceedingly picturesque, forming a succession of beautiful grassy downs, open glades, and clumps of forest-trees, resembling the finest park-scenery in Europe.

The next ridge in succession has three rather marked rocky peaks, the sides of which slope abruptly to the North and South, into two deep valleys, through which run the branches of the Svarnavati, or Haringi river. The scenery here also is very pleasing.

After this comes the table-land of Mercara, which is terminated on the South, by a sharp declivity of 500 or 600 feet, forming the northern boundary of the great valley between Mercara and Nalkanadu. The valley is about 18 miles in length by 13 miles in breadth, and consists of a succession of low narrow ridges, with fertile valleys interposed. The lowest and central valley forms the bed of the river Kaveri. At the north-west angle of this valley there is a break in the line of ghatts, forming, what is called, the Sampaji valley which leads by a gradual slope into the low country. An excellent road has been constructed on this line, by which Mercara and Mangalore are connected. The southern termination of the valley, however, becomes abrupt, a ridge in the direction rising suddenly to the height of about 1,000 feet; and on the west it plunges still more suddenly into Malabar, by a fall of between 4,000 and 5,000 feet. It is crowned by several peaks, the most remarkable of which is the Tadianda Mol, the highest point in Coorg. [Mol means hill, mountain.]

A continuation of the valley to the South-east leads into the talook of Kiggattnád, which is of considerable extent, but much overgrown with jungle. Further to the south-east rise the Brahmagiri mountains, which form the boundary of the country in this direction. They are of great height, covered with forest trees, and abound with game. Like the other mountains of Coorg, their ridge on the top is very narrow.

The aspect of Coorg presents an entire forest. The long and narrow cultivated valleys enchased in it, serve but to render the vast woods more striking. The whole of the eastern boundary exhibits an almost uninterrupted and impervious forest from the Brahmagiri Hills to the banks of the Kávéri. This tract is wholly uninhabited. Advancing westward, the woods decrease in density as the country improves in cultivation, and become gradually thinner, till they reach the western ridges, the summits of which are partially bare of wood, and clothed with a luxuriant herbage. South of Vìrarájéndrapett the jungle become less impenetrable, and the whole of Kigattnádu, with the exception of the Eastern parts, including the Brahmagiri mountains, is comparitively open, at least when contrasted with the deep forests of the contiguous districts. Approaching to the North, the thick umbrageous woods of the central parts give way to the date, sandal and other trees, and shrubs of a more meagre soil, leaving Yelusavirashime an almost perfectly champaign country.

But a small portion of the summits of the ghatts is free from jungle. Their western face is covered with a continued forest of immense stature, partially subsiding at some distance from their base. Still wood is the unvaried feature of these regions. The general aspect of the country varies considerably in the different districts. In the vicinity of Sómavàrapett the hills are gently rounded, alternating with sloping glades, interspersed with clumps of forest trees. Near Mercara the hills are closer together, and more abrupt, the ravines deeper and wilder, and the jungle in the hollows much thicker. South of Mercara the country, seen from a distance, appears covered with wood, the only naked spots being the rice fields of the valleys; on descending into it, however, it is found to contain numerous open spaces, the woods being neither very dense nor very lofty. The scenery along the ridge of the ghatts to the westward is very beautiful, and may well compete with the Nilagiri; it is bold and varied in a high degree, the vegetation of the richest description and the forest trees of magnificent growth. The valleys, though varying in extent and depth, having the same general direction, *i. e.* from North-west to South-east, with the prevailing winds, the temperature of the country is thereby considerably moderated and rendered equable.

The waters of Coorg, as has been observed above, fall into the sea, washing both coasts of the Peninsula, the Kaveri with its tributaries flowing into the Bay of Bengal, while the rest, after a short and rapid course to the Western Coast, are lost in the Indian Ocean.

Coorg has, of course, no large river. Even the Kàveri has neither breadth nor depth during the dry seasons. Still they have generally an abundant and constant supply of water. Their sources being high up in the mountains, and the whole country almost consisting of steeps declivities, the streams are impelled with rapidity. The minor streams intersecting Coorg, vary only in size, which depends upon the length of their course, their general characteristies being the same. They swell in the early part of June and flow with a violent and boisterous rapidity till October, when they gradually diminish and become placid. The Western monsoon carries into the Hills of Coorg such a flood of water, that during its prevalence small rills, out of which a thirsty horse in April does not stoop to drink, rise into streams impassable for days. Every rivulet roughens into a wild torrent. With the monsoon all these rivers disappear and leave only small streams partially to occupy the immense chasms lately filled to the brim by the floods of the rainy season.

Of the rivers, that flow to the westward, the Barpolle is the most considerable. It rises in Kiggattnád, and through rocky ravines, in one of which it forms a superb cascade two or three hundred feet high, flows along the base of the hills, by the Heggada pass, where it is known as the Stony River, and disembogues itself into the sea to the North of Cannanore.

The Káveri, however, is the Queen of the Coorg waters. With its tributary the Kávëri drains nearly four fifths of the country. It rises in the Brahmagiri range, near the top of a hill, on the very verge of the Western Ghatts. Two streams, indeed, rise together at Tala Kaveri, where there is a temple of great celebrity among the people of the Kodagu, the Taulava and the Malayalam countries; but the Kanake, after a short run, joins the Kaveri again at Bhagamandala, a confluence marked likewise by some renowned temples. The Kaveri, as will be seen from the legend to be given in the following pages, is the holiest of rivers. The Ganges itself, that is the divinity of it, resorts to the all purifying floods of the Kaveri once a year, in Tulamasa (October—November) to wash away the pollution contracted from the crowds of sinners, who bathe in her waters.

Descending through the great valley between Mercara and Nalkanád, the Kaveri makes a sudden turn to the North, and flows for twenty or thirty miles along the Eastern frontier, receiving in its course several large tributaries, the principal of which is the Svarnavati, which drains the northern part of the country, and enters the Kaveri between Fraserpett and Ramasawmi-Kanave. Another large tributary of the Kaveri, is the Lakshmana-tirtha, which rises at the foot of the Brahmagiri, flows north-East into Mysore and joins the Kaveri in the talook of Mysore, a few miles from a village, which bears the name of Lakshamana-tirtha-katte. Also the Hemávati which is the northern boundry of Coorg, is absorbed by the Kaveri, into which it falls in the Yedatore talook of Mysore near the village of Tippur. The Kaveri is not rapid in any part of its course through Coorg. Its current, with the exception of a few passages, where it traverses beds of granite rock, is generally tranquil. In the dry season it is fordable at almost all points. But during the monsoon it runs by Fraserpett, for instance, in a stream two hundred and twenty to thirty feet deep."

The foregoing is an accurate and graphic description of the picturesque country, in which this hitherto unwritten Dialect is spoken by a peculiar and interesting race of people who, from their personal appearance and general habits and customs, would appear to have a distinct origin from the population both of Mysore and of the adjoining districts of Canara and Malayálam on the western coast;—and it is with the view of tracing their origin that I have been principally induced to venture on my labours and to offer this production for the consideration of those philologists, better able to draw such conclusions.

In conclusion I would offer a few remarks on the peculiar pronounciation in this dialect, which has been most difficult to convey, and on the apparent affinity of some of the words to other languages in Southern India.

I am aware that the Coorgs form but a very small portion of the population of Southern India, and that any knowledge of this dialect can never prove of any general use or importance; but it appears to me highly interesting and advisable, if not, indeed, imperative on the part of the Government, to trace out the affinity of such dialects to their cognate languages, and thereby throw a light on the origin and history of those minor races of India, which are fast disappearing or being swallowed up, amongst their more powerful and numerous neighbours.

The Coorgs themselves form an exemplification of these remarks. They are a small, but hardy, race, occupying a very limited tract of country. They were subjugated and their Rajahs were Lingayets and foreigners; but as yet they have preserved their nationality intact. Their costumes, their manners and customs are peculiar and different from those of the races, occupying the adjoining countries. They strongly object to any interference on the part of brahmins, and their religion is as simple and pure as any heathen religion can be. Children of the forests and mountains, placing an implicit belief in the legend of the origin of the rise of the Kávéri from the midst of their mountain homes, and in the power of those sylvan deities, which are supposed to occupy and rule over their dark and impenetrable forests, their religion but represents what ours was; when our ancesters roamed about the wilds of England, clad in the skins of wild beasts, before the gradual march of civilization and the light of true religion had so raised us above the other races of the world.

Such as we were in a still nearer period the Coorgs are now; and to our civilization and enlightenment are they fast approaching, thanks to the beneficence of our rule and to the exertions of those able and zealous men, who, by furthering the cause of education, have best promoted the interests of their Saviour.

I am much indebted to R. Belliapah, the Dep. Clerk of my Office, for much valuable aid and assistance in carrying out this work.

The peculiar difficulty of the dialect consists in the pronounciation of some of its vowels. The chief of which is the peculiar sound given to the vowel *u* in most of the words, in which that vowel is to be found. The pronounciation is as near as possible to that given to *u* in the word *creature,* and I have designated it as a half or silent *u,* and had wished to have it caused to be written in the Canarese character as follows ರು *ru,* and to have denoted it in the Roman character by placing a dot under the vowel; *but* the Press was not able to do so. This vowel has also another peculiar pronounciation, chiefly occurring in the Dative case in the affix of that case. This pronounciation is almost like that given by the French to *eu* in the word *queue.*

In many of the words, which are similar to corresponding words in the Canarese language, the initial ಹ *ha* of the Canarese is changed to ಫ *pha,* as Can. ಹೂವು, a flower, becomes in the Coorg dialect ಫೂವು: but this must be looked upon as a mere dialectic difference. To enable a comparison to be more clearly made between the Coorg dialect and other languages, I have drawn up a number of idiomatic sentences, containing pure Coorg words; and, under each word is entered its equivalent in other languages, if such equivalent is of the same sound or origin.

On comparing these sentences and words it will be seen that the Coorg words show a great affinity to the Tamul and Malayalum, and in many instances to the Canarese, especially in the " Hale Kannadi " or old Canarese. Literal changes are so similar in many languages and so numerous in old Canarese that they would be no evidence of distinct origin. *P.* and *h.* are almost always interchangeable ; *l* and *ḍ* (ಲ and ಡ) are often so. With these remarks I would commend my efforts to those more acquainted with the subject to trace out both the origin of the dialect and of these peculiar and interesting mountaineers.

R. A. COLE,
Supt. of Coorg.

FRASERPETT,
3*rd* *August,* 1867.

1. THE ALPHABET.

As already stated in the Preface, the Coorg Dialect has hitherto been only a spoken one, and I have adopted the Canarese character for the language, using the Roman character to convey the sound, or pronunciation.

2. Vowels.

Short	ಅ *a*,	ಇ *i*,	ಉ *u*,	ಋ *ṛi*,	ಎ *e*,	ಒ *o*,
Long	ಆ *á*,	ಈ *í*,	ಊ *ú*,	ೠ *ṛí*,	ಏ *é*,	ಓ *é*,
Diphthongs		ಐ *ei*,	ಔ *ou*,			

The following are either vowels or consonants. ಂ *m*, *n* or *ng*, according to position, and ಃ *aha*.

3. *Twenty-five* Classified *Consonants*.

	Unaspirated.	Aspirated.	Unaspirated.	Aspirated.	Nasal.
Guttural Class	ಕ *ka*	ಖ *kha*	ಗ *ga*	ಘ *gha*	ಙ *gna*.
Palatal	ಚ *cha*	ಛ *chcha*	ಜ *ja*	ಝ *jha*	ಞ *nya*.
Cerebral	ಟ *ṭa*	ಠ *ṭha*	ಡ *ḍa*	ಢ *ḍha*	ಣ *ṇa*.
Dental	ತ *ta*	ಥ *tha*	ದ *da*	ಧ *dha*	ನ *na*.
Labial	ಪ *pa*	ಫ *pha*	ಬ *ba*	ಭ *bha*	ಮ *ma*.

4. *Nine* unclassified *Consonants*.

ಯ *ya*, ರ *ra*, ಲ *la*, ವ *va*, ಶ *sha*, ಷ *ṣha*, ಸ *sa*, ಹ *ha*, ಳ *ḷa*.

The Compound Letter ಕ್ಷ *kṣha*, Compounded of ಕ *ka*, and ಷ *ṣha*.

TABULAR VIEW OF THE ALPHABET.

5. Vowels

Initial forms.	Medial and final forms.	Corresponding English Characters.	Power of the vowels.	Examples of Consonants and vowels united.
ಅ	˘	*a*	*like a in about*	ಕ್ *and* ಅ *becomes* ಕ *ka*
ಆ	ಾ	*á*	— *á* ,, *far*	ಕ — ಆ ,, ಕಾ *ká*
ಇ	ಿ	*i*	— *i* ,, *him*	ಗ — ಇ ,, ಗಿ *gi*
ಈ	ೀ	*í*	— *ee* ,, *deep*	ದ — ಈ ,, ದೀ *dí*
ಉ	ು	*u*	— *oo* ,, *wool*	ನ — ಉ ,, ನು *nu*
ಊ	ೂ	*ú*	— *oo* ,, *cool*	ಪ — ಊ ,, ಪೂ *pú*
ಉ್		*ú*	— *u* ,, *creature*	
ಋ	ೃ	*ṛi*	} *not in use*	
ೠ	ೄ	*ṛí*		
ಎ	ೆ	*e*	— *e in met*	ಯ — ಎ ,, ಯೆ *ye*
ಏ	ೇ	*é*	— *a* ,, *mate*	ರ — ಏ ,, ರೇ *ré*
ಐ	ೈ	*ei*	— *y* ,, *my*	ಲ — ಐ ,, ಲೈ *lei*
ಒ	ೊ	*o*	— *o* ,, *not*	ಶ — ಒ ,, ಶೊ *sho*
ಓ	ೋ	*ó*	— *o* ,, *note*	ಸ — ಓ ,, ಸೋ *só*
ಔ	ೌ	*ou*	— *ow* ,, *owl*	ಹ — ಔ ,, ಹೌ *how*

The chief difference as regards pronunciation and in the letters of the Alphabet is merely in the addition of two *u s* in the vowels, the *u* designated by me the silent *ú* and proposed to be written as an affix, in which alone it has the peculiar sound alluded to, with the sign of the half letter over it, ರು; and the *u* in the affix of the Dative Cases, in which this vowel has the sound of *eu* in the French word *queue*, a tail.

6. Consonants.

Consonants with the inherent vowel ಅ a.	Corresponding English Characters.	Sound of the Consonants with the inherent vowel ಅ a.	Form and position when combined with other consonants.	EXAMPLES.	
ಕ	ka	like ka in kalender	—್ಕ	ಕಾಟ್ಕೋಳಿ	káṭkoḷi.
ಖ	kha	————			
ಗ	ga	— ga ,, gender	—್ಗ	ತಡ್ಗಿಣಿ	taḍgiṇi.
ಘ	gha	————			
ಙ	gna	————	—್ಙ	ಖಡ್ಙನೆ	khaḍgnane.
ಚ	cha	— cha ,, chapter	—್ಚ	ನಿಶ್ಚಯ	nischaya.
ಛ	chcha	— chch ,, ,,	—್ಛ	ಇಚ್ಛೆ	ichchhe.
ಜ	ja	— ja ,, jam			
ಝ	jha	————			
ಞ	nya	————			
ಟ	ṭa	— ta ,, martaban	—್ಟ	ಮೊರ್ಟೆ	morṭe.
ಠ	ṭha	————			
ಡ	ḍa	— da ,, cardamom	—್ಡ	ಮೊರ್ಡು	morḍu.
ಢ	ḍha	————			
ಣ	ṇa	— na ,, carnal	—್ಣ	ಯರ್ಣೆ	yarṇe.
ತ	ta	— ta ,, thank	—್ತ	ಕರ್ತಡು	kartadu.
ಥ	tha	— tha ,, that			
ದ	da	————			
ಧ	dha	————			
ನ	na	— na ,, natural	—್ನ	ಕುತ್ನಿ	kutni.
ಪ	pa	— pa ,, parrot	—್ಪ	ಕೊಳ್ಪೆ	koḷpe.
ಫ	pha	————			
ಬ	ba	— ba ,, barrow	—್ಬ	ನಾಡ್ಬಾಚೆ	náḍbáche.
ಭ	bha	————			
ಮ	ma	— ma ,, matter	—್ಮ	ಧರ್ಮ	dharma.
ಯ	ya	— ya ,, yam	—್ಯ	ಕುಪ್ಯ	kupya.
ರ	ra	— ra ,, rag	—್ರ	ಗ್ರಾಣ	gráṇa.
ಲ	la	— la ,, lack	—್ಲ	ತಪ್ಲೆ	taple.
ವ	va	— va ,, vam	—್ವ	ಬೊಗಳ್ವು	bogaḷvu
ಶ	sha	————			
ಷ	ṣha	————			
ಸ	sa	— sa ,, sab			
ಹ	ha	————			
ಳ	ḷa	— rḷa ,, moorland			
ಕ್ಷ	kṣha	————	—್ಕ್ಷ	ತಕ್ಷಣ	takṣhaṇa.

It will be observed that the guttural consonants are unknown and unused probably as it was not a grammatical language. The consonants ಹ *ha* is also unknown, ಪ *pa* always taking its place, or an initial ಅ *a*, or other vowel.

AN

ELEMENTARY GRAMMAR

OF

THE COORG LANGUAGE.

PARTS OF SPEECH.

There are eight Parts of Speech, Viz, Noun, Adjective, Pronoun, Verb, Adverb, Postposition, Conjunction and Interjection.

NOUN.

There are, 1. Common nouns; as ಫೂವು, *phúvu,* a flower. 2. Proper nouns; as, ಅಚ್ಚೈಯ, ಪೊನ್ನಪ್ಪ. *achcheiya, ponnappa,* men's names. 3. Verbal nouns; as, ಆಡುವದು, *áḍuvadu,* 4. Derivative nouns; as, ಊರುಕಾರು, *úru-káru,* a villager. 5. Compound nouns; as, ಮನೆ ಪಡಿ *mane-padi,* a house-door; ಮನೆ ಕೊರವುಕಾರು, *mane-koravukáru,* head of the house. 6. Nouns of relationship; as, ಅಪ್ಪು, *appu,* father.

Verbal nouns; are formed by adding to the roots of all verbs, ವದು *vadu,* thus from ಯೆಳದು, *yeḷadu,* write, is formed ಯೆಳದುವದು, *yeḷadu vadu,* the act of writing.

Derivative nouns are formed by adding certain affixes to the crude form of nouns.

1. ಆರು, *áru,* and ಕಾರು, *káru,* and ಗಾರು, *gáru,* denoting the agent or doer, ಕುಂಬ, *kumba,* an earthen vessel ಕುಂಬಾರು, *kumbaru,* a potter. ಅಂಗಡಿ, *angaḍi,* a shop ಅಂಗಡಿಕಾರು, *angaḍikáru,* a shop keeper. ಬೋಟೆ, *bóṭe,* hunting ಬೋಟೆಗಾರು, *bótegáru,* a hunter.

2. ಕಾರು, *káru,* ಗಾರು *gáru,* ವಂತು, *wantu,* denote possession; as, ಬುದ್ಧಿ *budhí,* wisdom ಬುದ್ಧಿಕಾರು, *budhikáru, budhiwanta,* a wise man, and ಪಣ wealth, ಪಣಗಾರು *paṇagáru,* ಪಣವಂತು *paṇawantu,* a wealthy person.

3. ಕಳಿ *kaḷi,* ಯಿಕೆ *ike,* and ತನ *tana,* form neuter and abstract nouns, as ಪುಚ್ಚಿ *puchchi,* foolish ಪುಚ್ಚಿಕಳಿ, *puchchikaḷi,* foolishness ಮಕ್ಕ *makka,* children ಮಕ್ಕಕಳಿ, *makkaḷi,* and ಮಕ್ಕಳಾಟಿಕೆ *mákkáḷaṭike,* childhood ಬಡ *baḍa,* poor ಬಡತನ *baḍatana,* poverty.

Compound nouns are formed by the union of two nouns; as ಬೊಳಿ ಪಣ *boḷi-paṇa,* a silver fanam, ಆಮಡೆಪೊನ್ನು *ámaḍe-ponnu,* a gold pagoda. Nouns are also formed from participles, by affixing the pronouns ಅವು *avu,* he, ಅವ *ava,* she, ಆದು *adu,* it ಅವು *avu,* they (Mas. & Fem.) andಅದು *adu,* they (Neut) to the relative participles. Thus ಯೆಳ್ದದು *yeḷadu,* who or which writes, and ಅವು *avu,* he, forms ಯೆಳ್ದುವವು *yeḷaduvawu,* writer, ಪಾಡುವ *páḍuwa,* who or which sings, and ಅವ *ava,* ಪಾಡುವವ *páḍuwawa,* a songstress. ಮಾಡುವು *máḍuwu,* who or which makes, and ಅವು *avu,* they ಮಾಡುವವು *máḍuvawu,* makers; ಪೋನು *pónu,* who or which went, ಪೋನವು *pónawu,* he who went, ಪೋನವ *pónava,* she who went.

LIST OF NOUNS OF RELATIONSHIP.

Masculine.

ಮುತ್ತಪ್ಪು *muttappu,* great grandfafather.

ಅಜ್ಜು *ajju,* grandfather.

ಅಪ್ಪು *appu,* father.

ಬಲ್ಯಪ್ಪು *balyappu,* father's elder brother.—Mother's elder sister's husband.

ಚಿಕ್ಕಪ್ಪು *chikkappu,* Do. younger brother, Do. younger sister's husband.

ಅಂಣು *annu,* elder brother.

ತಂಮಣು *tammaṇu,* younger brother.

ತಂಮಾವು *tammáwu,* maternal uncle.

ಮಾವು *mávu,* father in-law.

Feminine.

ಮುತ್ತವ್ವ-ಮುತ್ತಜ್ಜಿವು *muttawva muttajjiwu,* great grandmother.

ಅಜ್ಜವು-ತಾಯಿ *ajjawu tái,* grandmother.

ಅವ್ವು *awwu,* mother.

ಬಲ್ಯವ್ವು *balyawu,* mother's elder sister.—Father's elder brother's wife.

ಚಿಕ್ಕವ್ವು *chikkawu,* Do. younger sister, Do. younger brother's wife.

ಅಕ್ಕು *akku,* elder sister.

ತಂಗೆ *tange,* younger sister.

ತಂಮಾವಿ *tammávi,* father's sister.

ಮಾವಿ *mávi,* mother in-law.

ವೊಡೆಯ *woḍeya*, husband.

ಮೋವು *mówu*, son.

ಮಯಿಮು *maimu*, son in-law nephews. Includes his brothers &c.

ಮರುಮೋವು *maru-mówu*, grandson.

ಕಿರುಮೋವು *kiru mówu*, great grandson.

ಭಾವು *bháwu*, wife's elder brother. Son's wife's father.

ಮಚ್ಚಿಣು *machchiṇu*, husband's elder brother. wife's younger brother,

ಪೊಂಡಿ *ponḍi*, or ಪೊಂಣು *ponṇu*, wife.

ಮೋವ್ವ *mówwa*, daughter.

ಮಯಿಮ *maima*, daughter in-law. Includes her sister &c.

ಮರುಮೋವ *maru-mówa*, grand-daughter.

ಕಿರುಮೋವ *kiru mówa*, great grand-daughter.

ಮದೆಮ *madema*, sister-in-law &c.

ಮಚ್ಚಿಣಿ *machchiṇi*, husband's brother's wife.

ಮಾತಂಗೆ *mátange*, husband's [other wife.

Nouns are of the Masculine, Feminine and Neuter genders.

Men and gods are masculine, women and goddesses are feminine; animals and inanimate objects are neuter. The word ಆಣು *áṇu*, male, is prifixed to shew the male sex; and ಪೊಂಣು *ponṇu*, female to shew the female sex; as ಆಣುಕುಂಞ್ಞಿ *áṇukuṇyi*, a male infant; ಪೊಂಣುಕುಂಞ್ಞಿ *poṇukuṇyi*, a female infant; ಆಣುನರಿ *áṇu-nari*, a tiger; ಪೊಂಣುನರಿ *ponṇu-nari*, a tigress; ಆಣಾಳು *áṇáḷu*, a male servant; ಪೊಂಣಾಳು *ponṇáḷu*, a female servant.

Masculine nouns ending in ರು *ru*, form the feminine by the addition of ತಿ *ti* to the ರ; as ಮಂಗಲಕಾರು *mangalakáru*, a bridegroom; ಮಂಗಲಕಾರತಿ *mangalakárati*, a bride.

ಕಾಳೆ *káḷe*, a bull,
ಮಂಡು *manḍu*, a steir.
ಪೋರಿ *pṓri*, a he buffalo.
ತೈರು *teiru*, a cock.
ಪೋತು *pótu*, a he goat
ಕೊಂಬಕಡಮು *komba-kaḍamu*, a male samber.

ಪಯ್ಯು *paiu*, a cow.
ಪಯ್ಯುಕಡಚಿ *paiu-kaḍachi*, a heifer
ಎಮ್ಮೆ *yemme*, a she buffalo.
ಪೋಡೆ *póḍe*, a hen.
ಪೊಂಣಾಡು *ponṇáḍu*, a she goat.
ಮುಂಡಿಕಡಮು *munḍi-kaḍamu*, a female samber.

NUMBER OF NOUNS.

Nouns have two numbers; Singular and Plural.

The plural is formed by adding ಅಂಗ *anga,* ವು *vu,* or ಆ *á* or ಯಾ *yá,* to the singular ; as ಅಂಣು *aṇṇu,* elder brother ಅಂಣಂಗು *aṇṇangu,* elder brothers; ಯೆತ್ತು *yettu,* a bullock ಯೆತ್ತುಆ *yettuá,* bullocks; ತಂಗೆ *tange,* younger sister ತಂಗೆಯಾ *tangeyá,* younger sisters. ಕುಂಞಿ *kuṇyi,* a child, is an exception its plural is ಮಕ್ಕ *makka,* children.

When the cardinal numbers are used in reference to persons, the word ಆಳು *áḷu,* is added to all the numbers ; as ವರಾಳು *waráḷu,* one person ದಂಡಾಳು *danḍáḷu,* two persons. ಜನ *jana,* is sometimes used to denote multitude ; as ಅಲ್ಲಿ ಎಚ್ಚಕು ಜನ ಉಂಡು *alli yechchaku jana unḍu,* how many persons are there there?

DECLENSION OF NOUNS.

There are five declensions apparently in the Coorg Dialect, which are distinguished from each other by their terminations in the crude state. I have classed all ending in the silent *u* or in *u* as the 1st Declension ; those in ಅ as of the 2nd ; those in ಇ as of the 3rd ; those in ಎ as of the 4th and Neuter nouns in ಅ as of the 5th Declension.

The last might be classed under the 2nd Declension, the only peculiarity being the introduction of a ತ as a penultimate in all the cases except Nominative, Dative and Vocative.

CASES OF NOUNS.

Nouns have eight cases, which are formed by the addition of the following affixes to the crude state of the noun.

The state of a noun without any affix is called its crude state.

CASES.	AFFIXES.	SIGNS.
1. Nominative.—	ಯು *yu,* and silent *u.*	a
2. Accusative.—	ಆ, ತುನ,ನ *á* and *tunana,*	a
3. Instrumental.—	ತಿಂಜಿ, ಇಂಜಿ-ಗೊಂಡು *tinji inji,* and *gonḍu,*	by
4. Dative.—	ಕು, ಗು *ku* and *gu,*	to
5. Ablative.—	ಚೆಲ್ಲಿತು *chellitu,*	from
6. Genitive.—	ಡ, ಅಂಡು *ḍa* and *anḍu,*	of
7. Locative.—	ಲು, ಪಕ್ಕ *lu,* and *pakka,*	in
8. Vocative.—	ಏ *yé,*	O!

In the Instrumental case ಯಿಂದ and ತಿಂದ are added to neuter nouns and ಗೊಂಡು to masculine and feminine nouns ; as ಮರ a tree, ಮರತಿಂದ by a tree ಅವು he ಅವನ ಗೊಂಡು by him. In some words the addition of ಗೊಂಡು to the accusative case of neuter nouns also forms the Instrumental case, as ಮರತುನ a tree ಮರತುನಗೊಂಡು by a tree.

In Dative cases the affix ಕು is used in nouns, of all genders and ಗು for masculine and feminine only.

In the locative case ಲು is used for neuter and ಪಕ್ಕ for masculine and feminine nouns.

1st. DECLENSION, MASCULINE NOUN ENDING in the silent *u*, (WHICH IS SOUNDED LIKE *eu*.)

CRUDE NOUN ಕುರುಬು.

	SINGULAR.	PLURAL.
No.	ಕುರುಬು *kurubu,* a shepherd.	ಕುರುಬ *kuruba,* shepherds.
Ac.	ಕುರುಬನ *kurubana.* ,,	ಕುರುಬರ *kurubara,* ,,
In.	ಕುರುಬನಗೊಂಡು *kurubanagonḍu,* by or from &c.	ಕುರುಬರಗೊಂಡು *kurubaragonḍu,* by or from &c.
Da.	ಕುರುಬಂಗು *kurubangeu,* to a &c.	ಕುರುಬಕು *kurubakeu,* to &c.
Ab.	ಕುರುಬನಚೆಲ್ಲಿತು *kurubana-chellitu,* from &c.	ಕುರುಬರಚೆಲ್ಲಿತು *kuruburu-chellitu,* from &c.
Ge.	ಕುರುಬಂಡ *kurubanḍa,* of &c.	ಕುರುಬಡ *kurubaḍa,* of &c.
Lo.	ಕುರುಬಂಡಪಕ್ಕ *kurubaḍa-pakka,* in &c.	ಕುರುಬಡಪಕ್ಕ *kurubaḍa-pakka,* in &c.
Vo.	ಕುರುಬನೇ *kurubané,* O &c.	ಕುರುಬರೇ *kurubaré,* O &c.

MASCULINE NOUNS ENDING in *u*.

CRUDE NOUN ಗುರು

	SINGULAR.	PLURAL.
No.	ಗುರು *guru,* a priest	ಗುರುವ *guruva,* priests
Ac.	ಗುರುನ *guruna,* ,, ,,	ಗುರುವಳ *guruvaḷa,* ,,
In.	ಗುರುನ ಗೊಂಡು ,, *gonḍu,* by or from ,,	ಗುರುವಳ ಗೊಂಡು ,, *gonḍu,* by or from
Da.	ಗುರುಕು *gurukeu,* to ,,	ಗುರುವಕು *guruvakeu,* to ,,

Feminine Nouns.

	Singular	Plural
Ab.	ಗುರುನ ಚೆಲ್ಲಿತು *guruna-chellitu,* from ,,	ಗುರುವಳ್ಳ ಚೆಲ್ಲಿತು *guruvaḷa-chellitu,* from ,,
Ge.	ಗುರುಡ *guruḍa,* of ,,	ಗುರುವಡ *guruvaḍa,* of ,,
Lo.	ಗುರುಡ ಪಕ್ಕ ,, *pakka,* in ,,	ಗುರುವಡ ಪಕ್ಕ ,, *pakka,* in ,,
Vo.	ಗುರುವೇ *guruvé,* O ,,	ಗುರುವಳ್ಳೇ *guruvaḷé,* O ,,

FEMININE NOUNS ENDING IN ಯು.

Crude Noun ಪಯ್ಯು.

	Singular	Plural
No.	ಪಯ್ಯು *payu,* a cow	ಪಯ್ಯುವ *payuva,* cows.
Ac.	ಪಯ್ಯುನ *payuna,* ,,	ಪಯ್ಯುವಳ್ಳ *payuvaḷa,* ,,
In.	ಪಯ್ಯುನ ಗೊಂಡು ,, *gonḍu,*	ಪಯ್ಯುವಳ್ಳ ಗೊಂಡು ,, *gonḍu,* by or from.
Da.	ಪಯ್ಯುಕು *payukeu,* to ,,	ಪಯ್ಯುವಕು *payuvakeu,* to ,,
Ab.	ಪಯ್ಯುನ ಚೆಲ್ಲಿತು *payuna-chellitu,* from	ಪಯ್ಯುವಳ್ಳ ಚೆಲ್ಲಿತು *payuvaḷa-chellitu,* from
Ge.	ಪಯ್ಯುಡ *payuḍa,*	ಪಯ್ಯುವಡ *payuraḍa,* of ,,
Lo.	ಪಯ್ಯುಡ ಪಕ್ಕ ,, *payuda-pakka,*	ಪಯ್ಯುವಡ ಪಕ್ಕ ,, *pakka,* in ,,
Vo.	ಪಯ್ಯುವೇ *payuvé,* O ,,	ಪಯ್ಯುವಳ್ಳೇ *payuvalé,* O ,,

This plural form is seldom used, the affix ತ being used instead of ವ in common conversation. Again in the western Talooks ತ is used, whilst in the southern Talooks ವ is made use of.

NEUTER NOUNS ENDING IN *u.*

Crude Noun ಕುರು.

No. ಕುರು *kuru,* seed.

Ac. ಕುರುನ *kuruna,* ,,

In. ಕುರುವಿಂಜಿ *kuruvinji,*
ಕುರುವಿನ ಗೊಂಡು *kuruvina-gonḍu,* } by or from ,,

Da. ಕುರುಕು *kurukeu,* to ,,

Ab. ಕುರುನ ಚೆಲ್ಲಿತು *kuruna-chellitu,* from ,,

Ge. ಕುರುರ *kurura,* of ,,

Lo. ಕುರುಲು *kurulu,* in ,,

Vo. ಕುರುವೇ *kuruvé,* O ,,

The Instrumental case in such nouns is formed by the insertion of ವ between the crude noun and the ordinary affix.

2nd DECLENSION. NOUNS ENDING in ಅ.

FEMININE NOUN ENDING IN ಅ.

CRUDE NOUN ಮೋವ.

	SINGULAR.	PLURAL.
No.	ಮೋವ *móva,* a daughter.	ಮೋಳಿಯ *móḷiya,* daughters.
Ac.	ಮೋವಳ *móvaḷa,* ,,	ಮೋಳಿಯಳ *móḷiyaḷa,* ,,
In.	ಮೋವಳಗೊಂಡು *móvaḷagonḍu,* by or from.	ಮೋಳಿಯಳಗೊಂಡು *móḷiyaḷa-gonḍu,* by or from.
Da.	ಮೋವಕು *móvakeu,* to ,,	ಮೋಳಿಯಕು *móḷiyakeu,* to ,,
Ab.	ಮೋವಳ ಚೆಲ್ಲಿತು *móvaḷa-chellitu,*	ಮೋಳಿಯಳ ಚೆಲ್ಲಿತು *móḷiyaḷa-chellitu*
Ge.	ಮೋವಡ *móvaḍa,* of ,,	ಮೋಳಿಯಡ *móḷiyaḍa,* of ,,
Lo.	ಮೋವಡ ಪಕ್ಕ *móvaḍa-pakka,* in	ಮೋಳಿಯಡ ಪಕ್ಕ *móḷiyaḍa-pakka,* in
Vo.	ಮೋವಳೇ *móvaḷé,* O ,,	ಮೋಳಿಯಳೇ *móḷiyaḷé,* O ,,

These nouns form the plural by changing the singular affix of ವ into ಳಿ ಯ; and accusative in both numbers by the addition of ಳ.

3rd DECLENSION. NOUNS ENDING in *i.*

MASCULINE NOUN ENDING IN *i.*

CRUDE NOUN ಪೋರಿ.

	SINGULAR.	PLURAL.
No.	ಪೋರಿ *póri,* male buffalo.	ಪೋರಿಯ *póriya,* buffaloes.
Ac.	ಪೋರಿನ *pórina,* Do.	ಪೋರಿಯಳ *póriyaḷa,* Do.
In.	ಪೋರಿನ ಗೊಂಡು *pórina-gonḍu,* by or from.	ಪೋರಿಯಳ ಗೊಂಡು *póriyaḷagonḍu,* by or from.
Da.	ಪೋರಿಕು *pórikeu,* to Do.	ಪೋರಿಯಕು *póriyakeu,* to Do.
Ab.	ಪೋರಿನ ಚೆಲ್ಲಿತು *pórina-chellitu,* from.	ಪೋರಿಯಳ ಚೆಲ್ಲಿತು *póriyaḷachellitu,* from.
Ge.	ಪೋರಿರ *pórira,* of Do.	ಪೋರಿಯಡ *poriyaḍa,* of Do.
Lo.	ಪೋರಿರ ಪಕ್ಕ *pórira-pakka,* in Do.	ಪೋರಿಯಡ ಪಕ್ಕ *póriyaḍa-pakka,* in Do.
Vo.	ಪೋರಿಯೇ *póriyé,* O Do.	ಪೋರಿಯಳೇ *póriyaḷé,* O Do.

The plural nominative is formed by adding ಯ to the singular; and the ನ in the singular cases is changed to ಳ in the plural with ಯ; evidently introduced for the sake of euphony.

MASCULINE NOUNS ENDING in *i*.

CRUDE NOUN ಪರಧಾನಿ.

	SINGULAR.	PLURAL.
No.	ಪರಧಾನಿ *paradháni,* a minister	ಪರಧಾನಿಯು *paradhániya,* ministers
Ac.	ಪರಧಾನಿನ *paradhánina,* ,,	ಪರಧಾನಿಯುಳ್ಳ *paradhániyaḷa,* ,,
In.	ಪರಧಾನಿನ ಗೊಂಡು ,, *gonḍu,* by or from	ಪರಧಾನಿಯುಳ್ಳ ಗೊಂಡು ,, *gonḍu,* by or from ,,
Da.	ಪರಧಾನಿಕು *paradhánikeu,* to ,,	ಪರಧಾನಿಯುಕು *paradhániyakeu,* to ,,
Ab.	ಪರಧಾನಿನ ಚೆಲ್ಲಿತು *paradhánina-chellitu,* from ,,	ಪರಧಾನಿಯುಳ್ಳ ಚೆಲ್ಲಿತು *paradhániyaḷa-chellitu,* from ,,
Ge.	ಪರಧಾನಿರ *paradhánira,* of	ಪರಧಾನಿಯುಡ *paradhániyaḍa,* of ,,
Lo.	ಪರಧಾನಿರ ಪಕ್ಕ ,, *pakka,* in ,,	ಪರಧಾನಿಯುಡಪಕ್ಕ ,, *pakka,* in ,,
Vo.	ಪರಧಾನಿಯೋ *paradhániyé,* O ,,	ಪರಧಾನಿಯುಳ್ಳೇ *paradhániyaḷé,* O

FEMININE NOUNS ENDING IN *i*.

CRUDE NOUN ಮೂಡಿ.

	SINGULAR.	PLURAL.
No.	ಮೂಡಿ *múḍi,* a girl.	ಮೂಡಿಯು *múḍiya,* girls.
Ac.	ಮೂಡಿನ *múḍina,* ,,	ಮೂಡಿಯುಳ್ಳ *múḍiyaḷa,* ,,
In.	ಮೂಡಿನ ಗೊಂಡು *múḍina-gonḍu,* in from.	ಮೂಡಿಯುಳ್ಳ ಗೊಂಡು *múḍiyaḷa-gonḍu,* by or from.
Da.	ಮೂಡಿಕು *múḍikeu,* to ,,	ಮೂಡಿರಿಯುಕು *múḍiyakeu,* to ,
Ab.	ಮೂಡಿನ ಚೆಲ್ಲಿತು *múḍina-chellitu,* from.	ಮೂಡಿಯುಳ್ಳ ಚೆಲ್ಲಿತು *múḍiyaḷa-chellitu* from.
Ge.	ಮೂಡಿರ *múḍira,* of ,,	ಮೂಡಿಯುಡ *múḍiyaḍa,* of ,,
Lo.	ಮೂಡಿರ ಪಕ್ಕ *múḍira-pakka,* in ,,	ಮೂಡಿಯುಡ ಪಕ್ಕ *múḍiyaḍa-pakka,* in ,,
Vo.	ಮೂಡಿಯೋ *múḍiyé,* O ,,	ಮೂಡಿಯುಳ್ಳೇ *múḍiyaḷé,* O ,,

Masculine and feminine nouns ending in *i* form their cases in the same manner.

NEUTER NOUN ENDING IN *i*.

CRUDE NOUN ಪೊಟ್ಟಿ.

No. ಪೊಟ್ಟಿ *poṭṭi,* a box.

Ac. ಪೊಟ್ಟಿನ *poṭṭina,* ,,
In. ಪೊಟ್ಟಿಂಜಿ *poṭṭinji,* ,, } by or from ,,
ಪೊಟ್ಟಿನ ಗೊಂಡು *poṭṭina-gonḍu,*
Da. ಪೊಟ್ಟಿಕು *poṭṭikeu,* to ,,
Ab. ಪೊಟ್ಟಿನ ಚೆಲ್ಲಿತು *poṭṭina-chellitu,* from ,,
Ge. ಪೊಟ್ಟಿರ *poṭṭira,* of ,,
Lo. ಪೊಟ್ಟಿಲು *poṭṭilu,* in ,,
Vo. ಪೊಟ್ಟಿಯೇ *poṭṭiyé,* O ,,

As before remarked, neuter nouns in the Coorg dialect have no plural number; the singular cases being also used in the plural with the several numbers of the article pre-fixed.

4th DECLENSION. NOUNS ENDING in *e.*

FEMININE NOUN ENDING IN *e.*

Crude Noun ಸೂಳೆ.

	Singular	Plural
No.	ಸೂಳೆ *súḷe,* a dancing girl	ಸೂಳೆಯು *súḷeya,* dancing girls,
Ac.	ಸೂಳೆನ *súḷena,* ,,	ಸೂಳೆಯುಳ್ಳ *súḷeyaḷa,* ,,
In.	ಸೂಳೆನ ಗೊಂಡು ,, *gonḍu,* by or from.	ಸೂಳೆಯುಳ್ಳ ಗೊಂಡು ,, *gonḍu,* by or from.
Da.	ಸೂಳೆಕು *súḷekeu,* to ,,	ಸೂಳೆಯುಕು *súḷeyakeu,* to ,,
Ab.	ಸೂಳೆನ ಚೆಲ್ಲಿತು *súḷena-chellitu,* from.	ಸೂಳೆಯುಳ್ಳ ಚೆಲ್ಲಿತು *súḷeyaḷa-chellitu,* from.
Ge.	ಸೂಳೆರ *súḷera,* of ,,	ಸೂಳೆಯುಡ *súḷeyaḍa,* of ,,
Lo.	ಸೂಳೆರಪಕ್ಕ ,, *pakka,* in	ಸೂಳೆಯುಡ ಪಕ್ಕ ,, *pakka,* in
Vo.	ಸೂಳೆಯೇ *súḷeyé,* O ,,	ಸೂಳೆಯುಳೇ *suḷeyaḷé,* O ,,

FEMININE NOUN ENDING in *e.*

Crude Noun ಯೆಂಮೆ.

	Singular.	Plural.
No.	ಯೆಂಮೆ *yeme,* she buffalo	ಯೆಂಮೆಯು *yemeya,* she buffaloes.
Ac.	ಯೆಂಮೆನ *yemena* ,, ,,	ಯೆಂಮೆಯುಳ್ಳ *yemeyaḷa,* ,,
In.	ಯೆಂಮೆನಗೊಂಡು ,, *gonḍu,* by or from.	ಯೆಂಮೆಯುಳ್ಳಗೊಂಡು ,, *gonḍu* by &c.
Da.	ಯೆಂಮೆಕು *yemekeu,* to ,,	ಯೆಂಮೆಯುಕು *yemeyakeu,* to ,,
Ab.	ಯೆಂಮೆನ ಚೆಲ್ಲಿತು *yemena-chellitu,* from ,,	ಯೆಂಮೆಯುಳ್ಳ ಚೆಲ್ಲಿತು *yemeyaḷachellitu,* from ,,

Ge.	ಯೆಂಮೆರ *yemera*, of ,,	ಯೆಂಮೆಯುಡ *yemeyaḍa*, of ,,
Lo.	ಯೆಂಮೆರ ಪಕ್ಕ ,, *pakka*, in ,,	ಯೆಂಮೆಯುಡ ಪಕ್ಕ ,, *pakka*,
Vo.	ಯೆಂಮೆಯೇ *yemeyé*, O ,,	ಯೆಂಮೆಯುಳೇ *yemeyaḷé*, O ,,

The plural is formed by the addition of ಯು to the singular nominative. The plural of the names of all quadrupeds would seem to be thus formed; as ನಾಯಿ, a dog, ನಾಯಿಯು, dogs; ಕುದ್ರೆ a horse ಕುದ್ರೆಯು horses; ಪಂದಿ a hog ಪಂದಿಯು hogs.

ಕುಟ್ಟಿ and ಮರಿ *kuṭṭi, mari* are used to denote the young of animals; and they form the plural by the addition of ಯು also to their singular; as ನಾಯಿಕುಟ್ಟಿ a pup; ನಾಯಿಕುಟ್ಟಿಯು pups.

NEUTER NOUNS ENDING IN *e*.

CRUDE NOUN ಮನೆ.

No. ಮನೆ *mane*, a house.
Ac. ಮನೆನ *manena*, ,,
In. ಮನೆಯಿಂಜಿ *maneinji*, ಮನೆನ ಗೊಂಡು *manena-gonḍu*, } by or from ,,
Da. ಮನೆಕು *manekeu*, to ,,
Ab. ಮನೆನ ಚೆಲ್ಲಿತು *manena-chellitu*, from ,,
Ge. ಮನೆರ *manera*, of ,,
Lo. ಮನೆಲು *manelu*, in ,,
Vo. ಮನೆಯೇ *maneyé*, O ,,

MASCULINE NOUNS ENDING in *e*.

CRUDE NOUN ದೊರೆ.

No.	ದೊರೆ *dore*, a master	ದೊರೆಯು *doreya*, masters
Ac.	ದೊರೆನ *dorena*, a ,,	ದೊರೆಯುಳ *doreyaḷa*, ,,
In.	ದೊರೆನ ಗೊಂಡು ,, *gonḍu*, by or from	ದೊರೆಯುಳ ಗೊಂಡು,,*gonḍu*, by or from ,,
Da.	ದೊರೆಕು *dorekeu*, to a	ದೊರೆಯುಕು *doreyakeu*, to ,,
Ab.	ದೊರೆನ ಚೆಲ್ಲಿತು *dorena-chellitu*, from	ದೊರೆಯುಳ ಚೆಲ್ಲಿತು ,, *chellitu*, or from
Ge.	ದೊರೆರ *dorera*, of ,,	ದೊರೆಯುಡ *doreyaḍa*, of ,,
Lo.	ದೊರೆರ ಪಕ್ಕ *dorera-pakka*, in	ದೊರೆಯುಡ ಪಕ್ಕ *doreyaḍa-pakka*, in ,,
Vo.	ದೊರೆಯೇ *doreyé*, O ,,	ದೊರೆಯುಳೇ *doreyaḷé*, O ,,

It will be seen by the above examples that nouns ending in *u* form the plural by the addition of ವ, and those terminating in *i* form the plural by the addition of ಯು; and that the accusative singular is formed by the additions of ನ to the nominative, and the accusative plural by the addition of ಳ to the nominative plural.

5th. DECLENSION NEUTER NOUNS ENDING IN ಅ.

CRUDE NOUN ಪೊಲ.

No. ಪೊಲ *pola,* a dry field.

Ac. ಪೊಲತ್ನ *polatuna,* ,,

In. ಪೊಲತ್ನಗೊಂಡು *polatuna gondu,* } by or from a field.
ಪೊಲತಿಂಜಿ *polatinji,*

Da. ಪೊಲಕು *polakeu,* to a field.

Ab. ಪೊಲತ್ನ ಚೆಲ್ಲಿತು *polatuna-chellitu,* from a field.

Ge. ಪೊಲತ್ರ *polatura,* of a field.

Lo. ಪೊಲತ್ಲು *polatulu,* in a ,,

Vo. ಪೊಲವೇ *polavé,* O ,,

It will be seen that in words in the Coorg dialect, which are similar to those in Canarese, the initial ಹ of the Canarese is changed to ಪ in Coorg.

NEUTER NOUN in ಅ.

CRUDE NOUN ಮರ.

No. ಮರ *mara,* a tree.

Ac. ಮರತ್ನ *maratuna,* a tree.

In. ಮರತಿಂಜಿ *maratinji,* by or from a tree.

Da. ಮರಕು *marakeu,* to tree.

Ab. ಮರತ್ನಚೆಲ್ಲಿತು *maratuna-chellitu,* from a tree.

Ge. ಮರತ್ರ *maratura,* of a tree.

Lo. ಮರತ್ಲು *maratulu,* in a tree.

Vo. ಮರವೇ *maravé,* O tree.

Neuter nouns have no plural, In the Instrumental case sometimes ಗೊಂಡು is affixed to the accusative case and affix, as ಮರತ್ನಗೊಂಡು. In the Locative case sometimes ಲಕ್ಕ is used by adding it to the Genitive case, the ರ of which is sometimes changed into ದ or either are used indifferently.

NOUNS OF RELATIONSHIP.

Nouns of relationship of both genders ending in what I have termed the silent *u* form their plural by dropping the *u* and adding ಂಗ and are declined in other respects like nouns of the first declension; as.

CRUDE NOUN ಅಪ್ಪು a father.

	SINGULAR.	PLURAL.
No.	ಅಪ್ಪು *appu*, a father.	ಅಪ್ಪಂಗ *appanga*, a fathers.
Ac.	ಅಪ್ಪನ *appana*, ,,	ಅಪ್ಪಂಗಳ *appangaḷa*, ,,
In.	ಅಪ್ಪನ ಗೊಂಡು ,, *goṇḍu*, by ,,	&c. &c. &c.

The plural of such nouns ending in *e* and in *i* is formed by the addition of ಯ to the singular; as;

CRUDE NOUN ತಂಗೆ Younger sister.

	SINGULAR.	PLURAL.
No.	ತಂಗೆ *tange*.	ತಂಗೆಯ *tangeya*.
Ac.	ತಂಗೆನ *tangena*.	ತಂಗೆಯಳ *tangeyaḷa*.
	&c. &c.	&c. &c.

ಮೋವ, a Daughter, however, has a different form in the plural; the final ವ being changed into ಳಿ ಯ; as.

CRUDE NOUN ಮೋವ a Daughter.

	SINGULAR.	PLURAL.
No.	ಮೋವ *móva*.	ಮೋಳಿಯ *móḷiya*.
Ac.	ಮೋವಳ *móvaḷa*.	ಮೋಳಿಯಳ *móḷiyaḷa*.
	&c.	&c.

It is declined in other respects like nouns of the 2nd declension. It may be remarked that feminine nouns ending in ಅ, form the Accusative by the addition of ಳ to the Nominative. Feminine nouns of relationship ending in the vowel ಅ form the plural by the addition of ಕ್ಕ to the singular; as.

CRUDE NOUN ಮೈಮ Daughter-in-law.

	SINGULAR.	PLURAL.
No.	ಮೈಮ *meima*.	ಮೈಮಕ್ಕ *meimakka*.

Ac. ಮೈಮಳ *meimaḷa.* ಮೈಮಕ್ಕಳ *meimakkaḷa.*
&c. &c.

NOUNS OF QUALITY.

Neuter nouns of quality have the final syllable, before the affix, in the Accusative, Instrumental, Dative, Ablative, and Genitive, cases lengthened. Masculine and Feminine nouns of quality have not this peculiarity and are declined like other nouns, and pronouns.

ಬೊಳ್ತದು *boḷtadu,* a white thing.

No. ಬೊಳ್ತದು *boḷtadu.*
Ac. ಬೊಳ್ತಾನ *boḷtána.*
In. ಬೊಳ್ತಾನ ಗೊಂಡು ,, *gonḍu.*
Da. ಬೊಳ್ತಾಂಗು *boḷtángeu.*
Ab. ಬೊಳ್ತಾನ ಚೆಲ್ಲಿತು *boḷtána-chellitu.*
Ge. ಬೊಳ್ತಾಂದ *boḷtánḍa.*
Lo. ಬೊಳ್ತದಲು, ಬೊಳ್ತಾಂದ ಪಕ್ಕ *boḷtánḍa pakka.*
Vo. ಬೊಳ್ತದೆ *boḷtade.*

VERBAL NOUNS.

The different cases of the verbal nouns are formed in the same manner, as other nouns except that the ವ of the present participle is lengthened into ವಾ in the Accusative, Instrumental, Ablative, Genitive and Locative cases.

No. ನೋಡುವದು *nóḍuvadu,* the act of seeing.
Ac. ನೋಡುವಾನ *nóḍuvána.*
In. ನೋಡುವಾನ ಗೊಂಡು ,, *gonḍu.*
Da. ನೋಡುವಕು *nóḍuvakeu.*
Ab. ನೋಡುವಾನ ಚೆಲ್ಲಿತು *nóḍuvána-chellitu.*
Ge. ನೋಡುವಾಂದ *nóḍuvánḍa.*
Lo. ನೋಡುವಾಲು *nóḍuválu.*
Vo. none.

ADJECTIVES.

Adjectives precede the nouns to which they belong; as ನಲ್ಲಮರ *nallu-mara,* a good tree; ಪುದಿಯ ಪೊಟ್ಟಿ, *pudiya-poṭṭi,* a new box; ಚೆರಿಯ ಮರ *cheriya-mara,* a young tree.

ಕುಟ್ಟಿ *kuṭṭi,* a young animal, is added to express the young of quadrupeds; as ಆನೆ ಕುಟ್ಟಿ *áne-kuṭṭi,* a young elephant, ಕುದ್ರೆ ಕುಟ್ಟಿ a colt; but for the young of cows and buffaloes ಕಡಚಿ *kaḍachi,* is added; as ಯೆಮ್ಮೆ ಕಡಚಿ *yemme-kaḍachi,* a young buffalo; ಪಯ್ಯು ಕಡಚಿ *paiyu-kaḍachi,* a calf.

ಕುಂಞ್ಞಿ *kuṇyi,* is added to denote the young of all birds, and ಮರಿ *mari,* is sometimes, but seldom used; as ಕೋಳಿ ಕುಂಞ್ಞಿ *kóḷi-kuṇyi,* a chicken, ಮರಿ *mari,* is also added to denote the young of fishes; ಕುಂಞ್ಞಿ *kuṇyi,* is also used, but seldom; as ಮೀನು ಕುಂಞ್ಞಿ *mínu-kuṇyi,* a young fish. Both these words are also added to denote the young of serpents; as ಪಾಂಬು ಕುಂಞ್ಞಿ *pámbu-kuṇyi,* a young serpent.

ಚೆರಿಯ *cheriya,* signifying small is added to denote the young of insects; as ಚೆರಿಯ ಪುಳು *cheriya-puḷu,* a young insect.

Relative participles are also used, like adjectives, before nouns, and in them the relative pronouns "who" and "which" are implied, as ಪೋಃಪಳ ಬಟ್ಟೆ *pópaḷa-baṭṭe,* the going pathway, the way in which he goes, or will go. ಬಂದು ಮನಷ್ಯ *bandu-manasha,* the man who has come, ಮಾಡತ ಪಣಿ *máḍatu-paṇi,* the work not done.

As in the Canarese language, there are not many adjectives in the Coorg dialect, and the defect is supplied by affixing to nouns the irregular participles, ಆನು,-ಉಳ್ಳು *ánu* and *uḷḷu,* as ಪಣ *paṇa,* money ಪಣಉಳ್ಳು *paṇauḷḷu,* rich; ಚಾಯಿ *chái,* beauty ಚಾಯಿಆನು *chdiánu,* beautiful.

COMPARISON OF ADJECTIVES.

There is no regular mode of comparing adjectives in the Coorg dialect but comparisons are generally made by the addition of ಇಂಜಿ *inji,* to the dative case; as ಯೇಡ ಕುದ್ರೆಕಿಂಜಿ ನೀಡ ಕುದ್ರೆ ಬಲ್ಯದು *yéḍa-kudre-kinji-níḍa kudre-balyadu,* your horse is larger than my horse.

Comparisons may also be expressed by using the plural Locative case without the addition of ಇಂಜಿ *inji*, as ಈ ಪೊಂಣ್ಣುಳ್ಳುಳು *í (ee) ponṇúḷuḷu*, ಅವ ನಲ್ಲವ *ava-nallava*, she is the best of these women, ಈ ಗುಂಪುಲು ಅವು ಬಲ್ಯವು *í ee gumpulu-avú-ballyavu*, he is the biggest in the crowd.

PRONOUNS.

There are seven descriptions of pronouns in the Coorg dialect, viz.— 1. Personal. 2. Demonstrative. 3. Reciprocal. 4. Numeral. 5. Intermediate. 6. Of Quantity. 7. Interrogative.

The pronouns of quantity are only of the neuter gender,

Pronouns are declined like nouns,

I. PERSONAL PRONOUNS.

CRUDE STATE, ನಾನು. I.

	SINGULAR.	PLURAL.
No.	ನಾನು *nánu*, I.	ಯೆಂಗ, *yenga*, we.
Ac.	ಯೆನ್ನ *yenna*, me.	ಯೆಂಗಳ *yengaḷa*, us.
In.	ಯೆನ್ನ ಗೊಂಡು *yenna-gonḍu.*	ಯೆಂಗಳ ಗೊಂಡು *yengaḷa-gonḍu.*
Da.	ಯೆನಕು *yenakeu.*	ಯೆಂಗಕು *yengakeu.*
Ab.	ಯೆನ್ನ ಚೆಲ್ಲಿತು *yenna-chellitu.*	ಯೆಂಗಳ ಚೆಲ್ಲಿತು *yengaḷa-chellitu.*
	ಯೇಡ ದೆಸೆಲು *yéḍa-deselu.*	ಯೆಂಗಡ ದೆಸೆಲು *yenḍa-deselu.*
Ge.	ಯೇಡ *yéḍa.*	ಯೆಂಗಡ *yengaḍa.*
Lo.	ಯೇಡ ಪಕ್ಕ *yéḍa-pakka.*	ಯೆಂಗಡ ಪಕ್ಕ *yengaḍa-pakka.*

In this pronoun the initial ನಾ is changed in to ಯೆ for the other cases, with the addition of ಂ in the Accusative, Instrumental, and Ablative, cases; and in the Genitive and Locative, cases the initial ಯೆ is lengthened in to ಯೇ. In the plural the initial ಯೆ remains throughout all the cases, with the addition of the ಂ.

This pronoun has also another plural; Viz.

No. ನಂಗ *nanga*,

Ac. ನಂಗಳ *nangaḷa*,

In. ನಂಗಳ ಗೊಂಡ *nangaḷa-gonḍu*,

&c. &c.

CRUDE STATE ನೀ thou.

	SINGULAR.	PLURAL.
No.	ನೀನು ***nínu,*** you, thou.	ನಿಂಗ ***ninga,*** ye or your.
Ac.	ನಿನ್ನ ***ninna,*** yours, thee.	ನಿಂಗಳ ***ningala,*** yours.
In.	ನಿನ್ನ ಗೊಂಡು ***ninna-gonḍu.***	ನಿಂಗಳ ಗೊಂಡು ***ningala-gonḍu.***
Da.	ನಿನಕು ***ninakeu.***	ನಿಂಗಕು ***ningakeu.***
Ab.	ನಿನ್ನ ಚೆಲ್ಲಿತು ***ninna-chellitu.***	ನಿಂಗಳ ಚೆಲ್ಲಿತು ***ningala-chellitu.***
	ನಿನ್ನಡ ದೆಸೆಲು ***ninaḍa-deselu.***	ನಿಂಗಡ ದೆಸೆಲು ***ningaḍa-deselu.***
Ge.	ನಿಂನಡ—ನೀಡ ***ninnaḍa, níḍa.***	ನಿಂಗಡ ***ningaḍa.***
Lo.	ನಿನ್ನಡ ಪಕ್ಕ—ನೀಡ ಪಕ್ಕ ***ninnaḍa-pakka, níḍa-pakka.***	ನಿಂಗಡ ಪಕ್ಕ ***ningaḍa-pakka.***

In ನೀ thee, the long ನೀ of the nominative is changed into the short ನಿ in the other cases and in the plural the initial is changed to ನಿಂ throughout the cases in that number, with ಗ in addition before the affixes.

II. DEMONSTRATIVE PRONOUNS. (REMOTE.)

CRUDE STATE. ಅವು *avu*, he.

	SINGULAR.	PLURAL.
No.	ಅವು ***avu,*** he.	ಅವು ***avu,*** they.
Ac.	ಅವನ ***avana,*** him.	ಅಯುನ ***ayana,*** them.
In.	ಅವನ ಗೊಂಡು ***avana gonḍu.***	ಅಯುನ ಗೊಂಡು ***ayana-gonḍu.***
Da.	ಅವಂಗು ***avangeu.***	ಅಯುಂಗು ***ayangeu.***
Ab.	ಅವನ ಚೆಲ್ಲಿತು ***avana-chellitu.***	ಅಯುನ ಚೆಲ್ಲಿತು ***ayana-chellitu.***
	ಅವಂಡ ದೆಸೆಲು ***avanḍa-deselu.***	ಅಯುಂಡ ದೆಸೆಲು ***ayanḍa-deselu.***
Ge.	ಅವಂಡ ***avanḍa.***	ಅಯುಂಡ ***ayanḍa.***
Lo.	ಅವಂಡ ಪಕ್ಕ ***avanḍa-pakka.***	ಅಯುಂಡ ಪಕ್ಕ ***ayanḍa-pakka.***

In the Dative, Genitive and Locative Cases, both Singular and Plural, ಂ (*am*) is introduced between the crude form of this pronoun and the affix. The plural noun is formed by changing the vowel from what I termed the silent *ú* to the vowel ು *u*, and in the other cases of the plural the ವ gives way to ಯು.

CRUDE STATE ಅವ. She.

SINGULAR.	PLURAL.
No. ಅವ *ava.*	ಅವು *avu.*
Ac. ಅವಳ *avaḷa.*	ಅಯನ *ayana.*
In. ಅವಳಗೊಂಡು *avaḷa-gonḍu.*	ಅಯನಗೊಂಡು *ayana-gonḍu.*
Da. ಅವಕು *avakeu.*	ಅಯಂಗು *ayangeu.*
Ab. ಅವಳಚೆಲ್ಲಿತು *avaḷa-chellitu.*	ಅಯನಚೆಲ್ಲಿತು *ayana-chellitu.*
Ge. ಅವಡ *avaḍa.*	ಅಯಂಡ *ayanḍa.*
Lo. ಅವಡಪಕ್ಕ *avaḍa-pakka.*	ಅಯಂಡಪಕ್ಕ *ayanḍa-pakka.*
Vo. ಅವಳೇ *avaḷé.*	

No. ಅವ *ava,* she.	ಅವು *avu.*
Ac. ಅವಳ *avaḷa,* Her.	ಅಯನ *ayana.*
In. ಅವಳ ಗೊಂಡು *avaḷaa-gonḍu,*	ಅಯನ ಗೊಂಡು *ayana-gonḍu.*
Da. ಅವಕು *avakeu,*	ಅಯಂಗು &c.
Ab. ಅವಳ ಚೆಲ್ಲಿತು *avaḷa-chellitu,*	The plural of this feminine pronoun is the same as the Masculine.
ಅವಡ ದೆಸೆಲು *avaḍa-deselu,*	
Ge. ಅವಡ *avaḍa,*	
Lo. ಅವಡ ಪಕ್ಕ *avaḍa-pakka,*	

In the Coorg dialect the silent ವು *u* denotes the masculine, ವ *va* the feminine and ದು *du* the neuter gender.

No. ಅಯಾಳು *ayáḷu,* he, that man.	ಅತ್ತಂಗ *uttanga,* they, those men.
Ac. ಅಯಾಳುನ *ayáḷuna,* him.	ಅತ್ತಂಗಳ *atangaḷa,* them.
&c. &c.	&c. &c.

This pronoun is derived from ಆ, that, and ಆಳು, a person.

CRUDE STATE ಅದು it.

No. ಅದು *adu,* it.

Ac. ಅದುನ *aduna,* it.

In. ಅದತಿಂಜಿ, ಅದನ ಗೊಂಡು *adatinji, adana-gonḍu.*

Da. ಅದಂಗು *adangeu.*

Ab. ಅದನ ಚೆಲ್ಲಿತು *adana-chellitu.*

Ge. ಅದಂಡ *adanḍa.*

Lo. ಅದುಲು *adulu.*

Indeterminate Pronouns.

The plural is formed by adding the word ಯೆಲ್ಲ all, to the singular form.

II. DEMONSTRATIVE PRONOUNS (proximate.)

	SINGULAR.	PLURAL.
No.	ಇವು *ivu*, he, this man.	ಇವು *ivu*, these men.
Ac.	ಇವನ *ivana*, ,,	ಇಯನ *iyana*, ,,
	ಇವ *iva*, she, this woman.	ಇವು *ivu*, these women.
	ಈಳು *íḷu*, this person.	ಇತ್ತಂಗ *ittanga*, these persons.
	ಇದು *idu*, it, this thing.	

These pronouns are declined in the same manner as the corresponding remote demonstrative pronouns.

III. RECIPROCAL PRONOUNS.

ತಾನು *tánu*.

	SINGULAR.	PLURAL.
No.	ತಾನು *tánu*, himself.	ತಂಗ *tanga*, themselves.
Ac.	ತನ್ನ *tanna*, himself & itself.	ತಂಗಳ *tangaḷa*, ,,

This pronoun is used with reference to some other noun or pronoun of the 3rd person preceding it; as ಅವು ತನ್ನಡ or ತಾಡ, ತಾಂಡ ಮನೆಕು ಪೋಚಿ *avu tannaḍa* or *táḍa*, or *tánḍa manekeu póchi*, he went to his house.

The plural is also used honorifically in the second person singular, when addressing a superior or one to whom you wish to shew respect, as ತಂಗ ಬಪ್ಪದಿಲ್ಲೆಯಾ *tanga bappadilleyá*, will you not come?

IV. INDETERMINATE PRONOUNS.

There is only one indeterminate pronoun; viz, ಯೆಲ್ಲ all, the nominative of which is the same in all three genders; but the declension is different between the masculine and feminine genders and the neuter; as,

	Mas. & Fem.	Neuter.
No.	ಯೆಲ್ಲ *yella*.	ಯೆಲ್ಲ *yella*.
Ac.	ಯೆಲ್ಲರ *yellara*.	ಯೆಲ್ಲಾನ *yellána*.

In.	ಯೆಲ್ಲರ ಗೊಂಡು	*yellara-gonḍu.*	ಯೆಲ್ಲಾನ ಗೊಂಡು	*yellána-gonḍu.*
Da.	ಯೆಲ್ಲಾಕು	*yelláku.*	ಯೆಲ್ಲಾಂಗು	*yellángu.*
Ab.	ಯೆಲ್ಲರ ಚೆಲ್ಲಿತು	*yellara-chellitu.*	ಯೆಲ್ಲಾನ ಚೆಲ್ಲಿತು	*yellána-chellitu.*
Ge.	ಯೆಲ್ಲಡ	*yellaḍa.*	ಯೆಲ್ಲಾಂಡ	*yellánḍa.*
Lo.	ಯೆಲ್ಲಾಡಲು	*yelláḍalu.*	ಯೆಲ್ಲಾಲು	*yellálu.*

V. NUMERAL PRONOUNS.

SINGULAR.			PLURAL.		
ಒಬ್ಬು	*wobbu,*	one man.	ಇಬ್ಬ	*ibba,*	two men.
ಒಬ್ಬ	*wobba,*	one woman.	ಇಬ್ಬ	*ibba,*	two women.
ಒಂದು	*wondu,*	one thing.	ದಂಡು	*danḍu,*	two things.

These pronouns are declined like the demonstrative pronouns of the several genders given under that head, except in the plural, which is formed by adding ರ, *r*, to the accusative and is declined like the 1st declension of nouns.

VI. PRONOUNS OF QUANTITY.

There are no pronouns of quantity relating to the masculine and femenine genders; but in the neuter gender are to be found;

Remote ಅಚ್ಚಕು *achchaku,* so much, in so many as those.
Proximate ಇಚ್ಚಕು *ichchaku,* so much, in so many as these.
These are declined like ಅದು *adu.*

VII. INTEROGATIVE PRONOUNS.

SINGULAR.		PLURAL.	
ಯೇವು *yévu,* who, what man?		ಆರು *áru,*	what men?
ಯೇವ *yéva,* who, what woman?		ಆರು *áru,*	,, women?
ಯೇದು *yédu,* which thing?		plural.	none.

Interogative Pronouns.

These pronouns are declined in the same manner as the demonstrative pronouns.

ಎನ್ನು *yennu,* what ?

No. ಎನ್ನು *yennu,* what?
Ac. ಎನ್ನತಾನ *yennatána.*
In. ಎನ್ನತಾನ ಗೊಂಡು *yennatána-goṇḍu.*
Da. ಎನ್ನತಾಂಗು, ಎನ್ನಂಗು *yennatángeu, yennangeu.*
Ab. ಎನ್ನತಾನ ಚೆಲ್ಲಿತು *yennatána-chellitu.*
Ge. ಎನ್ನತಾಂಡ *yennatánḍa.*
Lo. ಎನ್ನತಾಲು *yennatálu.*

ಯೆಚ್ಚಕು *yechchakeu,* How much? This pronoun is declined like ಅದು *adu.*

Some of the demonstrative, numeral, and other pronouns are abbreviated, or changed, when they form the first member of a compound word ; as.

ಅದು *adu,* that	becomes	ಆ *á.*
ಇದು *idu,* this,	,,	ಈ *í.*
ಯೇದು *yédu,* which,	,,	ಯೇ *yé.*
ಒಂದು *wondu,* one,	,,	ಒರು *woru.*
ದಂಡು *danḍu,* two,	,,	ದಂಡಾ *danḍá.*
ಮೂಂದು *múndu,* three,	,,	ಮೂಂದಾ *múnḍá.*
ಪತ್ತು *pattu,* ten,	,,	ಪಂನು ಪದಿ *pannu, padi.*
ನಡುವು *naḍuvu,* middle,	,,	ನಡು *naḍu.*
ಮೇಕೆ *méke,* upper,	,,	ಮೇ *mé.*
ಕೀದ *kída,* under,	,,	ಕೀ *kí.*
ಪೋರಮೆ *pórame,* outside,	,,	ಪೊರ *pora.*
ಮಿಂಣೆ *minṇe,* front,	,,	ಮಿಂಣೆ *minṇe.*
ವೊಳು *woḷu,* inside,	,,	ವೊಳ *woḷa.*

EXAMPLES.

ಅದು *adu,* and ಮನೆ *mane,* becomes, ಆ ಮನೆ *á-mane,* that house.

ಒಂದು *wondu,* ,,	ಕಂಣು *kaṇṇu,*	,,	ಒರು ಕಂಣು *woru-kaṇṇu,* one eye.
ಪತ್ತು *pattu,*	ಒಂದು *wondu,*	,,	ಪಂನೊಂದು *pannondu,* eleven.
ಪತ್ತು *pattu,*	ನಾಲು *nálu,*	,,	ಪದಿನಾಲು *padinálu.*
ಪೊರಮೆ *porame,*	ಮನೆ *mane,*	,,	ಪೊರಮನೆ *poramane,* out house.
ಯೇದು *yédu,*	ಪೊಟ್ಟಿ *poṭṭi,*	,,	ಯೇ ಪೊಟ್ಟಿ *yé-poṭṭi,* which box?
ಇದು *idu,*	ಬಟ್ಟೆ *baṭṭe,*	,,	ಈ ಬಟ್ಟೆ *í-baṭṭe,* this road.

VERBS.

Verbs are divided, as in Canarese, into Active, Neuter, and Causal; *but* the Passive form is unknown.

The root of the verb is generally the same as the 2nd person singular Imperative.

The roots of verbs generally terminate in the silent *u* or half *u*, in ಎ *e*; in ಅ *a*; and in ಇ *i*.

The Conjugations have been classed accordingly and distinguished from each other by these four several endings of the roots of the verbs.

Viz.	1st	Conjugation	ending	in	ು silent	*u.*
	2nd.	,,	,,	,,	ಎ	*e.*
	3rd.	,,	,,	,,	ಅ	*a.*
	4th.	,,	,,	,,	ಇ	*i.*

There are four simple, moods viz. the infinitive, imperative, negative, and affirmative; the potential and subjunctive moods being compounds.

In the affirmative mood there are only three simple and six compound tenses. The future tense being also much in the same sense as the 2nd or contingent future in Canarese.

The infinitive mood is impersonal. The other simple moods and tenses are formed by the addition of certain personal affixes to the Roots Participles and Gerunds.

THE FOLLOWING ARE THE PERSONAL AFFIXES USED IN THE CONJUGATION OF VERBS.

	Imperative.	Negative.	Affirmative Mood — Present Tense.	Past Tense.	1st. Future Tense.
SINGULAR.					
1st. Person.	ಅಡು. *aḍu.*	ಅ, ಉಲೆ, ಇಲ್ಲೆ *a* or *ule-ille*	ಇ, ಉವಿ, ವಳೆ *i, uvi-vaḷe*	ನೆ, ನು, ಎ, *ne, nu, e.*	ಉ *vu.*
2nd. „		ಉಲೆ. ...	ಇಯು, ಉವಿಯು *uviya.*	ಇಯು *iya.*	ವಿಯು *viya.*
3rd. Masculine.	ಅಡು. ...	ಉಲೆ. ...	ವ, ವಳ *va, vaḷa.*	ಇಚಿ *ichi.*	ಉ *u.*
3rd. Feminine.	ಅಡು. ...	ಉಲೆ. ...	ವ, ವಳ	ಇಚಿ ...	ಉ ...
3rd. Neuter.	ಅಡು. ...	ಉಲೆ. ...	ವ, ವಳ	ಇಚಿ ...	ಉ ...
PLURAL.					
1st. Person.	ಅಡು. ...	ಉಲೆ. ...	ವ, ವಳ	ಇಚಿ ...	ಉ ...
2nd. „	ಇ. *i*	ಉಲೆ. ...	ಇರ, ವಿರ *ira, vira.*	ಇರ *ira.*	ವಿರ, ಇರ *vira, ira.*
3rd. M. and F.	ಅಡು. *aḍu.*	ಉಲೆ. ...	ವ, ವಳ *va, vaḷa.*	ಇಚಿ *ichi.*	ಉ *u.*

I. CONJUGATION, OR VERBS ENDING IN SILENT *u*.

Root ಮಾಡು *máḍu.*

Gerunds or Verbal Participles.

		Compounded of the root and
Present.	ಮಾಡಿ ಯೆಂಡು *máḍiyanḍu,* doing.	ಇಯೆಂಡು *iyanḍu.*
Past.	ಮಾಡಿತು *máḍitu,* having done.	ಇತು *itu.*
Negat.	ಮಾಡತ್ತೆ *máḍatte,* not having done.	ಅತೆ *ate.*

Relative Participles.

		The root and
Present and Future.	ಮಾಡುವು *máḍuwu,* who or which does or will do.	ವು *wu.*
Past.	ಮಾಡುನು *máḍunu,* who are which did.	ನು *nu.*
Nagative.	ಮಾಡತು *máḍatu,* who are which does not, did not or will not do.	ಅತು *atu.*

Compound Relative Participles.

		The *present* gerund and
Present.	ಮಾಡಿಯೆಂಡುಳ್ಳು *máḍiyenḍuḷḷu,* who or which, is or will be doing.	ಉಳ್ಳು *uḷḷu.*
Future.	ಇಪ್ಪು *ippu.*	ಇಪ್ಪು *ippu.*
Past.	ಮಾಡಿಯೆಂಡಿಂಜು *máḍiyenḍinju,* who or which was doing.	ಇಂಜು *inju.*

		The *past* gerund and
Perfect.	ಮಾಡತುಳ್ಳು *máḍutuḷḷu,* who or which has done or will have done.	ಉಳ್ಳು *uḷḷu.*
Future perf.	ಇಪ್ಪು *ippu.*	ಇಪ್ಪು *ippu.*
Pluperfect.	ಮಾಡಿತ್ತಿಂಜು *máḍitinju,* who or which had done.	ಇಂಜು *inju.*

INFINITIVE MOOD.

	The root and
ಮಾಡುವಕೆು *máḍuvakeu.*	ವಕೆು *vakeu.*

IMPERATIVE MOOD.

(Root and personal affixes.)

	SINGULAR.	PLURAL.
1st person.	ಮಾಡದು *máḍaḍu,* let me do.	ಮಾಡದು *máḍaḍu,* let us do.
2nd ,,	ಮಾಡು *máḍu,* do thou.	ಮಾಡಿ *máḍi,* do ye.
3rd Mas. / 3rd Fem. / 3rd Neu.	ಮಾಡದು *máḍaḍu,* let him, her or it do.	ಮಾಡದು *máḍaḍu,* let them do.

NEGATIVE MOOD.

(Root and personal affixes.)

I &c. do not.

1st person.	ಮಾಡುಲೆ	*maḍule.*
2nd ,,	ಮಾಡುಲೆ	,,
3rd Mas.	ಮಾಡುಲೆ	,,
3rd Eem.	ಮಾಡುಲೆ	,,
3rd Neu.	ಮಾಡುಲೆ	,,

The same form is used for the plural, with the several personal pronouns going before.

AFFIRMATIVE MOOD.

Present Tense I do &c.

(Present relative participle ಮಾಡುವು and personal affixes.)

	Singular	Plural
1st person.	ನಾನು ಮಾಡುವಿ *nánu máḍuvi,* or ವಳ್ಳೆ or *máḍuwaḷe,* I do.	ಮಾಡುವ *máḍuwa,* we or ವಳ್ಳೆ or ,, *máḍuwaḷe,* we do.
2nd ,,	ನೀನು ಮಾಡುವಿಯು *nínu máḍuviya,* thou.	ಮಾಡುವೀರ *máḍuvíra,* ye do.
3rd Mas.	ಮಾಡುವ ವಳ್ಳ *máḍuwa,* or *máḍuwaḷa,* He.	ಮಾಡುವ *máḍuwa,* ವಳ್ಳ *máḍuwaḷa,*
3rd Fem.	ಮಾಡುವು She	ವಳ್ಳ ,, she ಮಾಡುವ ,,
3rd Neu.	ಮಾಡುವ It	ವಳ್ಳ ,, it ,,

Past Tense. I did &c.

(Past relative participle ಮಾಡುನು *máḍunu,* and personal affixes.)

	SINGULAR.		PLURAL.	
1st person.	ಮಾಡುನೆ *mádune*, ,, *nú*,	I did.	ಮಾಡಿಚಿ *mádichi*,	we did.
2nd ,,	ಮಾಡಿಯ *mádiya*,	thou.	ಮಾಡಿರ *mádira*,	ye ,,
3rd Mas.	ಮಾಡಿಚಿ *mádichi*,	he.	ಮಾಡುಚಿ *máduchi*,	they,,
3rd Fem.	ಮಾಡುಚಿ ,,	she.	ಮಾಡುಚಿ ,,	,, ,,
3rd Neu.	ಮಾಡುಚಿ ,,	it	,,	,, ,,

1ST FUTURE TENSE. I shall or will do &c.

(Future relative perticiple ಮಾಡುವು *máduwu*, and personal affixes.)

1st person.	ಮಾಡುವು *máduwu*.	ಮಾಡು *mádu*.
2nd ,,	ಮಾಡುವಿಯ *máduviya*.	ಮಾಡುವಿರ *máduvira*.
3rd Mas.	ಮಾಡು *mádu*.	ಮಾಡು *mádu*.
3rd Fem.	ಮಾಡು ,,	ಮಾಡು ,,
3rd Neu.	ಮಾಡು ,,	

COMPOUND TENSES.

The Coorg dialect also comprises six compound tenses in the Affirmative mood. The present, past and future tenses are formed by adding to the present gerund of the verbs, the present, past and future tenses of the Verb ಇರು *iru*, to be. The addition of the same tenses to the past gerund forms the perfect, pluperfect and future perfect tenses of the verb.

PRESENT TENSE. I am doing &c.

(Present gerund ಮಾಡಿಯಂಡು *mádiyandu*, and the present tense of ಇರು *iru*.)

	SINGULAR.	PLURAL.
1st person.	ಮಾಡಿಯಂಡುಳ್ಳೆ *mádiyandulle*, or *mádiyandullu*.	ಮಾಡಿಯಂಡುಂಡು *mádiyandundu*.
2nd person.	ಮಾಡಿಯಂಡುಳ್ಳಿಯ *mádiyandulliya*.	ಮಾಡಿಯಂಡುಳ್ಳಿರ *mádiyandullira*.
3rd Mas.	ಮಾಡಿಯಂಡುಂಡು *mádiyandundu*,	ಮಾಡಿಯಂಡುಂಡು } Same as 1st person plural.
3rd Fem.	ಮಾಡಿಯಂಡುಂಡು ,,	ಮಾಡಿಯಂಡುಂಡು
3rd Neu.	ಮಾಡಿಯಂಡುಂಡು ,,	

Perfect Tense.

PAST TENSE I was or would have been, doing &c.

(Present gerund ಮಾಡಿಯೊಂಡು *máḍiyanḍu,* and the past of ಇರು *iru.*)

	SINGULAR.	PLURAL.
1st person.	ಮಾಡಿಯೊಂಡಿಂಜೆ *máḍiyanḍinje.*	ಮಾಡಿಯೊಂಡಿಂಜತು *máḍiyanḍinjatu.*
2nd person.	ಮಾಡಿಯೊಂಡಿಂಜಿಯ *máḍiyanḍinjiya.*	ಮಾಡಿಯೊಂಡಿಂಜಿರ *máḍiyanḍinjira.*
3rd Mas.	ಮಾಡಿಯೊಂಡಿಂಜತು *máḍiyenḍinjatu.*	ಮಾಡಿಯೊಂಡಿಂಜತು } Same as 1st person Plural.
3rd Fem.	,, ,, ,,	
3rd Neu.	,, ,, ,,	

FUTURE TENSE. I shall or will be doing &c.

(Present gerund ಮಾಡಿಯೊಂಡು *máḍiyanḍu,* and the Future tense of ಇರು *iru.*)

1st person.	ಮಾಡಿಯೊಂಡಿಪ್ಪು *máḍiyanḍippu.*	ಮಾಡಿಯೊಂಡಿಕ್ಕು *máḍiyanḍikku.*
2nd person.	ಮಾಡಿಯೊಂಡಿಪ್ಪಿಯ *máḍiyanḍippiya.*	ಮಾಡಿಯೊಂಡಿಪ್ಪಿರ *máḍiyanḍippira.*
3rd Mas.	ಮಾಡಿಯೊಂಡಿಕ್ಕು *máḍiyanḍikku.*	ಮಾಡಿಯೊಂಡಿಕ್ಕು. } Same as 3rd person singular.
3rd Fem.	ಮಾಡಿಯೊಂಡಿಕ್ಕು ,,	,, ,,
3rd Neut.	ಮಾಡಿಯೊಂಡಿಕ್ಕು ,,	

PERFECT TENSE, I have done &c.

(Past gerund ಮಾಡಿತು *máḍitu,* and past tense of ಇರು *iru.*)

1st person.	ಮಾಡಿತ್ತುಳ್ಳಿಯು *máḍittuḷḷiyu.*	ಮಾಡಿತುಂಡು *máḍitunḍu.*
2nd ,,	ಮಾಡಿತ್ತುಳ್ಳಿಯ *máḍittuḷḷiya.*	ಮಾಡಿತುಳ್ಳಿರ *máḍituḷḷira.*
3rd Mas.	ಮಾಡಿತುಂಡು *máḍitunḍu.*	ಮಾಡಿತುಂಡು. } Same as 3rd person singular.
3rd Fem.	ಮಾಡಿತುಂಡು ,,	,, ,,
3rd Neut.	ಮಾಡಿತುಂಡು ,,	

PLUPERFECT TENSE, I had done &c.

(Past gerund ಮಾಡಿತು *máḍitu,* and past Tense of ಇರು *iru,*)

1st person.	ಮಾಡಿತ್ತಿಂಜೆ *máḍittinje.*	ಮಾಡಿತ್ತಿಂಜತು *máḍittinjatu.*

2nd ,,	ಮಾಡಿತ್ತಿಂಜಿಯ *máḍittinjiya,*	ಮಾಡಿತ್ತಿಂಜಿರ *máḍittinjira.*
3rd Mas.	ಮಾಡಿತ್ತಿಂಜತು *máḍittinjatu,*	ಮಾಡಿತ್ತಿಂಜತು } Same as Singular.
3rd Fem.	ಮಾಡಿತ್ತಿಂಜತು ,,	,, ,,
3rd Neu.	ಮಾಡಿತ್ತಿಂಜತು ,,	

Future Perfect Tense, I shall or will, or would have done &c.

(Past gerund ಮಾಡಿತು *máḍitu,* and future tence of ಇರು *iru.*)

1st person.	ಮಾಡಿತು ಇಪ್ಪು *máḍitu-ippu.*	ಮಾಡಿತು ಇಕ್ಕು *máḍitu-ikku.*
2nd person.	ಮಾಡಿತು ಇಪ್ಪಿಯ *máḍitu-ippiya.*	ಮಾಡಿತು ಇಪ್ಪಿರ *máḍitu-ippira.*
3rd Mas.	ಮಾಡಿತು ಇಕ್ಕು *máḍitu-ikku.*	ಮಾಡಿತು ಇಕ್ಕು *máḍituikku.*
3rd Fem.	ಮಾಡಿತು ಇಕ್ಕು ,,	,, ,, ,, ,,
3rd Neu.	ಮಾಡಿತು ಇಕ್ಕು ,,	,, ,, ,, ,,

In the 1st Person of each tense, ಎ *e* or the silent *u* are indieffrently used as the final vowel of the affix.

Whenever the past gerund is followed by a long vowel the Coorgs pronounce the single ತ; but whenever the past gerund precedes a short vowel the ತ is doubled

---

POTENTIAL MOOD.

The Potential mood is formed by the addition of certain affixes to the root and to the Infinitive, and in two tenses by the addition of the verbs ಕೈಯ್ಯು *keiyu,* to be able, and ಅರಿಯು, *ariyu,* to know.

Affirmative, May.	Negative May not.
(Root in silent *ú* and ಅಲು *alu.*)	(Inflnitive in ವಕು *waku,* and ಆಗ *ága.*)
I &c. may do ; or am at liberty to do.	I &c. may not do ; or am not at liberty to do.
ನಾನು ಮಾಡಲು *nánu máḍalu.*	ಮಾಡುವಕು ಆಗ *máḍuwaku ága.*
(Infinitive in ವಕು *wakeu,* ಕೈಯ್ಯು, *keiyu.*)	Infinitive in ವಕು *wakeu,* ಕೈಯ್ಯು *keiya.*

Potential Mood.

I &c. may or am at liberty to do. — I am may not, or, am not at liberty to do.

ಮಾಡುವಕು ಕೈಯು *máḍuwakeu keiyu.* — ಮಾಡುವಕು ಕೈಯು *máḍuwakeu keiya.*

By omitting the silent *ú,* the *k* may be doubled and pronounced as if one word.

Must.

Root in *ú* and ಅಂಡು *anḍu.*

I &c. must or need to do.

ಮಾಡಂಡು *máḍanḍu.*

Must not.

Root in *ú* and ಅಂಡ *anḍa.*

I &c. must not or need not do.

ಮಾಡಂಡ *máḍanḍa.*

Ought.

Root in *ú* ಅಂಡಿಯದು *anḍiyadu.*

I &c. ought to do; or it is proper for me to do.

ಮಾಡಂಡಿಯದು *máḍanḍiyadu.*

Ought not.

The negative is formed by ಅಂಡಿಯದಲ್ಲ, *anḍiyadalla.*

Can.

(Infinitive in ವಕು *waku,* and) ಅರಿಯು *ariyu.*

I, &c. can do; or I know to do.

ಮಾಡುವಕು ಅರಿಯು *máḍuwaku-ariyu,*

Cannot.

Infinitive in ವಕು *waka,* ಅರಿಯ *ariyu.*

I, &c. cannot or know not to do.

ಮಾಡುವಕು ಅರಿಯ *máḍuwaku-ariya.*

The vowal *u* gives an affirmative and the vowal "*a*" a negative Signification.

SUBJUNCTIVE MOOD.

Aorist Tense. Impersonal.

Root ಮಾಡು *máḍu,* and the affixes ಚೆಂಗಿ *chengi,* ಚೆಂಗೂ *chengú,* and ತೆಂಗಿ *tengi,* ತೆಂಗೂ *tengú,* and ಯೆಂಗಿ *yengi,* ಯೆಂಗೂ *yengú,* ಮಾಡು ಚೆಂಗಿ *máḍu-chengi,* if I. &c. do, shall or should do.

ಮಾಡು ಚೆಂಗೂ *máḍu-chengú,* Although I do, shall or should do. &c.

The other affixes are simliarly used with roots of other terminations, as ಬಾ ತೆಂಗಿ if I shall come.

PRESENT AND FUTURE TENSE. IMPERSONAL.

(Present and Future relative part. ಮಾಡುವು *máḍuwu,* and ಅನೆಕೆ *aneke* or ಅಂನನೆ *annane,* that, so that.)

ಮಾಡುವು ಅನೆಕೆ *máḍuwu-aneke.* that I, &c. may or might do.

NEGATIVE. IMPERSONAL.

(Negative Relative participle ಮಾಡತು *máḍatu,* and ಅನೆಕೆ *aneke,* that so that.)

ಮಾಡತು ಅನೆಕೆ *máḍatu-aneke,* that I, &c. may not or might not do.

SUBJUNCTIVE COMPOUND TENSE.

Formed by adding the subjunctive aorist tense of ಇರು *iru,* to the present, participle and negative gerunds of the verbs.

PRESENT TENSE. IMPERSONAL.

(Present gerund ಮಾಡಿಯಂಡು *máḍiyanḍu* and ಉಂಡೆಂಗಿ *undengi.*)

ಮಾಡುಯಂಡು ಉಂಡೆಂಗಿ *máḍuyanḍu-unḍengi.* ಮಾಡಿಯಂಡುಂಡೆಂಗಿ *máḍiyanḍunḍengi.*	} If I, &c. am doing.

PERFECT TENSE. IMPERSONAL.

(Past gerund ಮಾಡಿತು *máḍittu,* and ಉಂಡೆಂಗಿ *unḍengi.*)

ಮಾಡಿತು ಉಂಡೆಂಗಿ *máḍitu-unḍengi.* ಮಾಡಿತ್ತುಂಡೆಂಗಿ *máḍittunḍengi.*	} If I &c. have done.

NEGATIVE. IMPERSONAL.

(Negative gerund ಮಾಡತ್ತೆ *máḍatte,* and ಉಂಡೆಂಗಿ *undengi.*)

ಮಾಡತ್ತೆ ಉಂಡೆಂಗಿ *máḍatte-unḍengi.* ಮಾಡತ್ತುಂಡೆಂಗಿ *máḍattunḍengi.*	} If I, &c. do not, did not, or, will not do.

2nd CONJUGATION or a verb ending in ಎ *e.*

Root ಒಡೆ *woḍe,* Break.

GERUNDS OR VERBAL PARTICIPLES.

The root, ಒಡೆ *woḍe,* break.

Present. ಒಡೆತೆಂಡು *woḍetunḍu,* breaking. The root, and ತಂಡು *tanḍu.*

Imperative Mood.

Past.	ಒಡೆತಿತ್ತ್	*wodetittu.*	ತಿತ್ತ್	*tittu.*
Negative.	ಒಡೆಯತ್ತೆ	*wodeyatte.*	ಯತ್ತೆ	*yatte.*

Relative Participles.

			The root and
Present and Future	ಒಡೆಪು *wodepu,*	who or which broke or will break.	ಪು *pu.*
Past.	ಒಡೆತು *wodetu,*	who or which broke.	ತು *tu.*
Negative.	ಒಡೆಯತು *wodeyatu,*	who or which breaks not, broke not, or will not break.	ಯತು *yatu.*

Compound Relative Participle.

			Present Gerund and
Present.	ಒಡೆತಂಡು ಉಳ್ಳು *wodetandu-ullu,*	who or which is or will be breaking.	ಉಳ್ಳು *ullu.*
Future.	,, ಇಪ್ಪು *ippu.*		ಇಪ್ಪು *ippu.*
Past.	ಒಡೆತಂಡು ಇಂಜು *wodetandu-inju,*	who was breaking.	ಇಂಜು *inju.*

			Past Gerund and
Perfect.	ಒಡೆತಿತ್ತ್ ಉಳ್ಳು *wodetittu-ullu.*	who and those or will have broke.	ಉಳ್ಳು *ullu.*
Fut. perf.	,, ಇಪ್ಪು *ippu.*		ಇಪ್ಪು *ippu.*
Pluperfect.	ಒಡೆತಿತು ಇಂಜು *wodetitu-inju,*	who and had broke.	ಇಂಜು *inju.*

INFINITIVE MOOD.

ಒಡೆಪಕು *wodepaku,* — The root and ಪಕು *paku.*

IMPERATIVE MOOD.

(Root and personal affixes.)

Let me &c. break.

	Singular.	Plural.
1st person.	ಒಡೆಯಡು *wodeyadu.*	ಒಡೆಯಡು *wodeyadu.*
2nd ,,	ಒಡೆ *wode.*	ಒಡೆ ಇರ *wodeire.*
3rd Mas. 3rd Fem. 3rd Neu.	ಒಡೆಯಡು *wodeyadu.*	ಒಡೆಯಡು *wodeyadu.*

In speaking the ಯು becomes changed to ಕ, as ಒಡೆಕಡು *woḍekaḍu.*

NEGATIVE MOOD.

(Root and the Negative affix.)

I, &c. call not, will not call.

1st person.	ಒಡೆಪ್ಪುಲೆ *woḍepule.* or ಒಡೆಪೆಲೆ *woḍepele.*	ಒಡೆಪೆಲೆ *woḍepele.*
2nd ,,	,, ,,	,, ,,
3rd Mas.	,, ,,	,, ,,
3rd Fem.	,, ,,	,, ,,
3rd Neut.	,, ,,	,, ,,

AFFIRMATIVE MOOD.

Present Tense. I break.

(Present and Future Relative Participle ಒಡೆಪ್ಪು *woḍepu,* and personal affixes.

	Singular.	Plural.
1st person.	ಒಡೆಪೆ *woḍepe,* or ಒಡೆಪಳೆ *waḍepaḷe.*	ಒಡೆಪ *woḍepa,* or ಪಳ *paḷa.*
2nd ,,	ಒಡೆಪೆಯ *woḍepeya.*	ಒಡೆಪೆರ *woḍepera.*
3rd Mas. 3rd Fem. 3rd Neut.	ಒಡೆಪ *waḍepa,* or ಒಡೆಪಳ *waḍepaḷu.*	ಒಡೆಪ *waḍepa,* or ಪಳ *paḷa.*

It will be noticed that these tenses are formed with the Relative participle and personal affixes, and not with the present gerunds as in the Canarese language.

Past Tense. I broke &c.

(Past relative participle ಒಡೆತು *woḍetu,* and personal affixes.)

1st person.	ಒಡೆತೆ *woḍete.*	ಒಡೆತತ್ತು *woḍetattu.*
2nd ,,	ಒಡೆತಿಯ *woḍetiya.*	ಒಡೆತಿರ *woḍetira.*
3rd Mas. 3rd Fem. 3rd Neut.	ಒಡೆತತ್ತು *woḍetattu.*	ಒಡೆತತ್ತು *waḍetattu.*

Compound Tense.

1st Future Tense. I shall or will break &c.

(Future relative participle ಒಡೆಪು *woḍepu,* except in 3rd person singular and plural and 1st person plural., in which the final ಪು, is changed into ಕ್ಕೂ *kkú.*)

	Singular.	Plural.
1st person.	ಒಡೆಪು *woḍepu.*	ಒಡೆಕ್ಕೂ *woḍekkú.*
2nd ,,	ಒಡೆಪೆಯ *woḍepeya.*	ಒಡೆಪೆರ *waḍepera.*
3rd Mas. / 3rd Fem. / 3rd Neut.	ಒಡೆಕ್ಕೂ *woḍekkú.*	ಒಡೆಕ್ಕೂ *woḍekkú.*

COMPOUND TENSES.

There are six compound tenses in the affirmative mood. (See note in the 1st conjugation.)

Present Tense. I am breaking &c.

(Present gerund ಒಡೆತಂಡು *woḍetanḍu,* and the present tense of ಇರು *iru,* be.)

ಒಡೆತಂಡು ಉಳ್ಳಿಯು *woḍetanḍu-uḷḷiyu.* — ಒಡೆತಂಡು ಉಂಡು *woḍetanḍu-unḍu.*

ಒಡೆತಂಡುಳ್ಳಿಯು *woḍetanḍuḷḷiyu.* — ಒಡೆತಂಡುಂಡು *woḍetanḍunḍu.*

Past Tense. I was breaking &c.

(Present gerund ಒಡೆತಂಡು *woḍetanḍu,* and the past tense ಇರು *iru.* be.)

ಒಡೆತಂಡು ಇಂಜೆ *woḍetanḍu-inje.* — ಒಡೆತಂಡು ಇಂಜತು *woḍetanḍu-injutu.*

ಒಡೆತಂಡಿಂಜೆ *woḍetanḍinje.* — ಒಡೆತಂಡಿಂಜತು *woḍetanḍinjatu.*

Future Tense. I shall or will be breaking.

(Present gerund ಒಡೆತಂಡು *woḍetanḍu,* and the future tense of ಇರು *iru.*)

ಒಡೆತಂಡು ಇಪ್ಪು *woḍetanḍu-ippu.* — ಒಡೆತಂಡು ಇಕ್ಕು *woḍetanḍu-ikku.*

ಒಡೆತಂಡಿಪ್ಪು *woḍetanḍippu.* — ಒಡೆತಂಡಿಕ್ಕು *woḍetanḍikku.*

Perfect Tense. I have broken.

(Past gerund ಒಡೆತಿತ *woḍetitu,* and persent tense of ಇರು *iru.*)

ಒಡೆತಿತು ಉಳ್ಳಿಯು *woḍetitu-uḷḷiyu.* — ಒಡೆತಿತು ಉಂಡು *woḍetitu-unḍu.*

ಒಡೆತಿತ್ತುಳ್ಳಿಯು *woḍetittuḷḷiyu.* — ಒಡೆತಿತ್ತುಂಡು *woḍetittunḍu.*

PLUPERFECT TENSE I had broken &c.

(Past gerund ಒಡೆತಿತು *woḍetitu,* and past tense of ಇರು *iru.*)

ಒಡೆತಿತು ಇಂಜು *woḍetitu-inju,* | ಒಡೆತಿತು ಇಂಜತು *woḍetitu-injatu.*

ಒಡೆತಿತ್ತಿಂಜು *woḍetittinju,* | ಒಡೆತಿತ್ತಿಂಜತು *woḍetittinjatu.*

FUTURE PERFECT TENSE I shall or will, or would have broken &c.

(Past gerund ಒಡೆತಿತು *woḍetitu,* and future tense of ಇರು *iru.*)

ಒಡೆತಿತು ಇಪ್ಪು *woḍetitu-ippu,* | ಒಡೆತಿತ್ತು ಇಕ್ಕು *woḍetittu-ikku.*

ಒಡೆತಿತ್ತಿಪ್ಪು *woḍetittippu,* | ಒಡೆತಿತ್ತಿಕ್ಕು *woḍetittikkú.*

POTENTIAL MOOD.

(See notes on the 1st Conjugation.)

AFFIRMATIVE. MAY.

(Root in ಎ *e* and ಕಲು *kalu.*)

I &c. may break or am at liberty to break.

ಒಡೆಕಲು *woḍekalu,*

(Infinitive in ಪಕು *paku,* and ಕೈಯು *keiyu.*)

I &c. may or am at liberty to break.

ಒಡೆಪಕು ಕೈಯು *woḍcpaku-keiyu,*

NEGATIVE. MAY NOT.

(Infinitive in ಪಕು *paku,* ಆಗ *dga.*

I &c. may not break or am not at liberty to break.

ಒಡೆಪಕು ಆಗ *woḍepaku-dga.*

(Infinitive in ಪಕು *paku,* and ಕೈಯ *keiya.*)

I &c. may not or am not at liberty to break.

ಒಡೆಪಕು ಕೈಯ *woḍepaku-keiya.*

In speaking the ultimate ಕ of the Infinitive is dropped and the two component parts blended together.

MUST.

(Root in ಒಡೆ *woḍe,* and ಕಂಡು *kanḍu.*)

I &c. must or need to break.

ಒಡೆಕಂಡು *woḍekanḍu,*

MUST NOT.

(Root in ಒಡೆ *waḍe,* and ಕಂಡ *kanḍa.*)

I &c. must not, or, need not break.

ಒಡೆಕಂಡ *woḍekanḍa.*

OUGHT.

(Root in ಒಡೆ *woḍe,* and ಕಂಡಿಯದು *kanḍiyaḍu,*

I &c. ought to break ; or it is proper for me to break

ನಾನು ಒಡೆಕಂಡಿಯದು *nánu woḍekanḍiyaḍu,*

The Negative is formed by ಕಂಡಿಯದಲ್ಲ *kanḍiyadalla.*

Compound Tense.

CAN.	CANNOT.
(Infinitive in ಪಕು *paku,* and ಅರಿಯು *ariyu.*)	(Infinitive in ಪಕು *paku,* and ಅರಿಯ *ariya.*)
I &c. can break or I know to break.	I &c. cannot or know not to break.
ಒಡೆಪಕು ಅರಿಯು *wodepaku-ariyu,*	ಒಡೆಪಕು ಅರಿಯ *wodepaku-ariya.*

SUBJUNCTIVE MOOD.

AORIST TENSE IMPERSONAL.

(Past rel. part. ಒಡೆತು *woḍetu,* and the affixes ತೆಂಗಿ *tengi,* and ತೆಂಗೂ *tengú.*)

ಒಡೆತು ತೆಂಗಿ *woḍetutengi,* If I &c. break, shall or should break.

ಒಡೆತು ತೆಂಗೂ *woḍetutengú,* Although I break &c.

PRESENT AND FUTURE TENSE IMPERSONAL.

(Present and fut. rel. part. ಒಡೆಪು *woḍepu,* and ಅನಕೆ *anake,* that, so that.)

ಒಡೆಪು ಅನಕೆ *woḍepu-anake,* that I &c. may break.

NEGATIVE IMPERSONAL.

(Negative rel. part. ಒಡೆಯತು ಅನಕೆ *woḍeyatu-anake,* that, so that.)

ಒಡೆಯತು ಅನಕೆ *woḍeyatu-anake,* That &c. may not break.

In speaking the final ಕೆ *ke,* is often changed to ತೆ *te.*

COMPOUND TENSE.

Formed by adding the Subjunctive Aorist Tense of ಇರು *iru,* to the present, past, and negative gerunds of the principal verb.

PRESENT TENSE IMPERSONAL.

(Present gerund ಒಡೆತಂಡು *woḍetanḍu,* and ಉಂಡೆಂಗಿ *unḍengi.*)

ಒಡೆತಂಡು ಉಂಡೆಂಗಿ *woḍetanḍu-unḍengi,*
ಒಡೆತಂಡುಂಡೆಂಗಿ *woḍetanḍu-ḍunḍengi,* } If I &c. am breaking.

PERFECT TENSE IMPERSONAL.

(Present gerund ಒಡೆತಿತು *woḍetitu,* and ಉಂಡೆಂಗಿ *unḍengi.*)

ಒಡೆತಿತು ಉಂಡೆಂಗಿ *woḍetitu-unḍengi,*
ಒಡೆತಿತ್ತುಂಡೆಂಗಿ *woḍetittunḍengi,* } If I &c. have or had broken.

NEGATIVE IMPERSONAL.

(Negative gerund ಒಡೆಯುತೆ *wodeyate,* and ಉಂಡೆಂಗಿ *undengi.*)

ಒಡೆಯುತೆ ಉಂಡೆಂಗಿ *woḍeyote-unḍengi,* ಒಡೆಯುತುಂಡೆಂಗಿ *woḍeyatunḍengi,*	If I &c. break not, broke not, or shall not break.

3rd CONJUGATION or a verb ending in ಅ *a.*

Root ನಡ *naḍa,* walk.

GERUNDS, OR VERBAL PARTICIPLES.

		The Root and
Present.	ನಡಂದಂಡು *naḍandanḍu,*	ಅಂದಂಡು *andanḍu.*
Past	ನಡಂದಿತು *naḍanditu,*	ಅಂದಿತು *anditu.*
Negative.	ನಡಯುತೆ *naḍayate,*	ಯತ್ತೆ *yatte.*

RELATIVE PARTICIPLE.

		The Root and
Present & Future.	ನಡಪು *naḍapu,*	ಪು *pu.*
Past.	ನಡಂದು *naḍandu,*	ಅಂದು *andu.*
Negative.	ನಡಯುತು *naḍayatu,*	ಯುತ್ತು *yattu.*

COMPOUND RELATIVE PARTICIPLE.

			Present Gerund and
Present.	ನಡಂದಂಡು ಉಳ್ಳು	*naḍandanḍu-uḷḷu,*	ಉಳ್ಳು *uḷḷu.*
Future.	,, ಇಪ್ಪು	,,	ಇಪ್ಪು *ippu.*
Past.	ನಡಂದಂಡು ಇಂಜು	,,	ಇಂಜು *inju.*
			Past Gerund and
Perfect.	ನಡಂದಿತು ಉಳ್ಳು	*naḍanditu-uḷḷu,*	ಉಳ್ಳು *uḷḷu.*
Fut. perf.	,, ಇಪ್ಪು	,,	ಇಪ್ಪು *ippu.*
Pluperfect.	ನಡಂದಿತು ಇಂಜು	,,	ಇಂಜು *inju.*

INFINITIVE MOOD.

	The Root and
ನಡಪಕು *naḍapaku,*	ಪಕು *paku.*

IMPERATIVE MOOD.

(Root and personal affixes.)

Let me &c. walk.

Affirmative Mood.

	SINGULAR.	PLURAL.
1st person.	ನಡಕಡು *naḍakaḍu,*	ನಡಕಡು *naḍakaḍu.*
2nd ,,	ನಡ *naḍa,*	ನಡಯಿರಿ *naḍairi.*
3rd Mas. 3rd Fem. 3rd Neu.	ನಡಕಡು *naḍakaḍu,*	ನಡಕಡು *naḍakaḍu.*

In the 2nd person plural the ಇ *i* is omitted and ಡ is changed into ಡೆ *ḍe.*

NEGATIVE MOOD.

(Root and personal affixes.)

I &c. walk not, will not walk.

ನಡಪುಲೆ *naḍapule.*

or ನಡಪಿಲೆ *naḍapile.*

The letter ಕ *k,* is evidently introduced in the penultimates of the 1st and 3rd persons of the singular and plural of the Imperative mood for the sake of euphony, the ultimate ಡು *du,* being the same in all four conjugations.

AFFIRMATIVE MOOD.

PRESENT TENSE. I &c. walk.

(Present rel. part. ನಡಪು *naḍapu,* and personal affixes.)

1st person.	ನಡಪುಳೆ *naḍapuḷe,* or ನಡಪೆ *naḍape,*	ನಡಪಳ *naḍapaḷa.*
2nd ,,	ನಡಪಯು *naḍapaya,*	ನಡಪರ *naḍapara.*
3rd Mas. 3rd Fem. 3rd Neu.	ನಡಪಳ *naḍapaḷa,*	ನಡಪಳ *naḍapaḷa.*

PAST TENSE. I &c. walked.

(Past rel. part. ನಡಂದು *naḍandu,* and personal affixes)

	SINGULAR.	PLURAL.
1st per.	ನಡಂಡೆ *naḍunde,* or ನಡಂದು *naḍandu,*	ನಡಂದತು *naḍandatu.*
2nd.	ನಡಂದಿಯು *naḍandiya,*	ನಡಂದಿರ *naḍandira.*
3rd Mas. 3rd Fem. 3rd Neut.	ನಡಂದತು *naḍandatu,*	ನಡಂದತು *naḍandatu.*

1st Future Tense. I shall or will, walk.

(Future rel. part. ನಡಪು *naḍapu,* and personal affixes.)

1st. per.	ನಡಪು *naḍapu,*	ನಡಕ್ಕು *naḍakku.*
2nd. ,,	ನಡಪಿಯ *naḍapiya,*	ನಡಪಿರ *naḍapira.*
3rd Mas. / 3rd Fem. / 3rd Neut.	ನಡಕ್ಕು *naḍakku,*	ನಡಕ್ಕು *naḍakku.*

The 1st person singular of the present tense is also used for the 1st person singular of this tense.

COMPOUND TENSES.

There are six Compound Tenses in the Affirmative Mood.

Present Tense. I am walking &c.

(Present gerund ನಡಂದಂಡು *naḍandanḍu* and the present Tense of ಇರು *iru.*)

ನಡಂದಂಡು ಉಳ್ಳಿಯು *naḍandanḍu-uḷḷiyu,* ನಡಂದಂಡು ಉಂಡು *naḍandanḍu-unḍu.*
ನಡಂದಂಡುಳ್ಳಿಯು *naḍandanḍuḷḷiyu,* ನಡಂದಂಡುಂಡು *naḍandanḍunḍu.*

Past Tense. I was walking &c.

(Present gerund ನಡಂದಂಡು *naḍandanḍu,* and the past Tense of ಇರು *iru.*)

Singular.	Plural.
ನಡಂದಂಡು ಇಂಜು *naḍandanḍu-inju,*	ನಡಂದಂಡು ಇಂಜತು ,, *injatu.*
ನಡಂದಂಡಿಂಜು *naḍandanḍinju,*	ನಡಂದಂಡಿಂಜತು *naḍandanḍinjatu.*

Future Tense. I shall or will be walking &c.

(Present gerund ನಡಂದಂಡು *naḍandanḍu,* and the future Tense of ಇರು *iru.*)

ನಡಂದಂಡು ಇಪ್ಪು *naḍandanḍu-ippu,* ನಡಂದಂಡು ಇಕ್ಕೂ ,, *ikkú.*
ನಡಂದಂಡಿಪ್ಪು *naḍandanḍippu,* ನಡಂದಂಡಿಕ್ಕೂ *naḍandanḍikkú.*

Perfect Tense. I have walked &c.

(Past gerund ನಡಂದಿತು *naḍanditu,* and present tense ಇರು *iru.*)

ನಡಂದಿತ್ತು ಉಳ್ಳಿಯು *naḍandittu-uḷḷiyu,* ನಡಂದಿತು ಉಂಡು ,, *unḍu.*
ನಡಂದಿತ್ತುಳ್ಳಿಯು *naḍandittuḷḷiyu,* ನಡಂದಿತ್ತುಂಡು *naḍandittunḍu.*

Pluperfect Tense. I had walked &c.

(Past gerund ನಡಂದಿತು *naḍanditu,* and past tense of ಇರು *iru.*)

Potential Mood.

ನಡಂದಿತು ಇಂಜು *naḍanditu-inju*, ನಡಂದಿತು ಇಂಜತು ,, *injatu.*
ನಡಂದಿತ್ತಿಂಜು *naḍandittinju*, ನಡಂದಿತ್ತಿಂಜತು *naḍandittinjatu.*

FUTURE PERFECT TENSE. I shall or will or would have walked &c.
(Present gerund ನಡಂದಿತು *naḍanditu*, and future tense of ಇರು *iru.*)

ನಡಂದಿತು ಇಪ್ಪು *naḍanditu-ippu*, ನಡಂದಿತು ಇಕ್ಕು *naḍanditu-ikku.*
ನಡಂದಿತ್ತಿಪ್ಪು *naḍandittippu*, ನಡಂದಿತ್ತಿಕ್ಕೂ *naḍandittikkú.*

POTENTIAL MOOD.

The tenses of this mood, as also of the Subjunctive mood, are conjugated in the same manner as those of the 2nd Conjugation.

4th CONJUGATION or verbs ending in ಇ *i*,

(Root ಪೊಯಿ *poi*, Beat.)

GERUNDS OR VERBAL PARTICIPLES.

		The Root and
Present.	ಪೊಜ್ಜಂಡು *pojjanḍu*,	ಜ್ಜಂಡು *jjanḍu.*
Past.	ಪೊಜ್ಜಿತು *pojjitu*,	ಜ್ಜಿತು *jjitu.*
Negative.	ಪೊಯತು or ಪೊಯ್ಯತು *poyatu*, or *poyiyatu*,	ಯತು *yatu.*

In forming the gerunds the final vowel of the root, being followed by another vowel, is converted into ಜ *ja*, for euphony's sake.

RELATIVE PARTICIPLE.

		The Root and
Present & Future.	ಪೊಯಿವು *poivu*,	ವು *wu.*
Past.	ಪೊಜ್ಜು *pojju*,	ಜ್ಜು *jju*,
Negative.	ಪೊಯಿಯತು or ಪೊಯ್ಯತು *poiyatu*, or *poyyatu*,	ಯತ್ತು *yattu.*

In the past participle the final vowel of the root is also left out for euphony's sake.

COMPOUND RELATIVE PARTICIPLES.

		Present Gerund and
Present.	ಪೊಜ್ಜಂಡು ಉಳ್ಳು *pojjanḍu-uḷḷu*,	ಉಳ್ಳು *uḷḷu.*
Future.	ಪೊಜ್ಜಂಡು ಇಪ್ಪು ,, *ippu*,	ಇಪು *ipu.*
Past.	ಪೊಜ್ಜಂಡು ಇಂಜು ,, *inju*,	ಇಂಜು *inju.*

			Past Gerund and
Perfect.	ಪೊಜ್ಜಿತು ಉಳ್ಳು	*pojjitu-uḷu,*	ಉಳ್ಳು *uḷḷu*
Future.	ಪೊಜ್ಜಿತು ಇಪ್ಪು	*pojitu-ippu.*	ಇಪ್ಪು *ipu.*
Pluferfect.	ಪೊಜ್ಜಿತು ಇಂಜು	,, *inju.*	ಇಂಜು *inju.*

The omission of the final vowel of the root in these participles will also be noticed.

INFINITIVE MOOD.

ಪೊಯಿವಕು *poiwaku.* — The Root and ವಕು *waku.*

IMPERATIVE MOOD.

(Root and personal affixes.)

Let me beat &c.

	SINGULAR.	PLURAL.
1st person.	ಪೊಯಿ ಅಡು *poi-aḍu,*	ಪೊಯಿ ಅಡು *poi-aḍu.*
2nd ,,	ಪೊಯಿ *poi,*	ಪೊಯಿರಿ *poiri.*
3rd Mas. / 3rd Fem. / 3rd Neu.	ಪೊಯಿ ಅಡು *poi-aḍu,*	ಪೊಯಿ ಅಡು *poi-aḍu.*

NEGATIVE MOOD.

(Root and personal affixes.)

I &c. beat not, will, not beat.

ಪೊಯಿ ಉಲೆ or *poiy-ule,* or

ಪೊಯ್ಯುಲೆ *poyyule.*

AFFIRMATIVE MOOD.

PRESENT TENSE. I beat.

(Present rel. part. ಪೊಯಿವು *poiwu,* and personal affixes.)

	SINGULAR.	PLURAL.
1st per.	ಪೊಯಿವಳೆ *poiwaḷe,*	ಪೊಯಿವಳ *poivaḷa.*
	or ಪೊಯಿವಿ *poivi,*	
2nd.	ಪೊಯಿವಿಯ *poiviya,*	ಪೊಯಿವಿರ *poivira.*

Affirmative Mood.

	Singular	Plural
3rd Mas. 3rd Fem. 3rd Neut.	ಪೊಂಯಿವಳ *poivaḷa,*	ಪೊಂಯಿವಳ *poivaḷa.*

The final vowel (ಯು) of the root in this tense is often turned into double ಯ್ಯು *yyu.*

PAST TENSE. I &c. beat.

(Past rel. part. ಪೊಜ್ಜು *pojju,* and personal affixes.)

	SINGULAR.	PLURAL.
1st per.	ಪೊಜ್ಜೆ *pojje,*	ಪೊಜ್ಜತು *pojjatu.*
2nd.	ಪೊಜ್ಜಿಯ *pojjiya,*	ಪೊಜ್ಜಿರ *pojjira.*
3rd Mas. 3rd Fem. 3rd Neut.	ಪೊಜ್ಜತು *pojjatu,*	ಪೊಜ್ಜತು *pojjatu.*

1st FUTURE TENSE. I shall or will beat &c.

(Future rel. part. ಪೊಂಯಿವು *poiwu,* and personal affixes.)

1st per.	ಪೊಂಯಿ ಉ *poiwu,*	ಪೊಂಯಿ ಉ or *poiyu.* ಪೊಂಯ್ಯು *poyyu.*
2nd.	ಪೊಂಯಿವಿಯ *poiviya,*	ಪೊಂಯಿವಿರ *poivira.*
3rd Mas. 3rd Fem. 3rd Nent.	ಪೊಂಯಿವು *poiwu,* or ಪೊಯ್ಯು *poyyu,*	ಪೊಂಯಿ ಉ *poiwu.* ,, *poyyu.*

In the 1st person singular of all such tenses ಎ *e* is equally used, at the option of the speaker, with the silent *u* in the ultimate vowel or syllable.

The different tenses of the potential and subjunctive **Moods** are conjugated in the same manner as those of the 1st Conjugation.

It will have been noticed that the 1st person plural and 3rd person singular and plural in all the tenses are of the same form and termination.

In the present and perfect tenses of all the conjugations, the ultimate ಳೆ *ḷe* may be changed to ಳಿ *ḷi,* and ಯು *yu,* added.

In the past negative gerunds and Relative participles, and in all tenses, in which such gerunds and participles form component parts, the ultimate ತ *t* may be doubled.

Similarly the ultimate ಕ *k* of the Infinitive mood of all the conjugations may be doubled.

In the 1st person plural and 3rd person singular and plural of the several future tenses, the ultimate vowel ಉ *u* may be either long or short, and the ultimate vowel of the 2nd person, singular is also often lengthened.

The Coorgs, in speaking, often change the ultimate vowel, silent *u* of the root in verbs of the 1st conjugation into ಇ *i*; and the ultimate vowel ಎ *e* of the roots of verbs of the 2nd conjugation in to ಅ *a*.

In the Imperative mood of the 3rd Conjugation the consonant ರ would seen to have been introduced between the root and affixes for the sake of euphony; the affixes being the same in all four Conjugations.

CAUSAL VERBS.

Causal verbs are generally formed by the additions of ಚಿರು *chiru,* to the root of any verb ; as ಮಾಡು *máḍu,* to do ; ಮಾಡು ಚಿರು *máḍu-chiru,* to cause to do; but in very many verbs ಪಿ *pi* is inserted between the root and the affix, as

ಕೊಡು *koḍu,*	to give	ಕೊಡುಪಿಚಿರು *koḍupichiru,*	to cause to give
ಯೆಳ್ಳೆ *yeḷe,*	,, sit	ಯೆಳ್ಳೆಪಿ ಚಿರು	to cause to sit.
ನಡ *naḍa,*	,, walk	ನಡಪಿಚಿರು	,, ,, ,, walk.
ಕುದಿ *kuḍi,*	,, drink	ಕುದಿಪಿಚಿರು	,, ,, ,, drink.
ಒಡೆ *woḍe,*	,, beak	ಒಡೆಪಿಚಿರು	,, ,, ,, break.
ಪೋಉ *póu,*	,, to go	ಪೋಪಿ ಚಿರು	,, ,, ,, go.

But for this there would appear to be no fixed rule, and it could only be learnt by practice.

Root ಮಾಡು ಚಿರು *máḍuchiru.*

GERUNDS.

Present.	ಮಾಡು ಚೆಂಡು	*máḍuchenḍu.*
Past.	ಮಾಡುಚಿತು	*máḍuchitu.*
Negative.	ಮಾಡು ಚಿರತೆ	*máḍuchirate.*

These gerunds are compounded in the same manner as those of the Active verbs, the ultimate ರ *r* of the root being omitted in the present and past gerunds.

Infinitive Mood.

RELATIVE PARTICIPLES.

Present & Future.	ಮಾಡು ಚಿರುವು *máḍuchiruvu.*	Compounded in the same manner as those of Active verbs, except that in the past ಟ *ṭ* is used instead of ತ *t.*
Past	ಮಾಡು ಚಿಟ್ಟು *máḍuchiṭṭu.*	
Negative.	ಮಾಡು ಚಿರತು *máḍuchiratu* or ಮಾಡು ಚೆತ್ತು *máḍuchettu.*	

COMPOUND RELATIVE PARTICIPLES.

			Present gerund and
Present.	ಮಾಡುಚೆಂಡು ಉಳ್ಳು	*máḍuchenḍu-uḷḷu,*	ಉಳ್ಳು *uḷḷu.*
Future.	ಮಾಡುಚೆಂಡು ಇಪ್ಪು	,,	ಇಪ್ಪು *ippu.*
			The past gerund and
Perfect.	ಮಾಡುಚಿತು ಉಳ್ಳು	*máḍuchitu-uḷḷu,*	ಉಳ್ಳು *uḷḷu.*
Fut. perf.	ಮಾಡುಚಿತು ಇಪ್ಪು	,,	ಇಪ್ಪು *ippu.*
Pluperfect.	ಮಾಡುಚಿತು ಇಂಜು	,,	ಇಂಜು *inju.*

INFINITIVE MOOD.

ಮಾಡುಚಿರುವಕು *máḍuchiruwaku,* — The root and ವಕು *waku.*

IMPERATIVE MOOD.

Let me &c. cause to do.

(Root and personal affixes.)

	SINGULAR.	PLURAL.
1st person.	ಮಾಡುಚಿರುಡು *máḍuchiruḍu,*	ಮಾಡಿಚಿರಡು *máḍichiraḍu.*
2nd ,,	ಮಾಡುಚಿರು *máḍuchiru,*	ಮಾಡುಚಿರಿ *máḍuchiri.*
3rd Mas. 3rd Fem. 3rd Neu.	ಮಾಡುಚಿರುಡು *máḍuchiruḍu,*	ಮಾಡಿಚಿರಡು *máḍichiraḍu.*

In the 1st person plural and 3rd persons singular and plural the penultimate may be either ರ *r,* or ರು *ru.* The second syllable ಡು *ḍu,* may be changed into ಡಿ *ḍi,* throughout the conjugation.

NEGATIVE MOOD.

I, &c. do not or will not, cause to do.

(Root and personal affixes.)

ಮಾಡುಚಿರು ಉಲೆ *máḍuchiru-ule,* or ಮಾಡುಚಿರುವುಲೆ *máḍuchiruvule.*

AFFIRMATIVE MOOD.

PRESENT TENSE. I &c. Cause to do.

(Present rel. part. ಮಾಡುಚಿರುವು *máḍuchiruvu*, and personal affixes.)

SINGULAR.	PLURAL.
ಮಾಡುಚಿರುವಿ *máḍuchiruvi*, or	ಮಾಡುಚಿರುವಳ *máḍuchiruvaḷa*.
ಮಾಡುಚಿರುವಳೆ *máḍuchiruvaḷe*,	

PAST TENSE. I &c. caused to do.

(Past rel. part. ಮಾಡುಚಿಟ್ಟು *máḍuchiṭṭu*, and personal affixes.)

SINGULAR.	PLURAL.
ಮಾಡುಚಿಟ್ಟೆ *máḍuchiṭṭe*,	ಮಾಡುಚಿಟ್ಟತು *máḍuchiṭṭatu*.

1ST FUTURE TENSE. I, &c. shall or will cause to do.

(Future relative part. ಮಾಡುಚಿರುವು *máḍuchiruvu*, and personal affixes.)

SINGULAR.	PLURAL.
ಮಾಡುಚಿರುವು *máḍuchiruvu*, or	ಮಾಡುಚಿರು *máḍuchiru*.
ಮಾಡುಚಿರುವೆ *máḍuchiruve*,	

The compound tense of this mood as also those of the potential and subjunctive moods, are formed in the same manner as those of the regular verbs of the 1st conjugation.

The Coorgs, when speaking, often convert the ultimate ರು *ru*, of the root into ಡು *ḍu*, in causal verbs; and also double the penultimate ಚಿ *chi*, of the root.

PASSIVE VERBS.

There is no form of the passive verb in the Coorg dialect, the active form being invariably used.

IRREGULAR VERBS.

There are a few verbs, which are irregular in the formation of their present and past gerunds, and also of their present and past tenses. The irregularity in the gerunds would appear to consist in the insertion of certain consonants between the root of the verb and the affixes of the gerunds, or in the changing of the ultimate consonants of the roots into other consonants, apparently for the sake of euphony.

These remarks are also applicable to the irregular formation of the present and past tenses ; as for example the present and past tenses of the verb ನಿಲ್ಲು *nillu,* to stop, ought to be, according to the regular formation of such tenses of the first conjugation, ನಿಲ್ಲುವಳೆ *nilluvaḷe,* and ನಿಲ್ಲುನೆ *nillune,* respectively ; instead of which these verbs forms ನಿಪ್ಪಳೆ *nippaḷe,* for it's 1st person singular in the present tense, and ನಿಂಡೆ *nin-de,* for it's past tense.

LIST OF IRREGULAR VERBS.

Root.	Present Gerund.	Past Gerund.	Present Tense.	Past Tense.
			1st person singular.	1st person sing.
ನಿಲ್ಲು *nillu*, to stop.	ನಿಂದಂಡು *nindaṇḍu*,	ನಿಂದಿತು *ninditu*,	ನಿಪ್ಪಳೆ *nippaḷe* or ನಿಪ್ಪಿ *nippi*	ನಿಂದೆ *ninde* or ನಿಂದಿಯು *nindiyu*.
ಪೊಲ್ಲು *pollu*, to stitch.	ಪೊಂದಂಡು *pondaṇḍu*,	ಪೊಂದಿತು *ponditu*,	ಪೊಲ್ಲುವಳೆ *polluwaḷe*,	ಪೊಂದೆ *ponde*.
ಕೇಳು *kéḷu*, „ ask.	ಕೇಟ್ಟಂಡು *kéṭṭaṇḍu*,	ಕೇಟ್ಟಿತು *kéṭṭitu*,	ಕೇಪಳೆ *képaḷe*,	ಕೇಟ್ಟೆ *kéṭṭe*.
ಊಳು *úḷu*, „ plough.	ಉತ್ತಂಡು *uttaṇḍu*,	ಉತ್ತಿತು *uttitu*,	ಉಪ್ಪಳೆ *uppaḷe*,	ಉತ್ತೆ *utte*.
ಇರು *iru*, „ be.	ಇಂಜಂಡು *injaṇḍu*,	ಇಂಜಿತು *injitu*,	ಉಳ್ಳೆ *ulḷé* or ಇಪ್ಪಳೆ *ippa-*[*ḷe*,	ಇಂಜೆ *inje*.
ಇಡು *iḍu*, „ put.	ಇಟ್ಟಂಡು *iṭṭaṇḍu*,	ಇಟ್ಟಿತು *iṭṭitu*,	ಇಡುವಳೆ *iḍuvaḷe*,	ಇಟ್ಟೆ *iṭṭe*.
ಕೊಲ್ಲು *kollu*, „ kill.	ಕೊಂದಂಡು *kondaṇḍu*,	ಕೊಂದಿತು *konditu*,	ಕೊಲ್ಲುವಳೆ *kolluvaḷe*,	ಕೊಂದೆ *konde*.
ಚುಡು *chuḍu*, „ burn.	ಚುಟ್ಟಂಡು *chuṭṭaṇḍu*,	ಚುಟ್ಟಿತು *chuṭṭitu*,	ಚುಡುವಳೆ *chuḍuvaḷe*,	ಚುಟ್ಟೆ *chuṭṭe*.
ಕಾಯು *káyu*, „ wait, guard.	ಕಾತಂಡು *kátaṇḍu*,	ಕಾತಿತು *kátitu*,	ಕಾಪಳೆ *kápaḷe*,	ಕಾತೆ *káte*.
ನಡು *naḍu*, „ plant.	ನಟ್ಟಂಡು *naṭṭaṇḍu*,	ನಟ್ಟಿತು *naṭṭitu*,	ನಡುಪಳೆ *naḍupaḷe*,	ನಟ್ಟೆ *naṭṭe*.
ಬುಡು *buḍu*, „ let go, leave alone.	ಬುಟ್ಟಂಡು *buṭṭaṇḍu*,	ಬುಟ್ಟಿತು *buṭṭitu*,	ಬುಡುವಳೆ *buḍuvaḷe*,	ಬುಟ್ಟೆ *buṭṭe*.
ಕಾಣು *káṇu*, „ appear.	ಕಂಡಂಡು *kaṇḍaṇḍu*,	ಕಂಡಿತು *kaṇḍitu*,	ಕಾಂಬಳೆ *kámbaḷe*,	ಕಂಡೆ *kaṇḍe*.
ಚಾಳು *cháḷu*, „ die.	ಚತ್ತಂಡು *chattaṇḍu*,	ಚತ್ತಿತು *chattitu*,	ಚಾವಳೆ *cháveḷe*,	ಚತ್ತೆ *chatte*.
ಪೊರಡು *poraḍu*, make.	ಪೊರಟ್ಟಂಡು *poraṭṭaṇḍu*	ಪೊರಟ್ಟಿತು *poraṭṭitu*,	ಪೊರಡುವಳೆ *poraḍuwaḷe*,	ಪೊರಟೆ *poraṭe*.
ಯೇಳು *yéḷu*, „ get up.	ಯೆದ್ದಂಡು *yeddaṇḍu*,	ಯೆದ್ದಿತು *yedditu*,	ಯೇವಳೆ *yévaḷe*,	ಯೆದ್ದೆ *yedde*.
ಉಂಣು *uṇu*, „ to eat.	ಉಂಡಂಡು *uṇḍaṇḍu*,	ಉಂಡಿತು *uṇḍitu*,	ಉಂಬಳೆ *umbaḷe*,	ಉಂಡೆ *uṇḍe*.

The pronounciation of the verb ಕೇಳ್ಳು must be noted, the long *e* in this word is pronounced between the sound of the silent *u* and that given by the French to the vowels *eu*.

ADVERBS.

Adverbs are generally formed by the addition ಆಯಿತು *áyitu*, to noun and adjectives ; as,

ಚಾಯಿ *chái*, beauty.	ಚಾಯಿ ಆಯಿತು *chaiáyitu*, beautiful.
ಗುಟ್ಟು *guṭṭu*, secret.	ಗುಟ್ಟಾಯಿತು *guṭṭáitu*, secretly.
ನೇರೆ *nére*, straight.	ನೇರೆ ಆಯಿತು *néreáitu*, straightly.
ಉದ್ದ *udda*, long.	ಉದ್ದಆಯಿತು *uddaáitu*, longly.
ಬಲ *bala*, strong.	ಬಲವಾಯಿತು *balaváitu*, strongly.

Some adverbs are declined like nouns in the singular number ; as,

ಅಕ್ಕ *akka*, then, that time.

No.	ಅಕ್ಕ *akka*, or ಅಕ್ಕಲೆ *akkale.*
Ac.	ಅಕ್ಕಲೆತಾನ *akkletána.*
In.	ಅಕ್ಕಲೆತಾನಗೊಂಡು ,, *gonḍu.*
Da.	ಅಕ್ಕಲೆಕು *akkaleku*, or ಅಕ್ಕತಾಂಗು *akkatángu.*
Ab.	ಅಕ್ಕಲೆತಾನಚೆಲ್ಲಿತು *akkaletána-chellitu.*
Ge.	ಅಕ್ಕಲೆತಾಂಡ *akkaletánḍa.*
Lo.	ಅಕ್ಕಲೆತಾಲು *akkaletálu.*

In like manner are declined ಇಕ್ಕ *ikka*, now, ಯೆಕ್ಕ *yekka*, when, ಯೆಕ್ಕಲು *yekkalu*, every day ಅಂನತು *annatu*, such or that kind ಯೆಂನತು *yennatu*, which ಅಕ್ಕಕ್ಕ *akkakka*, now then or ಅಕ್ಕಕ್ಕಲು *akkakkalu*, ಇಂನತು *innatu*, this kind ಪೊಲಾಕ *poláka*, morning ಪಕ್ಕ *pakka*, near. ಪೊಲಚೆ *polache*, early morning.

ನಿಂನಾಂದು *ninnándu*, yesterday.

No.	ನಿಂನಾಂದು *ninnándu.*
Ac.	ನಿಂನಾಂದುತಾನ ,, *tána*, or ನಿಂನಾಂದುನ *ninnánduna.*
In.	ನಿಂನಾಂದುತೊಟ್ಟು ,, *toṭṭu*, or ನಿಂನಾಂದಿಂಜಿ *ninnándinji.*

Da. ನಿಂನಾಂದೆಕು *ninnándeku.*

Ab. ನಿಂನಾಂದುತಾನ ಚೆಲ್ಲಿತು *ninnándutána-chellitu.*

Ge. ನಿಂನಾಂದುತಾಂಡ *ninnándutánḍa.*

Lo. ನಿಂನಾಂದುಲು *ninnándulu.*

In like manner are declined ಮೊನೆಯಾಂದು *moneyándu,* day before yesterday: ಮತ್ತಿಯಾಂದು *mattiyándu,* day after tomorrow ಪೊಲಂಜತ್ತಿ *polanjatti,* dawn ಮಜ್ಜಣ *majjaṇa,* noon ಬಯಿಟ್ಟು *baiṭṭu,* evening ಅಂದು *andu,* that day ; and ಇಂದು *indu,* this day.

ನಾಳೆ *náḷe,* tomorrow.

No. ನಾಳೆ *náḷe.*

Ac. ನಾಳೆಯತಾನ *náḷeyatána,* or ನಾಳೆತುನ *náḷetuna.*

In. ನಾಳೆಯಿಂಜಿ *náḷeinji,* or ನಾಳೆತ್ತೊಟು *náḷettoṭu.*

Da. ನಾಳೆಕು *náḷeku.*

Ab. ನಾಳೆನ ಚೆಲ್ಲಿತು *náḷena-chellitu.*

Ge. ನಾಳೆರ *náḷera,* or ನಾಳೆಯತಾಂಡ *náḷeyatánḍa.*

Lo. ನಾಳೆಲು *náḷelu,* ನಾಳೆಯ ತಾಲು *náḷeyatálu.*

ಅಲ್ಲಿ *alli,* there.

No. ಅಲ್ಲಿ *alli.*

Ac. ಅಲ್ಲಿಯತಾನ *alliyatána.*

In. ಅಲ್ಲಿಂಜಿ *allinji.*

Da. ಅಲ್ಲಿಕು *alliku.*

Ab. ಅಲ್ಲಿಯತಾನ ಚೆಲ್ಲಿತು *alliyatána-chellitu.*

Ge. ಅಲ್ಲಿಯತಾಂಡ *alliyatánḍa.*

Lo. ಅಲ್ಲಿಯತಾಲು *alliyatálu.*

In like manner are declined ಇಲ್ಲಿ *illi,* here ; ಎಲ್ಲಿ *yelli,* where ; ಪೊರಮೆ *porame,* out ; ನಡುಲು *naḍulu,* middle ; ಕೀದಲು *kídalu,* dim ; ಮೀದಲು *mídalu,* upper ; ಬಯ್ಯ *bayya,* after or behind ಮಿಂಞಾಲು *minnyalu,* before ಎದಿಕೆ *yedike,* opposite.

The following are some of the indeclinable adverbs.

ಅಂನನೆ *annaṇe,* some manner.

ಅಲ್ಲತೆ *allate,* except.

ಅಲ್ಲೆಂಗಿ *allengi,* or, else.

Adverbs.

ಅಕ್ಕಲೆ *akkale,* that Instant.

ಅಕ್ಕಕ್ಕಲು *akkakkalu,* from time to time, gradually.

ಆನಕಲು *ánakalu,* though, notwithstanding.

ಅನಕೆ *anake,* just the same.

ಆಚೆಂಗೂ *áchengú,* however.

ಇಂಜಿ *inji,* than.

ಇಂನನೆ *innane,* In this manner.

ಇಕ್ಕಾಯಿತು *ikkáyitu,* Instantly.

ಎಂದೂ *yendú,* at any time.

ಎಂನನೆ *yennane,* In what manner.

ಎಂತೂ *yentú,* however.

ಎಕ್ಕಲು *yekkalu,* every day.

ಎಕ್ಕಾಲು *yekkálu,* ,,

ಎಕ್ಕೆಕ್ಕಲು *yekkekkalu,* ,,

ಎಕ್ಕಾನಕ *yekkánaka,* at any time.

ಎಕ್ಕಾಚೆಂಗಿ *yekkáchengi,,,* ,, ,,

ಎಕ್ಕಾಚೆಂಗೂ *yekkáchengú,,,* ,,

ಎಂದು *yendu,* so that, and.

ಒಂಮ *womma,* once.

ಅಕ್ಕೆಂನೆ *akkenne,* that very time.

ಪಿಂಞೇ *pinnyé,* afterwards.

ನೇರೆ *nére,* straight.

ನೆಯಿಂಗನೆ *neingane,* smoothly.

ಮಿನುಂಗನೆ *minungane,* ,,

ಮುಂಡತೆ *mundate,* for nothing, in vain.

ಪೆರ್ತ *perta,* many, much.

ಪೆರ್ತಾಯಿತು *pertáitu,* abundantly.

ಬೆರಿಯ *beriya,* quickly.

ಮಿಂಞೇ *minnye,* In front, before.

ಗೊಂಡು *gondu,* by means of, through.

ಮಿಂಞೆ ಆಯಿತು *minnyeáitu,* In front before.

ಮೆಲ್ಲೆ *melle,* slowly, gently.

ಯೆಕ್ಕಾನಕಲು *yekkánakalu,* always, at any time.

ಬೋರೆ ಆಯಿತು *bóreditu,* separately.

ಬೆರಿಯ ಆಯಿತು *beriyaditu,* swiftly.

ಕೂಡ *kúda,* also, together.

ಅಕ್ಕೆಂನೆ *akkenne,* immediately.

ಅಂನನೆ ಆಚೆಂಗೂ *annane-áchengú,* at least, although.

ಅಂನನೆ ಆನಕಲು *annane-ánakalu,* ,, ,,

ಇಂನನೆ *innane,* In this manner.

ಯೆಂನನೆ *yennane,,* what ,, have.

ಯೆಂನನೆಯು *yennaneyu,* by any means.

ಯೆಂನನೆ ಆಚೆಂಗೂ *yennane-áchengú,* ,,

POSTPOSITIONS.

The following postpositions govern the accusative and genitive cases of nouns and pronouns.

ಕೂಡೆ *kúḍe,* with, along with.

ಕೀದಲು *kídalu,* down.

ಪೆಂಣ್ಯೆ *peṇnyé,* after.

ಮಿಂಣ್ಯೆ *minṇyé,* before, front.

ಬಯ್ಯ *bayya,* after, behind.

ಯೆತ್ತನಕೆ *yettanake,* until, till.

ಚೆಲ್ಲಿತು *chellitu,* on account of.

ಅಲ್ಲತ್ತೆ *allatte,* besides.

ಅಳತೆಕು *aḷateku,* as far as.

ಮೇಲೆ *méle,* above, upon.

ಮೇಕೆ *méke,* ,, ,,

ಬೊಂಡಿತು *bonḍitu,* for, on account of.

The following govern the dative case.

ಅಂಗಾಯಿತು *angáitu,* for.

ಬಯ್ಯ *bayya,* after, behind.

ಮಿಂಣ್ಯೆ *minṇyé,* before, front.

ಮೇಕೆ *méke,* above, upon.

ಅಲ್ಲತೆ *allate,* besides.

ಬೊಂಡಿತು *bonḍitu,* for, on account of.

ಚೆಲ್ಲಿತು *chellitu,* ,, ,, ,, ,,

CONJUNCTIONS.

ಆಚೆಂಗಿ *áchengi,* or, even, any.

ಆನಕ್ಕ *ánakka,* but.
ಆಡು *áḍu,* be it so.
ಆನಗೊಂಡು *ánagonḍu,* on account of that.
ಅದನಗೊಂಡು *adana-gonḍu,* ,, ,,
ಇಂನ್ಯೂ *innyú,* yet, still.
ಅಲ್ಲತೆ *allate,* besides.
ಊ *óó,* and, also, even.
ಯೆಂನೊ *yenno,* whether it is or not.
ಕೂಡ *kúḍa,* also
ಊ ಇಲ್ಲೆ *ú-ille.* neither, nor.
ಊ ಅಲ್ಲ *ú-alla,*

INTERJECTIONS.

ಅಯ್ಯೋ *ayyó,* ಅಹಾ *ahhá,* ಅಯ್ಯಯ್ಯೋ *ayayayyó,* ಉಯಿ *wui,* ಉಯ್ಯೊ *wuyyó,*	Oh ! expressive of sorrow and pain.
ಅಃ *aha,* ಆಂ *án,* ಅಹ *ahha,*	Expressiveof surprise, pleasure admiration, and reproach.
ಒಹೊ *wohhó,*	O ! oh !
ಛೇ *chhé,* ಛೀ *chhí,*	expressive of. disgust.

PARTICLES.

There are only two particles, ಯೇ *yé,* which denotes doubt and is negative, and ಉಂ *um,* which denotes the affirmative.

The Rules of syntax are identical with those of the Canarese language.

VOCABULARY.

A.	ಕನ್ನಡ ಭಾಷೆ.	ಕೊಡಗು ಭಾಷೆ.
Rice, food,	ಅನ್ನ *an-na,*	ಕೂಳು *kúḷu.*
A Shop,	ಅಂಗಡಿ *angaḍi,*	ಅಂಗಡಿ *angaḍi.*
An Elder brother,	ಅಂಣ *aṇ-ṇa,*	ಅಣ್ಣು *aṇṇu.*
The Post,	ಅಂಚೆ *anche,*	ಅಂಚೆ *anche.*
An Estimate,	ಅಂದಾಜು *andáju,*	ಅಂದಾಜು *audáju.*
Breadth,	ಅಗಲ *agala,*	ಅಗಲ *agala.*
A Washerman,	ಅಗಸ *agasa,*	ಮಡಿಯಳು *maḍiyaḷu.*
A Petition,	ಅರ್ಜಿ *arji,*	ಅರ್ಜಿ *arji.*
To Examine,	ಅಜಮಾಯಿಸು *ajamáyisu,*	ನೋಟು, ತುಡುಕು *nóṭu, tuḍuku.*
To Drive,	ಅಟ್ಟು *aṭṭu,*	ವೋಡಿಚಿರು, ದವುತು *wóḍichiru, davutu.*
A river dam,	ಅಣ್ಣೆ *aṇṇe,*	ಕಟ್ಟೆ *katte.*
Half a fanam,	ಅಡ್ಡ *aḍḍa,*	ಅರೆಪಣ *are-paṇa.*
An alarm,	ಅಡಾವುಡಿ *aḍávuḍi,*	ಅಡಾವುಡಿ *aḍúvuḍi.*
Hinderance,	ಅಡ್ಡಿ *aḍḍi,*	ತಡೆ *taḍe.*
A foot,	ಅಡಿ *aḍi,*	ಅಡಿ ಯಾ ಮೊಟ್ಟು *aḍi* or *moṭṭu.*
Arecanut,	ಅಡಿಕೆ *aḍike,*	ಅಡೆಕೆ *aḍeke.*
Cooking,	ಅಡಿಗೆ *aḍige,*	ಮನೆಪಣಿ *manepaṇi.*
A Country fig,	ಅತ್ತಿ *atti,*	ಅತ್ತಿಪಂಣು *atti-paṇṇu.*
A Civil Court,	ಅದಾಲತು *adálatu,*	ಅದಾಲತು *adálatu.*
Hatred,	ಅದಾವತು *adávatu,*	ಪಗೆ *page.*
Half,	ಅರ್ಧ *ardha,*	ಪಾದಿ *pádi.*
To Enjoy,	ಅನುಭವಿಸು *anubhavisu,*	ಸುಖಪಡು *sukha-paḍu.*
Suspicion,	ಅನುಮಾನ *anumána,*	ಅನುಮಾನ *anumána.*
To Say,	ಅನ್ನು *an-nu,*	ಯೆಂಣು, ಪರೆ *yeṇṇu, pare.*
Several, Many,	ಅನೇಕ *anéka,*	ಪೆರ್ತ *perta.*
Rarity,	ಅಪರೂಪ *aparúpa,*	ಅಪರೂಪ *aparúpa.*
An Order,	ಅಪ್ಪಣೆ *appaṇe,*	ಅಪ್ಪಣೆ *appaṇe.*

Vocabulary.

	ಕನ್ನಡ ಭಾಷೆ.	ಕೊಡಗು ಭಾಷೆ.
Irregularity,	ಅಬಂದರೆ *abandare,*	ಬರಾಬರಿ ಇಲ್ಲತು *barábai-* [*illatu.*
Tax on productive trees,	ಅಮರಾಯಿ *amaráyi,*	
District Revenue officer,	ಅಮಲ್ದಾರ *amaldára,*	ಸುಬೇದಾರು *subédáru*
On the part of Government,	ಅಮಾನಿ *amáni,*	ಅಮಾನಿ *amáni.*
Sir,	ಅಯ್ಯಾ *ayyá,*	ಅಯ್ಯಾ *ayyá.*
King,	ಅರಸು *arasu,*	ಧೊರೆ, ವಡೆಯು *dhore, wo-* [*ḍeyu.*
Half,	ಅರೆವಾಸಿ *arevási,*	ಪಾದಿ *pádi.*
Know,	ಅರಿಯು *ariyu,*	ಅರಿ *ari.*
First,	ಅವ್ವಲು *aw-valu,*	ಒಂದನೆ *ondane.*
Measurement,	ಅಳತೆ *aḷate,*	ಅಳತೆ *aḷate.*
Everlasting,	ಅಕ್ಷಯ *akṣhaya,*	ಎಕ್ಕಾಲು ಇಪ್ಪದು ಬಾವದು *yekkálu-ippadu, bávadu.*
Squirrel,	ಅಳಲು *aḷalu,*	ಕೊರಿಯು *koriyu.*
Thin Cake,	ಅಪ್ಪಳ *ap-paḷa,*	ಪಪ್ಪಡ *pappaḍa.*
Beat, To slap,	ಅಪ್ಪಳಿಸು *appaḷisu,*	ಜೆಪ್ಪು, ಎರಿ *jeppu, eri.*
Infamy,	ಅಪಖ್ಯಾತಿ *apakhyáti,*	ಅಪಕೀರ್ತಿ *apakírthi.*
Adoration,	ಅಲಂಕಾರ *alankára,*	ಚಾಯಿ *chái.*
Solicitation,	ಅರಿಕೆ *arike,*	ಅರಿಕೆ, ಎಂಣುಯೊ *arikey, eṇuyo.*
Necessary Ceremony,	ಅವಸರಪ್ರಸ್ತ *awasara-prasta,*	ಆಂಡಿಯ ಮಂಗಲ *áṇḍiya-mangala.*
Want,	ಅಪೇಕ್ಷೆ *apékṣhe,*	ಆಸೆ *áse.*
Always,	ಅನವರತ *anavarata,*	ಎಕ್ಕಾಲು *ekkálu.*
Kindness,	ಅಂತಃಕರಣ *antahkaraṇa,*	ಪ್ರೀತಿ *príti,* ಪಿರಿತ *pirita,* ಕೊ- [ಡಿ *kodi.*
Petitioner,	ಅರ್ಜಿದಾಷ್ತು *arjidaṣhtu,*	ಪ್ರಿಯದಾದಿಗಾರು *priyádigáru.*
Petition,	ಅರ್ಜಿ *arji,*	ಅರ್ಜಿ *arji.*
Tank belonging to Government,	ಅಮಾನಿ ತಲಾವು ಅಮಾನಿಕೆರೆ, *amáni-kere,*	ಸರಕಾರತು ಕೆರೆ, ಅರಮನೆ ಕೆರೆ *sarakáradu-kere, ara-mune kere.*
Yawning,	ಆಕಳಿಕೆ *ákaḷike,*	ಹಾವಳೆ *háwaḷe.*
End,	ಆಖೈರು *ákheiru,*	ಕಡೆ, ತುದಿ *kaḍe, tudi.*
Become,	ಆಗು *águ,*	ಆಪು ಆಡು *ápu, áḍu.*
Beyond,	ಆಚೆ *áche,*	ಅಪ್ಪುರತು *apparatu.*
Play,	ಆಟ *áṭa,*	ಕಳಿ *kaḷi.*

	ಕನ್ನಡ ಭಾಷೆ.	ಕೊಡಗು ಭಾಷೆ.
Outh, Anna,	ಆಣೆ *áṇe,*	ಆಣೆ *áṇe.*
Profit,	ಆದಾಯ *ádáya,*	ಬರುಬೈ *barubei,* ಬರು *baru*
Beginning,	ಆದಿ *ádi,*	ಆದಿ *ádi,* ಸುರು *suru.*
Respective,	ಆಯಾಯ *áyáya,*	ಅದದು *adadu.*
Sugar Mill,	ಆಲೆ *ále,*	ಆಲೆ *ále.*
Consider,	ಆಲೋಚಿಸು *álóchisu.*	ನಿರಿಚಿರು, ನಿರಿಚಿನೋಟು *nirichiru, nirichinóṭu.*
Individual,	ಆಸಾಮಿ *ásámi.*	ಆಸಾಮಿ *ásámi,* ಆಳು *aḷu.*
Estate,	ಆಸ್ತಿ *ásti,*	ಆಸ್ತಿ, ಬದ್ಕು *ásti, badku.*
Servant,	ಆಳು *áḷu,*	ಆಳು *áḷu.*
Reign,	ಆಳು *áḷu,*	ಬಾಳು *báḷu.*
Instant,	ಆಕ್ಷಣ *ákṣhṇa,*	ಅಕ್ಕೆಂಣೆ *akkenne.*
Collector of a small District,	ಆಮಿಲು *ámilu,*	ಸುಭೇದಾರು *subhédáru.*
Respect,	ಆದಾಬು *ádábu,*	ಮರಿಯಾದಿ *mariyádi.*
ಇ. I.	**ಇ.**	
Contract,	ಇಜಾರೆ *ijáre,*	ಗುತ್ತಿಗೆ *guttige.*
Put down,	ಇಡು *iḍu,*	ಬೆಯಿ *bei.*
Increase,	ಇಜಾಪೆ *ijápe,*	ಯೇರ *éra.*
Is,	ಇದೆ *ide,*	ಉಂಡು *unḍu.*
Be,	ಇರು *iru,*	ಇರು *iru.*
Go down,	ಇಳೇ ಬೀಳು *iḷé-bíḷu,*	ಕೀದಕುಪೋಉ *kidakupóu.*
Rat,	ಇಲಿ *ili,*	ಎಲಿ *yeli.*
Thus,	ಇಂತಿ *inti,*	ಇಂನೆನೆ *innene.*
U.	**ಉ.**	
There is,	ಉಂಟು *unṭu,*	ಉಂಡು *unḍu.*
Production,	ಉತ್ಪತ್ತಿ *utpatti,*	ಪುಟ್ಟುವಳಿ *puṭṭuvaḷi,* ಬೊಳಚಲು *boḷachalu.*
Situation, Occupation,	ಉದ್ಯೋಗ *udyóga,*	ಚಾಕ್ರಿ *chákri.*
A place where salt is manufactured,	ಉಪ್ಪಳ *uppaḷa,*	ಉಪ್ಪಾಳೆ *uppále.*
Cultivate,	ಉಳು *uḷu,*	ಊಳು *úḷu.*
On account of,	ಉದ್ದಿಶ್ಯ *ud-dishya,*	ಅಂಗಾಯಿತು *ángáitu.*
Uú.	**ಊ.**	
well,	ಊದು *údu,*	ಪುಡಪು *puḍupu.*

Vocabulary.

	ಕನ್ನಡ ಭಾಷೆ.	ಕೊಡಗು ಭಾಷೆ.
Meal,	ಊಟ *úṭa,*	ಊಣು *úṇu.*
Village,	ಊರು *úru,*	ಊರು *úru.* [*iru.*
Guess,	ಊಹಿಸು *úhisu,*	ನೆನೆ *nene,* ಬೇರಿಚೆರು *bérich-*
E.	ಎ.	
Front side,	ಎದುರು *eduru,*	ಮಿಣ್ಣೆ, ಎದಿಕೆ *miṇye, yeḍi-*
What sort,	ಎಂಥಾ *enthá,*	ಎನ್ನತು *yennatu.* [*ke.*
How much,	ಎಷ್ಟು *eṣhṭu,*	ಎಚ್ಚಕು *yechchaku.*
Eé.	ಏ.	
Union,	ಏಕ *éka,*	ಒಂದಾಯಿತು *wondáitu.*
Blow,	ಏಟು *éṭu,*	ಪೊಯಿತು *poitu,* ಕುತ್ತು, ಗುದ್ದು *kuttu, guddu.*
O.	ಒ.	
One man,	ಒಬ್ಬ *ob-ba,*	ಒಬ್ಬು, ಒರುಮನುಸು *wobḅu, woru-manasu.*
Oó.	ಓ.	
Read,	ಓದು *ódu,*	ಓದು *wódu.*
Run,	ಓಡು *óḍu,*	ಓಡು *wódu.*
Ka.	ಕ.	
Assessment land Tax,	ಕಂದಾಯ *kandáya,*	ಕಂದಾಯ *kandáya.*
Eye,	ಕಣ್ಣು *kaṇ-ṇu,*	ಕಣ್ಣು *kaṇṇu.*
Blanket,	ಕಂಬಳಿ *kambaḷi,*	ಕಂಬಳಿ *kambaḷi.*
Deficiency,	ಕಮ್ಮಿ *kam-mi,*	ಕಮ್ಮಿ *kammi,* ಕೊರಚಲು *ko-*
Office,	ಕಚ್ಚೇರಿ *kachchéri,*	ಕಚೇರಿ *kachéri.* [*rachalu.*
Construct,	ಕಟ್ಟಿಸು *kaṭṭisu,*	ಕಟ್ಟಿಚೆರು *kaṭṭichiru.*
Small shallow pond or dam,	ಕಟ್ಟೆ *kaṭṭe,*	ಕಟ್ಟೆ, ಕೂವ *kaṭṭe, kúva,* a well.
Ford,	ಕಡಗು *kaḍagu,*	ಕಡಲು *kaḍavu.*
Gutter,	ಕಡವು *kaḍavu,*	ಒಬ್ಬೆ *obbe.*
Kettle, pan,	ಕಡಾಯಿ *kaḍáyi,*	ಕಡಾಯ *ḳaddya.*
Cut,	ಕಡಿ *kaḍi,*	ಕೆತ್ತು *kettu.*
Side,	ಕಡೆ *kaḍe,*	ಬರಿ *bari.*
Deficiency, remnant,	ಕಡಮೆ *kaḍame,*	ಮಿಂಜುನದು *minjunadu.*
Valley,	ಕಣಾವೆ *kaṇave,*	ತಗ್ಗು *taggu.*
Cut,	ಕತ್ತರಿಸು *kattarisu,*	ಕೆತ್ತು *kettu,* ಮುರಿ *muri.*

	ಕನ್ನಡ ಭಾಷೆ.	ಕೊಡಗು ಭಾಷೆ.
Darkness,	ಕತ್ತಲೆ *kattale,*	ಇರಟು *iraṭu.*
Proprietor, lord,	ಕರ್ತ *karta,*	ಕೊರುಕಾರು, ಒಡೆಕಾರು *korukáru, waḍekáru.*
Story,	ಕಥೆ *kathe,*	ಪಡಿಮ *paḍima.*
Door,	ಕದ *kada,*	ಪಡಿ *paḍi.*
Regularity,	ಕ್ರಮ *krama,*	ನಡಪು *naḍapu.*
Melt,	ಕರಗು *karagu,*	ಕರಕು *karaku,* ಉರುಕು *uruku.*
Calf,	ಕರ *kara,*	ಕಡಚಿ *kaḍachi.*
Call,	ಕರೆಯು *kareyu,*	ಕಾಕು *káku.*
Head station of a District,	ಕಸಬಾ *kasabá,*	ಒಂದನೇಜಾಗ *ondané-jága.*
Steal,	ಕಳು *kaḷu,*	ಕಳು, ಕದಿ *kaḷu, kadi.*
Sugar Cane,	ಕಬ್ಬು *kabbu,*	ಕೈಬು *keibu.*
Send,	ಕಳುಹಿಸು *kaḷuhhisu,*	ಅಯೆ *aye.*
Difficult,	ಕಷ್ಟ *kashṭa,*	ಕಷ್ಟ, ಕಟ್ಟ *kashṭa, kaṭṭa.*
Proceedings of a suit,	ಕಟ್ಟು *kaṭ-ṭu,*	ಕಟ್ಟು *kaṭṭu.*
Debt,	ಕಡ *kaḍa,*	ಸಾಲ *sála.*
Thief,	ಕಳ್ಳ *kaḷḷa,*	ಕಳ್ಳು *kaḷḷu.*

Ká. ಕಾ.

Appear,	ಕಾಣು *káṇu,*	ಕಾಂಬು, ಕಾಣು *kámba, káṇu.*
Protect,	ಕಾಪಾಡು *kápáḍu,*	ಸಾಕು, ಚಾಕು *sáku, cháku.*
Public works,	ಕಾಮಗಾರಿ *kámagári,*	ಪಣಿ *paṇi.*
Permanency,	ಕಾಯಂ *káyam,*	ಯಕ್ಕಾಲು *yakkálu,* ಕಾಯಂ *kayam.*
Usage,	ಕಾಯಿದೆ *káyide,*	ನಡಪು *naḍapu.*
Sick,	ಕಾಯಿಲೆ *káyile,*	ನೊಂಬಲ *nombala.*
Reason,	ಕಾರಣ *káraṇa,*	ಮೊಳಿ *moḷi.*
Now in force,	ಕಾಲಪರಿವರ್ತಮಾನ *kála-parivartamána,*	ಇಕ್ಕನಡಪದು *ikka-naḍa-padu.*
Wet season,	ಕಾರು *káru,*	ಮಳೆಗಾಲ *maḷegála.*
Leg,	ಕಾಲು *kálu,*	ಕಾಲು *kálu.*
Watch guard,	ಕಾವಲು *kávalu,*	ಪಾರ *pára.*

Ki. ಕಿ.

Orange,	ಕಿತ್ತಲೆ *kit-tale,*	ಕಿತ್ತುಳಿ *kittuḷi,* ಈಳಿ *éli.*
Trifling trouble,	ಕಿರುಕುಳ *kirukuḷa,*	ಕಿರುಕುಳ *kirukuḷa.*
Commandant of a Fort,	ಕಿಲ್ಲೇದಾರು *killédáru,*	ಕಿಲ್ಲೇದಾರು *killédáru.*

	ಕನ್ನಡ ಭಾಷೆ.	ಕೊಡಗು ಭಾಷೆ.
Kí.	ಕೀ.	
Pull,	ಕೀಳು *kíḷu,*	ಬಲಿ, ಪೊರಿ *boli, pori.*
Ku.	ಕು.	
Assistance,	ಕುಮ್ಮಕು *kum-maku,*	ಕುಮ್ಮಕು, ವತ್ತಾಸ, ಸಕಾಯ *kummaku, vattása sakáya.*
Drink,	ಕುಡಿಯು *kuḍiyu,*	ಕುಡಿ *kuḍi.*
Reap,	ಕುಯಿ *kuyi,*	ಕೊಯಿ, ಪರಿ, ಅರು *koyi, pari, aru.*
Sheep,	ಕುರಿ *kuri,*	ಕೊರಿ *kori.*
Kú.	ಕೂ.	
Cry loud,	ಕೂಗು *kúgu,*	ಕೂತುಕೊಡು, ಮೊರೆಯಿಡು *kútu-koḍu, moreyiḍu.*
To Sit,	ಕೂಡು, ಕೂರು *kúḍu, kúru,*	ಎಳೆ *yeḷe.*
Join,	ಕೂಡು *kúḍu,*	ಕೂಟು *kúṭu,* ಕೂಡು *kúḍu.*
Ke.	ಕೆ.	
Ruby,	ಕೆಂಪು *kempu,*	ಕೆಂಪು, ಚೋಪು *kempu, chópu.*
To Spoil,	ಕೆಡು *keḍu,*	ಪಾಳಾವು *páḷávu.*
Tank,	ಕೆರೆ *kere,*	ಕೆರೆ *kere.*
Some,	ಕೆಲವು *kelavu,*	ಚೆಂನಂಗು *chennangu.*
Business,	ಕೆಲಸ *kelasa,*	ಪಣಿ *paṇi.*
Under,	ಕೆಳಗೆ *keḷage,*	ಕೀದಲು *kídalu.*
Ké.	ಕೇ.	
Ask or hear,	ಕೇಳು *kéḷu,*	ಕೇಳು *kéḷu.*
Thief, Prisoner,	ಕೈದಿ *keidi,*	ಕಳ್ಳ, ಕುಳ, ತಪ್ಪುಮಾಡುನವ *keḷḷa, kuḷa, tappumáḍunava.*
Hand,	ಕೈಯಿ *keiyi,*	ಕೈಯಿ *keiyi.*
Workman,	ಕೈವಾಡುಗಾರ *keiváḍugára,*	ಕೈವಾಡುಗಾರ, ಪಣಿಕಾರು *paṇikáru.*
Deposition,	ಕೈಪಿಯತು *keipiyatu,*	ಕೈಪಿಯತು ವಾಂಗ್ಮೂಲ *keipiyatu, vangmúla.*
Ko.	ಕೊ.	
Room,	ಕೊಠಡಿ *koṭhaḍi,*	ಕೋಂಬರೆ *kómbare.*
Give,	ಕೊಡು *koḍu,*	ಕೊಡು *koḍu.*
Axe,	ಕೊಡ್ಲಿ *koḍli,*	ಕೊಡ್ಲಿ *koḍli.*

	ಕನ್ನಡ ಭಾಷೆ.	ಕೊಡಗು ಭಾಷೆ.
Kill,	ಕೊಲ್ಲು ***kollu,***	ಕೊಲ್ಲು, ಕೊಂದುರು ***kollu, konduru.***
Buy,	ಕೊಳ್ಳು ***koḷ-ḷu,***	ಯೆಡು,ಕೊವ್ವು ***yaḍu, kovvu.***
Kó.	ಕೋ.	
Buffalo.	ಕೋಣ ***kóṇa,***	ಪೋರಿ ***póri.***
Anger,	ಕೋಪ, ***kópa,***	ಚೆಡಿ ***cheḍi.***
Kha.	ಖ.	
A measure of Capacity,	ಖಂಡಗ ***khanḍaga,***	ಖಂಡಗ ***khanḍaga.***
Expense,	ಖರ್ಚು ***kharchu,***	ಖರ್ಚು ***kharchu.***
Treasury,	ಖಜಾನೆ ***khajáne,***	ಖಜಾನೆ, ತೊಳಸೆಖಾನೆ ***khajáne toḷase-kháne.***
Instalment of Tax,	ಖಿಸ್ತು ***khistu,***	ಖಿಸ್ತು, ಕಂತು ***khistu kantu.***
Dry land,	ಖುಷ್ಕಿ ***khushki,***	ಪೊಲ ***pola.***
Imprisonment,	ಖೈದಿ ***kheidi,***	ಖೈದು ***kheidu.***
Census,	ಖಾನಿಸುಮಾರಿ ***khánisumári,***	ಖಾನಿಸುಮಾರಿ ***khánisumári.***
Ga.	ಗ.	
Sandal wood,	ಗಂಧ ***gandha,***	ಚಾಂದು ***chándu.***
Chatty, pot,	ಗಡಿಗೆ ***gaḍige,***	ಕರವ, ಕೈಪೆರಿ ***karava, keiperi.***
Wet land,	ಗದ್ದೆ ***gad-de,***	ಬೇಲು, ತೆವ ***bélu teva.***
House holder.	ಗ್ರುಹಸ್ತ ಯೆಜಮಾನ ***graha-sta, yajamána.***	ಕೊರವುಕಾರು, ಮನೆಕಾರು ***koravukáru, manekáru.***
Gá.	ಗಾ.	
Cart,	ಗಾಡಿ ***gáḍi,***	ಗಾಡಿ, ಬಂಡಿ ***gáḍi, banḍi.***
Oil mill,	ಗಾಣ ***gáṇa,***	ಎಂಣೆಗಾಣ ***yenṇe gáṇa.***
Village,	ಗ್ರಾಮ ***gráma,***	ಊರು ***úru.***
Leaves of a kind of intoxicating Indian plant,	ಗಾಂಜಾ,ಭಂಗಿ ***gánjá bhangi,***	ಭಂಗಿ ***bhangi.***
Gi.	ಗಿ.	
Tree,	ಗಿಡ ***giḍa***	ಮರ ***mara.***
Purchaser,	ಗಿರಾಕಿ ***giráki,***	ಕೇಪವು, ಕೊವ್ವವು ***képavu, kovvavu.***
Gí.	ಗೀ.	
Line or Stroke,	ಗೀಟು ***gíṭu,***	ಗೀಟು, ಗೆರೆ ***gíṭu, gere.***

	ಕನ್ನಡ ಭಾಷೆ.	ಕೊಡಗು ಭಾಷೆ.
Gu.	**ಗು.**	
Collection of a people,	ಗುಂಪು *gumpu,*	ಗುಡ್ಡೆ, ಗುಂಪು *guḍḍe gumpu.*
Tent,	ಗುಡಾರ *guḍára,*	ಗುಡಾರ, ತಂಬು *guḍára ta-mbu.*
Heap,	ಗುಡ್ಡೆ *guḍ-ḍe,*	ಗುಡ್ಡೆ *guḍḍe.*
Pit,	ಗುಣಿ *guṇi,*	ಕುಂಡು *kunḍu.*
Contract,	ಗುತ್ತಿಗೆ *guttige,*	ಗುತ್ತಿಗೆ *guttige.*
Aim,	ಗುರಿ *guri,*	ಕುರ್ರಿ, ಗುರಿ *kurri, guri.*
Mark,	ಗುರ್ತು *gurtu,*	ಗುರ್ತ *gurta.*
Uproar,	ಗುಲ್ಲು *gul-lu,*	ಗುಲ್ಲು, ಸದ್ದು *gullu, saddu.*
Year or month past,	ಗುಜಷ್ಟಾ ಗುದಸ್ತಾ *gujaṣhtá, gudastá,*	ಕೈಂಜು ತಿಂಗು or ಕಾಲ *kein-jutingu,* or *kála.*
Tent pin,	ಗೂಟ *gúṭa,*	ಗೂಟ ದರಿ *gúṭa, dari.*
Basket.	ಗೂಡೆ *gúḍe,*	ಪಚ್ಚಿಯ *pachchiya.*
Cultivate.	ಗೇಯು *géyu,*	ಕೆಯಿ *keyi.*
Firmness.	ಗೊತ್ತು *got-tu,*	ಗೊತ್ತು,ನೆಪ್ಪು *gottu,neppu.*
Manure.	ಗೊಬ್ಬರ *gob-bara,*	ಚಾಣ *cháṇa.*
Plain Ring,	ಗೋಲು *gólu,*	ಸುತ್ತು,ಉರುಟು,ಬಟ್ಟತೆ *suttu, uruṭu, baṭṭate.*
Abstract,	ಗೋಷ್ವಾರೆ *góṣhváre,*	ಗೋಷ್ವಾರೆ *góṣhváre.*
Head man of a Village,	ಗೌಡ *gouḍa,*	ಗೌಡ,ಪಟೇಲ *gouḍa,paṭéla.*
Ghurry,	ಘಂಟೆ *ghanṭe,*	ಘಂಟೆ, ಮಣಿ *ghanṭe,maṇi.*
Wound,	ಘಾಯ *gháya,*	ಗಾಯ, ಕಲೆ, ಮುರಿ *gháya, kale, muri.*
Cha.	**ಚ.**	
Flat thin brick,	ಚದರಬಿಲ್ಲೆ *chadara bille,*	ಚದರಬಿಲ್ಲೆ *chadara-bille.*
Service,	ಚಾಕರಿ *chákari,*	ಚಾಕರಿ *chákari.*
Calumny, slander,	ಚಾಡಿ *cháḍi,*	ಚಾಡಿ *cháḍi.*
Choultry,	ಚಾವಡಿ *chávaḍi,*	ಚಾವಡಿ *chávaḍi.*
Small,	ಚಿಕ್ಕ, ಸಣ್ಣ *chikka, saṇṇa,*	ಚೆರಿಯದು *cheriyadu.*
Chit,	ಚೀಟು *chíṭu,*	ಚೀಟು *chíṭu.*
Spot,	ಚುಕ್ಕಿ *chukki,*	ಚುಳ್ಳು *chuḷḷu.*
Interest,	ಚುಂಗಡಿ *chungaḍi,*	ಚುಂಗಡಿ, ಬಡ್ಡಿ *chungaḍi, ba-ḍḍi.*
Piece,	ಚೂರು *chúru,*	ಚೂರು,ತುಂಡು *chúru,tunḍu.*
Flint stone,	ಚಕ್ಮುಕಿ *chakmuki,*	ಚಕುಮುಕ್ಕಿ *chakumukki.*
Scorpion,	ಚೇಳು *chéḷu,*	ತೇಳು, ನಂಡುರಕು *téḷu, nan-ḍuraku.*

	ಕನ್ನಡ ಭಾಷೆ.	ಕೊಡಗು ಭಾಷೆ.
Pure,	ಚೊಕ್ಕಾ *chok-ká,*	ನಲ್ಲು ಅಂಜು *nallu-ánju.*
Theft,	ಚೋರಿ *chóri,*	ಕಳ್ಳತನ *kaḷḷatana.*
Concealment,	ಛಫಾವಣಿ *chhaphávaṇi,*	ವೊಳಿಪಿ ಚಿರುವು *voḷipichiru-vu.*
Settlement of Assessment,	ಜಮಾಬಂದಿ *jamábandi,*	ಜಮಾಬಂದಿ *jamábundi.*
Land,	ಜಮೀನು *jamínu,*	ಭೂಮಿ *bhúmi.*
People,	ಜನ *jana,*	ಮನಸ *manasa.*
Peon or Servant,	ಜವಾನ *javána,*	ಬಿಲ್ಲೆಕಾರು, ಕೋಲುಕಾರು *bi-llékáru, kólukáru.*
Presence,	ಜನಾಬು *jánabu,*	ಪಾದ *páda.*
Já.	ಜಾ.	
Quickness,	ಜಾಗ್ರತೆ *jágrate,*	ಚುರುಕು, ಬೆರಿಯ *churuku-beriya.*
Place,	ಜಾಗ *jága,*	ಜಾಗ *jága.*
Mark of a foot step,	ಜಾಡೆ *jáḍe,*	ಜಾಡು *jáḍu.*
Clever man,	ಜಾಣ *jáṇa,*	ಬುದ್ಧಿಕಾರು, ಚಾಲಾಕಾರು, ಕೆಣಿಯು *buddhikáru, chá lákáru, keṇiyu.*
Caste,	ಜಾತಿ *játi,*	ಕುಲ, ಜಾತಿ *kula, játi.*
Security,	ಜಾಮೀನು *jámínu,*	ತೊಣೆ *toṇe.*
Increase,	ಜಾಸ್ತಿ *jásti,*	ಪೆರ್ತ, ದೂತ *perta, dúta.*
Representation,	ಜಾಹಿರು *jáhiru,*	ಅರ್ಕೆ *arke.*
Estate,	ಜಿಂದಗಿ *jindagi,*	ವಡವೆ, ಸಾಮಾನ *vaḍave, sámána.*
Jealousy,	ಜಿದ್ದು *jid-du,*	ಮರ್ಮ *marma.*
Life,	ಜೀವ *jíva,*	ಜೀವ *jíva.*
Fine,	ಜುರ್ಮಾನೆ *jurmáne,*	ದಂಡ, ಪೊಳೆವಾಡು *daṇḍa, poḷeváḍu.*
Ta.	ತಂ.	
Lodge,	ತಂಗು *tangu,*	ಇಪ್ಪುದು *aippudu.*
Trouble,	ತಂಟೆ *tanṭe,*	ತಂಟೆ *tante.*
Father,	ತಂದೆ *tande,*	ಅಪ್ಪು *appu.*
Fit,	ತಕ್ಕ *tak-ka,*	ಬೋಂದಿಯಾನು *bónḍiyá-nu.*

Vocabulary.

	ಕನ್ನಡ ಭಾಷೆ.	ಕೊಡಗು ಭಾಷೆ.
Dispute,	ತಕರಾರು *takaráru,*	ತಕರಾರು *takaráru.*
Advance for cultivation,	ತಕಾವಿ *takávi,*	ಮುಂಗಡ *mungaḍa.*
Demand,	ತಕಾದೆ *takáde,*	ಕೇಪು ತಗಾದೆ *képu, tagáde.*
Hit,	ತಗಲು *tagalu,*	ಪಡು *paḍu.*
Dearness, high price,	ತಗ್ಗು *tag-gu,*	ತಗ್ಗು *taggu.*
Dismissal from service,	ತಗ್ಗೈರು *tageiru,*	ಬರತಪ್ರ್, ಎಡತುಬುಡುವು *baratarpu, yeḍatubuḍuvu.*
Fault,	ತಪ್ಪು *tap-pu,*	ತಪ್ಪು *tappu.*
Adoption of prompt measures,	ತರದೂದು *taradúdu,*	ಪೆಚಾಡುವು *pechádụvu.*
Sort,	ತರಹಾ *tarahá,*	ಮಾದ್ರಿ ತರ *mádri, tara.*
Wet land,	ತರಿ *tari,*	ಬೇಲು *bélu.*
To bring,	ತರು *taru,*	ಎಡುತಬಾ, ಕೊಂಡಾ *yeḍutabá, konḍá.*
Head,	ತಲೆ *tale,*	ಮಂಡೆ *manḍe.*
Peon attached to a village,	ತಳವಾರ *taḷavára,*	ಕುಳವಾಡಿ ಬಾರೀಕು *kuḷavádi, báríku.*
Immediately,	ತಕ್ಷಣ *takṣhaṇa,*	ಅಕ್ಕಂನೆ, ಒಡನೆ *akkenne, wodane.*
Quickness,	ತ್ವರೆ *tware,*	ಬೆರಿಯ *beriya.*
Tá.	ತಾ.	
Copper,	ತಾಂಬ್ರ *támbra,*	ಚೆಂಬು *chembu.*
To hit, to touch,	ತಾಕು *táku,*	ಪಡು, ತೊಡು, ತೂಂಡು *paḍu, toḍu, túnḍu.*
A Mandate, a written order,	ತಾಕೀದು *tákídu,*	ಉತ್ರ *utra.*
Grandfather,	ತಾತ *táta,*	ಅಜ್ಜಪು *aj-japu.*
Trouble,	ತೊಂದರೆ *tondare,*	ಕಷ್ಟ, ಕಟ್ಟ *kaṣhṭa, kaṭṭa.*
Garden,	ತೋಟ *tóṭa,*	ತೋಟ, ತೊಡಿಯ *tóta, toḍiya.*
Tope, Grove,	ತೋಪು *tópu,*	ತೋಪು *tópu.*
Show,	ತೋರಿಸು *tórisu,*	ಕಾಟ್ಟು *káṭṭu.*
Gun,	ತೋಪ್ *tóp,*	ಬಲ್ಯತೋಕು *balya-tóku.*
Da.	ದ.	
Army,	ದಂಡು *danḍu,*	ದಂಡು *danḍu.*
Cattle,	ದನ *dana,*	ಅತ್ತ *atta.*

	ಕನ್ನಡ ಭಾಷೆ.	ಕೊಡಗು ಭಾಷೆ.
Favour,	ದಯ daya,	ದಯೆ, ಕಿರುಬಿಯ daya, kirubiya.
Head Peon,	ದಫೇದಾರ daphéddra,	ದಪೇದಾರು, ಗೊತ್ತುಗಾರು dapédáru, gottugáru.
Enquiry, trial,	ದರ್ಯಾಫ್ತಿ darydpthi,	ವಿಚಾರ, ಇಚಾರ vichára, ichára.
Robbery,	ದರೋಡೆ daróḍe,	ಕಳ್ಳತನ kaḷḷatana.
Camp,	ದರಜಾಗ darajága,	ಮೊಖಾಂ ಉಳ್ಳ ಜಾಗ mokhám-uḷḷa jága.
Admission,	ದಾಖಲು dakhalu,	ಸೇರುವು séruvu.
Cousin,	ದಾಯಾದಿ dáyádi,	ದಾಯಾದಿ, ಸಂತಾನಗಾರು dáyádi, santánagáru.
Di.	**ದಿ.**	
Alarm, fear,	ದಿಗಲು digalu,	ಪೋದಿ póḍi.
A day,	ದಿವಸ divasa,	ನಾಳು, ವರುನಾಳು, ವಂನಾಂದು náḷu, varunáḷu, vannandu.
Du.	**ದು.**	
English penny, a pice,	ದುಡ್ಡು duḍ-ḍu,	ದುಡ್ಡು duḍḍu.
Second,	ದುಯಂ duyam,	ದಂಡನೆ danḍane.
Repair,	ದುರಸ್ತು durastu,	ಚಾಯಿಕೂಟುವು cháyi-kúṭuvu.
Dú.	**ದೂ.**	
Distance,	ದೂರ dúra,	ದೂರ dúra.
De.	**ಡೆ.**	
Blow,	ಡೆಬ್ಬೆ deb-be,	ಗುದ್ದು, ಪೊಯಿತು guddu, poitu.
Dé.	**ದೇ.**	
God,	ದೇವರು dévaru,	ದೇವ déva.
Lands belonging to the gods,	ದೇವಾದಯ dévádaya,	ದೆವಡಬೂಮಿ dévaḍa-búmi.
Country,	ದೇಶ désha,	ದೇಶ, ರಾಜಿಯ désha, rjiya.

Vocabulary.

	ಕನ್ನಡ ಭಾಷೆ.	ಕೊಡಗು ಭಾಷೆ.
Body,	ದೇಹ *déhha,*	ಮೇಲು, ಶರೀರ, ತಡಿ *mélu, sharíra taḍi.*
Do.	ಡೊ.	
Large,	ದೊಡ್ಡ *doḍḍa,*	ಬಲ್ಲಿಯು *balliyu.*
Cudgel,	ದೊಣ್ಣೆ *doṇ-ṇe,*	ದೊಂಣೆ *donṇe.*
Dó.	ಡೋ.	
Plunder,	ದೋಚು *dóchu,*	ಕೋತು, ಬಾತು *kótu, bátu.*
Dha.	ಧ.	
Master,	ಧಣಿ *dhaṇi,*	ಕೊರವುಕಾರು *koravukáru.*
Thickness,	ಧಪ್ಪ *dhap-pa,*	ಬಂಣ *baṇa.*
Voice,	ಧ್ವನಿ *dhwani,*	ಕೂತು *kútu.*
Courage,	ಧೈರ್ಯ *dheirya,*	ಧೈರ್ಯ *dheirya.*
Master or King,	ಧೊರೆ *dhore,*	ಧೊರೆ, ವಡೆಯು *dhore, vaḍeyu.*
Native wearing Cloth,	ಧೋತ್ರ *dhótra,*	ದೋತ್ರ *dótra.*
Negligence,	ಧೋರಣೆ *dhóraṇe,*	ದೋರಣೆ *dóraṇe.*
Na.	ನ.	
Prostration,	ನಮಸ್ಕಾರ *namaskára,*	ತೊಪ್ಪು, ಅಡ್ಡಬೂವು, ಕಾಲು ಪುದಿಪು *toppu, aḍḍabúvu, kálu-puḍipu.*
Loss,	ನಷ್ಟ *nashṭa.*	ಕೇಡು *kéḍu.*
Trust,	ನಂಬು *nambu,*	ನಂಬು *nambu.*
Capital,	ನಗರ *nagara,*	ಪಟ್ಟಣ *paṭṭaṇa.*
To proceed, to walk,	ನಡಿಯು *naḍiyu,*	ನಡ *naḍa.*
Middle,	ನಡುವೆ *naḍuve,*	ನಡೂಲು *naḍúlu.*
Specimen,	ನಮೂನೆ *namúne,*	ಮಾದ್ರಿ *mádri.*
Plan,	ನಕ್ಷೆ *nakṣhe,*	ಚಿತ್ರ *chitra.*
Ná.	ನಾ.	
Charge of money rupee, annas and pice,	ನಾಣ್ಯ *náṇya,*	ನಾಣ್ಯ *náṇya.*
Four in number,	ನಾಲ್ಕು *nálku,*	ನಾಲು *nálu.*
Justice,	ನ್ಯಾಯ *nyáya,*	ಞಾಯ *nyáya.*
Court of Justice,	ನ್ಯಾಯಸ್ಥಾನ *nyáyastána,*	ಞಾಯತೀಪಳ್ಳ ಜಾಗ *nyáya-típaḷa-jága.*

	ಕನ್ನಡ ಭಾಷೆ.	ಕೊಡಗು ಭಾಷೆ.
Written order,	ನಿರೂಪ *nirúpa,*	ಹುಕ್ಕುಂ, ಅಪ್ಪಣೆ *hukkum, appaṇe.*
Lime,	ನಿಂಬೆ *nimbe,*	ಚೋರಂಗೆಪುಳಿ *chórange-puḷi.*
Truth,	ನಿಜ *nija,*	ನೇರು *néru.*
Sleep,	ನಿದ್ದೆ *nidde,*	ವರಕು *varaku.*
Midnight,	ನಿಶಿ *nishi,*	ನಡಪಾದ್ರ *naḍapádra.*
Stand,	ನಿಲ್ಲು *nillu,*	ನಿಲ್ಲು *nillu.*
Water,	ನೀರು *níru,*	ನೀರು *níru.*
To enter by force,	ನುಗ್ಗು *nuggu,*	ನುಗ್ಗು, ಕೂಡು *nuggu, kúḍu.*
Hundred numeral,	ನೂರು *núru,*	ನೂರು *núru.*
Shove,	ನೂಕು *núku,*	ದೂಡು, ಉಂದು *dúḍu, undu.*
To Plant,	ನೆಡು *neḍu,*	ನಡು *naḍu.*
Think,	ನೆನಸು *nenasu,*	ನೆನೆ, ಬೇರಿಚೆರು *nene, béri-cheru.*
Neighbourhood,	ನೆರೆ *nere,*	ನೆರೆ, *nere.*
Pretence,	ನೆವ *neva,*	ನೆವನ *nevana.*
Pa.	ಪ.	
Five numeral,	ಪಂಚ *pancha,*	ಅಂಜಿ *anji.*
Torch,	ಪಂಜು *panju,*	ಪೊಂಜಿ, ದೀವಟಿಗೆ, ಪೊತ್ತೆ *ponji, dívaṭige, potte.*
Jury, arbitration,	ಪಂಚಾಯಿತ *panchâyita,*	ಪಂಚಾತಿಗಾರ, ಪಂಚಾತಿ *panchátigára, pancháti.*
Good Lot,	ಪುಣ್ಯ *puṇya,*	ಪುಣ್ಯ *puṇya.*
List,	ಪಟ್ಟಿ *paṭṭi,*	ಪಟ್ಟಿ *paṭṭi.*
Feel,	ಪಡು *paḍu,*	ತೊಡು *toḍu.*
Land Grant,	ಪಟ್ಟೆ *paṭṭe,*	ಪಟ್ಟೆ, ಸನ್ನದು *puṭṭe, sanna-du.*
Apprehension,	ಪತ್ತೆ *patte,*	ಪತ್ತೆ, ತೇಡಿಪುಡಿ ಪಡು *pa-tte téḍipuḍi-padu.*
Bond,	ಪತ್ರ *patra,*	ಪತ್ರ *patra.*
Usage, Custom,	ಪದ್ಧತಿ *pad-dhati,*	ನಡಪು *naḍapu.*
Acquaintance,	ಪರಿಚಿತಿ *parichiti,*	ಅರಿವು *arivu.*
Palanquiu,	ಪಲ್ಲಕ್ಕಿ *pallakki,*	ಪಲ್ಲೆಕಿ *palleki.*
Favor,	ಪಕ್ಷ *pakṣha,*	ಪಕ್ಷ, ಕಡೆ *pakṣha, kaḍe.*

	ಕನ್ನಡ ಭಾಷೆ.	ಕೊಡಗು ಭಾಷೆ.
Partiality,	ಪಕ್ಷಪಾತ *pakṣhapáta,*	ಪಕ್ಷಪಾತ, ಮೊಣ್ಣಾಯಿ *paksha_páta, monyáya.*
Separate,	ಪ್ರತ್ಯೇಕ *pratyéka,*	ಬೋರೆ *bóre.*
Defendant,	ಪ್ರತಿವಾದಿ *prativádi,*	ಪ್ರತಿವಾದಿ *prativádi.*
Stream,	ಪ್ರವಾಹ *praváha,*	ದುಂಬುನಪೊಳೆ,ಬೊಳ್ಳ *dumbuna-poḷe boḷḷa.*
Ceremony,	ಪ್ರಸ್ತ *prasta,*	ಮಂಗಲ *mangala.*
According to,	ಪ್ರಕಾರ *prakára,*	ಅಂನನೆ *annane.*
Utensil,	ಪಾತ್ರ *patra,*	ಪಾತ್ರ, ಕಲ *patra, kala.*
Waste,	ಪಾಳು *páḷu,*	ಪಾಳು *páḷu.*
Locality,	ಪ್ರಾಂತ *pránta,*	ಥಳ *thaḷa.*
Powder,	ಪುಡಿ *puḍi,*	ಪೊಡಿ *poḍi.*
Worship,	ಪೂಜೆ *púje,*	ಪೂಜೆ *púje.*
Crop,	ಪೈರು *peiru,*	ಬೊಳೆ *boḷe.*
Runaway,	ಪರಾರಿ *parári,*	ಪೋಡಿಪೋಪು, ಒಳಿಚಿಪೋಪು *vóḍipópu-voḷichipópu.*
Produce,	ಫಲ *phala,*	ಫಲ *phala.*
Yeild, grow,	ಫಲಿಸ *phalisa,*	ಬೊಳೆ *boḷe.*
Servant,	ಪಿದವಿ *pidavi,*	ಚಾಕ್ರಿ, ಆಳು *chákra, áḷu.*
Complaint,	ಪಿರ್ಯಾದಿ *piryádi,*	ಪಿರಿಯಾದಿ *piriyádi.*
Decision,	ಫೈಸಲು *pheisalu,*	ತೀರ್ಪು, ಕಡಕಟ್ಟು *tírpu, kaḍakaṭṭu.*
Ba.	ಬ.	
Waste land,	ಬಂಜರು ಭೂಮಿ *banjaru-bhúmi,*	ಪಾಳು ಭೂಮಿ *páḷubhúmi.*
Cloth,	ಬಟ್ಟೆ *baṭṭe,*	ತುಣಿ *tuṇi.*
Conceal,	ಬಚ್ಚು *bach-chu,*	ಒಳಿಪಿಚಿರು *voḷipichiru.*
Exchange,	ಬದಲಾಯಿಸು *badaláyisu,*	ಬದಲಾಯಿಚಿರು *badaláyichiru.*
Live,	ಬದುಕು *baduku,*	ಬಾಳು, ಬಾವು *báḷu, bávu.*
Dismissal from Service,	ಬರತರ್ಫ *baratarpu,*	ಭರತರ್ಫ, ಚಾಕ್ರಿಂಜಿಯೆಡುಪು *bharatarpu,chakrinji-yeḍupu.*
Write,	ಬರಿ *bari,*	ಎಳುದು *yaḷudu.*
Come,	ಬ *ba,*	ಬಾ *bá.*

	ಕನ್ನಡ ಭಾಷೆ.	ಕೊಡಗು ಭಾಷೆ.
Land belonging to the Brahmans,	ಬ್ರಂಹ್ಮಾದಾಯ *brammhádáya,*	ಪಟ್ಟಮಡಬೂಮಿ *paṭṭamaḍa-búmi.*
Compliment,	ಬಂದಗಿ *bandagi,*	ಸಲಾಂ, ಆಜಾರ *salám, ájára.*
Interest,	ಬಡ್ಡಿ *baḍḍi,*	ಚುಂಗಡಿ *chungaḍi.*
Very,	ಬಹಳ *bahaḷa,*	ಪೆರ್ತು *pertu.*
Item,	ಬಾಬು *bábu,*	ತರ *tara.*
Door,	ಬಾಗಲು *bágalu,*	ಪಡಿ *paḍi.*
Plantain,	ಬಾಳೆ *báḷe,*	ಬಾಳೆ *báḷe.*
Almond,	ಬಾದಂ *bádam,*	ಬಾದಮು *bádamu.*
Leave,	ಬಿಡು *biḍu,*	ಬುಡು *buḍu.*
The Sun,	ಬಿಸಲು *bisalu,*	ಬೆದು *bedu.*
Sow,	ಬಿತ್ತು *bittu,*	ಬಿತ್ತು *bittu.*
Fall,	ಬೀಳು *bíḷu,*	ಬೂಳು *búḷu.*
Lock,	ಬೀಗ *bíga,*	ಬೀಗ *bíga.*
Admiss of Seeds,	ಬೀಜವರಿ *bíjavari,*	ಬಿತ್ತುವರಿ *bittuvari.*
Throw,	ಬೀರು *bíru,*	ಕನಿ, ಚಾಡು *kani, cháḍu.*
Wisdom,	ಬುದ್ಧಿ *buddhi,*	ಬುದ್ಧಿ, ಮೂಲ *buddhi, múla.*
Fire,	ಬೆಂಕಿ *benki,*	ತಿತ್ತು *tittu.*
Hill,	ಬೆಟ್ಟ *beṭṭa,*	ಕುಂದು *kundu.*
Dry land,	ಬೆದ್ದಲು *beddalu,*	ಬಾಣೆ, ಪೊಲ *báṇe, pola.*
Jaggory,	ಬೆಲ್ಲ *bellá,*	ಬೆಲ್ಲ *bellá.*
Light,	ಬೆಳಕು *beḷaku,*	ಬೊಳಿ, ಬೊಪ್ಪು *boḷi, boppu.*
Grow,	ಬೆಳೆಯು *beḷeyu,*	ಬೊಳೆ *bóḷe.*
Crop,	ಬೆಳೆ *beḷe,*	ಬೊಳೆ *boḷe.*
Maragosa tree,	ಬೇವಿನ ಮರ *bévina-mara,*	ಬೇವುಮರ *bévu-mara.*
Want,	ಬೇಕು *béku,*	ಬೋಂಡು *bónḍu.*
Beg,	ಬೇಡು *béḍu,*	ಬೋಡು, ಯರೆ *bóḍu, yare.*
Abuse,	ಬೈಯು *beiyu,*	ಬೈಯಿ *beiyi.*
Teach or persuade,	ಬೋದಿಸು *bódisu,*	ಪಡಿಪಿಚಿರು *paḍipichiru.*
Idol,	ಬೊಂಬೆ *bombe,*	ಗೊಂಬೆ *gombe.*
Paddy,	ಭತ್ತ *bhatta,*	ನೆಲ್ಲು *nellu.*
Fear,	ಭಯ *bhaya,*	ಪೋಡಿ *póḍi.*
Devotee,	ಭಕ್ತ *bhakta,*	ಬಕ್ತು *baktu.*
Share,	ಭಾಗ *bhága,*	ಪಾಲು, ವೋದಿ *pálu, vódi.*

Vocabulary.

	ಕನ್ನಡ ಭಾಷೆ.	ಕೊಡಗು ಭಾಷೆ.
Condition of being,	ಭಾವ *bháva,*	ರೂಪು *rúpu.*
Well,	ಭಾವಿ *bhávi,*	ಕಣತರೆ, ಕೂವ *kaṇatare, kúva.*
Language,	ಭಾಷೆ *bháṣhe,*	ತಕ್ಕು *takku.*
Land,	ಭೂಮಿ *bhúmi,*	ಬೂಮಿ *búmi.*
Aloe plant,	ಭೂತಾಳೆ *bhútáḷe,*	ರಾಕ್ಷಸಕೈ *rákṣhasakei.*
Earthquake,	ಭೂಕಂಪ *bhúkampa,*	ಬೂಮಿ ನಡುಗುವದು *búmi-naḍuguvadu.*
Visit,	ಭೇಟಿ *bhéṭi,*	ಕಾಂಬು *kámbu.*
Purging,	ಭೇದಿ *bhédi,*	ತೂರುವು, ಕೆಲಯುಳವು *túru-vu, kelayaḷavu.*

Ma.

	ಮ.	
Understanding	ಮಂದಟ್ಟು *mandaṭṭu,*	ಗೊತ್ತು *gottu.*
Cot,	ಮಂಚ *mancha,*	ಕಟ್ಟು *kaṭṭu.*
Son,	ಮಗ *maga,*	ಮೋವು *móvu.*
Maund,	ಮಣ *maṇa,*	ಮಣ *maṇa.*
Marriage,	ಮದಿವೆ *madive,*	ಮಂಗಲ *mangala.*
House,	ಮನೆ *mane,*	ಮನೆ *mane.*
Tree,	ಮರ *mara,*	ಮರ *mara.*
Man,	ಮನುಷ್ಯ *manuṣhya,*	ಮನುಸು *manusu.*
Forget,	ಮರೆಯು *mareyu,*	ಮರೆಪು *marepu.*
Counsel, plot,	ಮಸಲತು *masalatu,*	ಬೇರ *béra.*
Sleep, lie down,	ಮಲಗು *malagu,*	ಬುದ್ದಾ *buddá.*
Rain,	ಮಳೆ *maḷe,*	ಮಳೆ *maḷe.*
Persons,	ಮಂದಿ *mandi,*	ಜನ *jana.*
Opinion come to by an arbitration,	ಮಹಜರು *mahajaru,*	ಮಾಜರು *májaru.*
To do, to make,	ಮಾಡು *máḍu,*	ಮಾಡು *máḍu.*
Land rent-free,	ಮಾನ್ಯ *mánya,*	ಮಾನ್ಯ *mánya.*
Sell,	ಮಾರು *máru,*	ಮಾರು *máru.*
Property,	ಮಾಲ್ *mál,*	ವಡ್ವೆ, ಪತ್ತು, ಬತ್ತು *vaḍve, pattu, battu.*
Representation,	ಮಾರೂಜು *márúju,*	ಹೋಲಿಕೆ, ದಿನಸು *hólike, dinasu,*
Season of thunder showers,	ಮುಂಗಾರು *mungáru,*	ಪುದುಮಳೆ ಬಪ್ಪುಕಾಲ *pudu-maḷe-bappukála.*

	ಕನ್ನಡ ಭಾಷೆ.	ಕೊಡಗು ಭಾಷೆ.
Face,	ಮುಖ *mukha,*	ಮೂಡು *múḍu.*
Touch,	ಮುಟ್ಟು *muṭṭu,*	ತೂಂಡು *túnḍu.*
Sink,	ಮುಳಗು *muḷagu,*	ಮುಳು *muḷu.*
Corner,	ಮೂಲೆ *múle,*	ಮೂಲೆ *múle.*
Amount of money,	ಮೊಬಲಗು *mobalagu,*	ವಟ್ಟು ಪಣ *vaṭṭu-paṇa.*
House tax,	ಮೊಹತರ್ಫಾ *mohatarp-ká,*	ಮನೆಪಣ *mane-paṇa.*
Seal, stamp,	ಮೊಹರು *moharu,*	ಮುದ್ರೆ *mudre.*
Cubit,	ಮೊಳ *moḷa,*	ಮೊಳ *moḷa.*
Deception,	ಮೋಸ *mósa,*	ಮೋಸ *mósa.*
Ya.	ಯ.	
Oil,	ಯೆಣ್ಣೆ *yen-ṇe,*	ಯುಂಣೆ *yunṇe.*
Bullock,	ಯತ್ತು *yattu,*	ಯುತ್ತು, ಮಂಡು *yuttu, manḍu.*
Endeavour,	ಯತ್ನಿಸು *yatnisu,*	ಪೇಚಾಡು *péchádu.*
Boundary,	ಯಲ್ಲೆ *yalle,*	ಅರ್ದಿ *ardi.*
Bund,	ಯೇರಿ *yéri,*	ಯೇರಿ *yéri.*
Ra.	ರ.	
Despatch,	ರವಾನ *raváná,*	ಅಯಪು *ayapu.*
Rágy,	ರಾಗಿ *rági,*	ಯೆರೆಯಿ *yereyi.*
Night.	ರಾತ್ರಿ *rátri,*	ಬೈಟು, ಇರುಟ್ಟು *beiṭu, ira-ṭṭu.*
Consent,	ರಾಜಿ *ráji,*	ರಾಜಿ *ráji.*
Custom,	ರಿವಾಜು *riváju,*	ನಡಪು *naḍapu.*
Signature,	ರುಜು *ruju,*	ರುಜು *ruju.*
Rupee,	ರೂಪಾಯಿ *rúpáyi,*	ಉರ್ಪಿಯ *urpiya.*
Silk,	ರೇಷ್ಮೆ *réshme,*	ಪಟ್ಟು *paṭṭu.*
Peasant,	ರೈತ *reita,*	ರೈತು *raitu.*
La.	ಲ.	
Account,	ಲೆಖ್ಖ *lek-kha,*	ಲೆಕ್ಕ, ಕಣಕು *lekká, kaṇa-ku.*

	ಕನ್ನಡ ಭಾಷೆ.	ಕೊಡಗು ಭಾಷೆ.
Va.	ವ.	
Merchant,	ವರ್ತಕ *vartaka,*	ಸೆಟ್ಟಿ *seṭṭi.*
Deduction, reduction,	ವಜಾ *vajá,*	ವಜಕೈಪು, ಕೈಪು *vajakeipu, keipu.*
A coin of ten fannams,	ವರಹಾ *varahá,*	ಬಿರಾಂ *birám.*
Accommodation,	ವಸತಿ *vasati,*	ಜಾಗ *jága.*
Handkerchief,	ವಸ್ತ್ರ *vastra,*	ವೈತ್ರ *veitra.*
Recovery,	ವಸೂಲು *vasúlu,*	ವಸೂಲು *vasúlu.*
Possession, care,	ವಶ *vasha,*	ಪಕ್ಕ *pakka.*
Year,	ವರ್ಷ *varsha,*	ಕಾಲ *kála.*
Information,	ವರ್ತಮಾನ *vartamána,*	ಸುದ್ದಿ *suddi.*
Quarrel, law suit,	ವ್ಯಾಜ್ಯ *vyájya,*	ವೇಜ್ಯ *vejya.*
Returning,	ವಾಪಸು *vápasu,*	ಬೈಯಕ್ಕು *beiyakku.*
Instalment,	ವಾಯಿದೆ *váyide,*	ಗಡಬ, *gaḍaba,*
Week,	ವಾರ *vára,*	ಏಳು ನಾಳು *yéḷu-náḷu.*
Inquiry,	ವಿಚಾರಣೆ *vichárane,*	ವಿಚಾರ *vichára,*
Division of property, &c.	ವಿಭಾಗ *vibhága,*	ಪಾಲು *pálu.*
Dispute,	ವಿವಾದ *viváda,*	ತಕರಾರು *takarárú.*
Kindness,	ವಿಶ್ವಾಸ *vishwása,*	ಪಿರಿತ *pirita.*
Betel,	ವೀಳ್ಳೆ *víḷḷe,*	ಕೊಡಿಯಲೆ *koḍiyale.*
Particulars,	ವಿವರ *vivara,*	ವಿವರ, ಇವುರ *vivara, ivura.*
Salt,	ಉಪ್ಪು *uppu,*	ಉಪ್ಪು *uppu.*
Physician,	ವೈದ್ಯ *veidya,*	ಮದ್ದುಗಾರು, ಬೈಚಿಯಕಾರು *maddugáru, beichiyakáru.*
Jewel,	ವೊಡವೆ *voḍave,*	ಪದುವೆಚ್ಚಿ, ಪದೀಚಿ *paduvechchi, padíchi.*
To Acknowledge,	ವೊಪ್ಪು *voppu,*	ವೊತ್ತ *votta.*
To dry, to bake,	ವೊಣಗು *voṇagu,*	ವಣಕು *vaṇaku.*
Sha.	ಶ.	
The loose roots,	ಶದೆ *shade,*	ಕಳೆ *kaḷe.*
Village accountant or clerk,	ಶಾನಭಾಗ *shánabhága,*	ಚೇನಬಾಯು *chénabáyu.*

	ಕನ್ನಡ ಭಾಷೆ.	ಕೊಡಗು ಭಾಷೆ.
To be caught,	ಶಿಕ್ಕು *shikku,*	ಕಿಟ್ಟು *kiṭṭu.*
Punishment,	ಶಿಕ್ಷೆ *shikṣhe,*	ಸೀಕ್ಷೆ *síkṣhe.*
Small pox,	ಶಿಡಬು *shiḍabu,*	ಅಂಮು, ಪುಂಣು *ammu, punnu.*
Chicken pox,	ಶಿತಾಳೆ *shitáḷe,*	ನೀಪರು *níparu.*
Persentage,	ಶೇಕಡ *shékaḍa,*	ನೂರಂಗು *núrangu.*
Bridge,	ಶೇತವೆ *ṣhétave,*	ಸೇತುವೆ *sétuve.*
Measure,	ಶೇರು *séru,*	ಸೇರು *séru.*
Concern,	ಷಾಮಿಲು *ṣhámilu,*	ಸಾಮಿಲು *sámilu.*
Beginning,	ಷುರು *ṣhuru,*	ಸುರು *suru.*
Sa.	ಸ.	
Circumstance,	ಸಂಗತಿ *sangati,*	ಸಂಗತಿ, ಮೊಳಿ *sangati, moḷi.*
Market,	ಸಂತೆ *sante,*	ಚತ್ತೆ *chatte.*
Repayment,	ಸಂದಾಯ *sandáya,*	ಕೊಡುಪು, *koḍupu.*
Wages, pay,	ಸಂಬಳ *sambaḷa,*	ಸಂಬಳ *sambaḷa.*
To happen,	ಸಂಭವಿಸು *sambhavisu,*	ಆಡು *áḍu.*
Consent,	ಸಂಮತಿ *sammati,*	ಒತ್ತಂಡದು *ottanḍadu.*
Intelligence,	ಸಮಾಚಾರ *samáchára,*	ವರ್ತಮಾನ, ಸುದ್ಧಿ *vartamána, suddhi.*
Goods,	ಸರಕು *saraku,*	ಸಾಮಾನ *sámána.*
Conveyance,	ಸವಾರಿ *savári,*	ಸವಾರಿ *savári.*
Also,	ಸಹಾ *sahá,*	ಕೂಡ *kúḍa.*
Now,	ಸಾಂಪ್ರತ *sámprata,*	ಇಕ್ಕಾ *ikká.*
Suffice,	ಸಾಕು *sáku,*	ಮದಿ *madi.*
To die,	ಸಾಯು *sáyu,*	ಚಾವು *chávu.*
A kind of spirituous liquor,	ಸಾರಾಯಿ *sáráyi,*	ಕಳ್ಳು *kaḷḷu.*
Delay,	ಸಾವಕಾಶ *sávakásha,*	ನಿದಾನ, ಮೆಲ್ಲೆ *nidána, melle.*
Witness,	ಸಾಕ್ಷಿ *sákṣhi,*	ಸಾಕ್ಷಿ *sákṣhi.*
To pour out,	ಸುರಿಯು *suriyu,*	ತೊರಿ *tori.*
Lie,	ಸುಳ್ಳು *suḷḷu,*	ಪೊಟ್ಟು *poṭṭu.*
Leaves,	ಸೊಪ್ಪು *soppu,*	ತೊಪ್ಪು *toppu.*

	ಕನ್ನಡ ಭಾಷೆ.	ಕೊಡಗು ಭಾಷೆ.
Ha.	ಹ.	
Day time,	ಹಗಲು *hagalu,*	ಪೋಲು *pólu.*
Money,	ಹಣ *haṇa,*	ಪಣ *paṇa.*
Fruit,	ಹಣ್ಣು *haṇṇu,*	ಪಂಣ್ಣು *panṇṇu.*
Ride, or ten,	ಹತ್ತು *hattu,*	ಪತ್ತು *pattu.*
Feast,	ಹಬ್ಬ *habba,*	ನಂಮೆ *namme.*
Obstacle,	ಹರಕತ್ತು *harakattu,*	ಅಡ್ಡಿ *aḍḍi.*
To tear,	ಹರಿಯು *hariyu,*	ಪರಿ, ಕೀತು *pari, kítu.*
Hunger,	ಹಶಿವು *hashivu,*	ಪದಿಪು, ಪದಿ *padipu, padi.*
Fine,	ಹಸನು *hasanu,*	ನಲ್ಲು *nallu.*
Cow,	ಹಸುವು *hasuvu,*	ಪಯ್ಯು *payyu.*
Village,	ಹಳ್ಳಿ *haḷḷi,*	ಊರು, ಕೇರಿ *úru, kéri.*
To throw,	ಹಾಕು *háku,*	ಇಡು, ಚಾಡು *iḍu, cháḍu.*
Readiness,	ಹಾಜರು *hájaru,*	ಹಾಜರ್ *hájar.*
Adultery,	ಹಾದರ *hádara,*	ಪುಲಿಯಾಟು *puliyáṭu.*
A road,	ಹಾದಿ *hádi,*	ಬಟ್ಟೆ *baṭṭe.*
A bed,	ಹಾಶಿಗೆ *háshige,*	ಕಡಕ್ಕೆ *kaḍakke.*
To spread,	ಹಾಸು *hásu,*	ಬಿರಿ *biri.*
Milk,	ಹಾಲು *hálu,*	ಪಾಲು *pálu.*
A snake,	ಹಾವು *hávu,*	ಪಾಂಬು *pámbu.*
To catch or apprehend.	ಹಿಡಿಯು *hiḍiyu,*	ಪುಡಿ *puḍi.*
An order,	ಹುಕುಂ *hukum,*	ಅಪ್ಪಣೆ *appaṇe.*
Straw,	ಹುಲ್ಲು *hullu,*	ಪಿಲ್ಲು *pillu.*
Toddy,	ಹೆಂಡ *henḍa,*	ಬೊಳ್ಳೆಕಳ್ಳು *boḷḷe-kaḷḷu.*
Wife,	ಹೆಂಡತಿ *henḍati,*	ಪೊಂಣು *ponṇu.*
Name,	ಹೆಸರು *hesaru,*	ಪೆದ *peda.*
To tell,	ಹೇಳು *héḷu,*	ಯೆಂಣು *yenṇu.*
To obtain,	ಹೊಂದು *hondu,*	ಸೇರು, ಸಂಪಾದಿಚಿರು *séru, sampádichiru.*
Smoke,	ಹೊಗೆ *hoge,*	ಪೊಗೆ *poge.*
To flog,	ಹೊಡಿಯು *hoḍiyu,*	ಪೊಯ್ಯಿ *poyyi.*
An ear of corn,	ಹೊಡೆ *hoḍe,*	ಪೊಡೆ *poḍe.*
Time,	ಹೊತ್ತು *hottu,*	ನೇರ *néra.*
Except,	ಹೊರ್ತು *hortu,*	ಅಲ್ಲತೆ *allate.*

	ಕನ್ನಡ ಭಾಷೆ.	ಕೊಡುಗು ಭಾಷೆ.
To start,	ಹೊರಡು *horaḍu,*	ಪೊರಡು *poraḍu.*
Burthen,	ಹೊರೆ *hore,*	ಮೊಟ್ಟೆ, ಕೆಟ್ಟು *moṭṭe, keṭṭu.*
Field,	ಹೊಲ *hola,*	ಪೊಲ *pola.*
River,	ಹೊಳೆ *hoḷe,*	ಪೊಳೆ *poḷe.*
Go,	ಹೋಗು *hógu,*	ಪೊ *po.*
Goat,	ಹೋತ *hóta,*	ಪೋತು *pótu.*
Yes,	ಹೌದು *haudu,*	ಅಕ್ಕು *akku.*

Kṣhe.

ಕ್ಷೆ.

Good health,	ಕ್ಷೇಮ *kṣhéma,*	ನಲ್ಲೊಣೆ, ಸುಗ ತೊಡೆ *nallone, suga-toḍe.*

A LIST OF IMPORTANT REVENUE TERMS.

ಇಜಾರೆ *ijáre*,
ಇನಾಂ *inám*,
ಕಂದಾಯ *kandáya*,
ಖುಷ್ಕಿ ಯಾ ಹೊಲ *khuṣhki* or *hola*,
ಛಪಾವಣೆ *chhapávaṇe*,
ಸಾಗುಸಂತು *ságusantu*,

ಜೋಡಿ ಉತ್ತಾರ *jóḍi-uttára*,
ಸೇಂದಿ *séndi*,
ಸಾರಾಯಿ *sáráyi*,
ಭಂಗಿ *bhangi*,
ಅಫೀಮು *aphímu*,
ಗೌಡುಂಬಳಿ *gouḍumbaḷi*,
ನಾಯಿ ಮಣ್ಣು ಉತ್ತಾರ *náyi maṇṇu uttára*,
ನೀರು ಕಂದಾಯ *nírukandáya*,
ಬಟಮಾನ್ಯ *baṭamánya*,
ವಾರ *vára*,

ಯಾಲ *yála*,
ಬಾಣೆ *báṇe*,

Contract ಇಜಾರೆ ಗುತ್ತಿಗೆ *ijáre, guttige.*

Lands rent free ದಯಬುಟ್ಟಿದು, ಇನಾಂ, ಜಾಗೀರು *dayabuṭṭadu, inám, jágíru.*

Money rent ಕಂದಾಯ *kandáya.*

Dry land ಪೊಲ *pola.*

Concealment of land ವೊಳಿಪಿಚಂಡದು, ಛಪಾವಣೆ, *woḷipichanḍadu, chhapávaṇe.*

An account shewing the species and quantity of seed sown, the extent of land under cultivation, and the quantity remaining. } ಸಾಗುಸಂತು *sagusuntu.*

Lands given to the Pagodahs ಜೋಡಿ ಉತ್ತಾರ *jóḍi-uttára.*

Toddy ಬೊಳ್ಳೆಕಳ್ಳು *boḷḷekaḷḷu.*

Liquor ಕಾಚಿಂಗಳ್ಳು *káchingaḷḷu.*

An intoxicating Indian plant so called ಭಂಗಿ *bhangi.*

Opium ಐಮದ್ದು *eimaddu.*

Gowdah Oombly ಗೌಡುಂಬಳಿ *gouḍumbaḷi.*

Land given to Village Watchmen.

Water tax ನೀರು ಕಂದಾಯ *níru kandáya.*

Lands given to Brahmans ಬಟಮಾನ್ಯ *baṭamánya.*

An equal division of the crop between the Government and the Ryot } ವಾರ *vára.*

Cardamom ಯಾಲ *yála.*

High ground attached to certain Paddy Fields ಬಾಣೆ *báṇe.*

ಒಳ್ಳೆ ಮೆಣಸು *volle menasu,*	Pepper	ನಲ್ಲ ಮಳವು ***nalla-maḷavu.***
ರಾಳು *rálu,*	Resin	ಬಂದ ***banda.***
ಅಡಿಕೆ *aḍike,*	Arecanut	ಅಡೆಕೆ ***aḍeke.***
(ತರಿ) ಬತ್ತದಗದ್ದೆ (*tari*) *battada-gadde,*	Wet land	ಬೇಲು ***bélu.***

ಮೊಹತರ್ಫಾ ***mohatarphá,*** — To this belong the following taxes, viz.

೧ ಮನೆ ಕಂದಾಯ *mane-kandáya*	Tax on houses	ಮನೆಪಣ ***mane-puṇa.***
೨ ದುಕಾನ್ ಕಂದಾಯ ***dukán-kandáya,***	Tax on shops	ಅಂಗಡಿ ಕಂದಾಯ ***angaḍi-kandáya.***
೩ ಮಗ್ಗ ಕಂದಾಯ ***magga-kandáya,***	Tax on looms	ಮಗ್ಗ ಕಂದಾಯ ***magga-kandáya.***
೪ ಗಾಣ ಕಂದಾಯ ***gáṇa-kandáya,***	Tax on oil	ಗಾಣ ಕಂದಾಯ ***gáṇa-kandáya.***

73 ಕಡ್ಡಿ ಅರಗು ***kaḍḍi-aragu,***	Sealing wax	ಅರಕು ***araku.***
ಅರಸಿನ ***arasina,***	Turmeric	ಮಂಜ ***manja.***
ಜೇನು ಮೇಣ *jénu-méṇa,*	Honey wax	ತೆಮೊಗ್ಗು *temoggu.*
ಹುಳಿಚಲುಹುಡಿ *hulichaluhuḍi,*	Red dye powder	ಹುಳಿಚಲು ಹುಡಿ *hulichalu-huḍi.*
ಹುಣಸೆ ಹಣ್ಣು ***huṇase-hanṇu,***	Tamarind	ಪುಳಿಜೆ *puḷije.*
ಗಂಧದ ಮರ ***gandada-mara,***	Sandalwood	ಚಾಂದು ಮರ *chándu-mura.*
ಸೀಗೇ ಕಾಯಿ ***sígé-káyi,***	Country soap nut	ಪುಳಂಗೋಡು *puḷungóḍu.*

K

GLOSSARY OF JUDICIAL WORDS.

Canarese.	*Coorg.*	*English.*
ಅಂಗೀಕಾರ *angíkára,*	ಒತ್ತವದು *ottavadu,*	Acceptance.
ಅಡಕ *aḍaka,*	ಅಡಕ *aḍaka,*	Commodiousness.
ಅರ್ಜೀದಾಸ್ತು *arjidástu,*	ಅರ್ಜೀಮಾಡಿಯಂಡು *arjimá-ḍiyanḍu,*	Petitioning.
ಅಡೆಚಣೆ *aḍachaṇe,*	ಅಡ್ಡಿ *aḍḍi,*	Obstruction.
ಅಮಲುಜಾರಿ *amalujári,*	ಅಮಲ್‌ಜಾರಿ *amaljári,*	Execution.
ಅಭಿಃಪ್ರಾಯ *abhhipráya,*	ಅಭಿಪ್ರಾಯ *abhipráya,*	Opinion.
ಅನುಮಾನ *anumána,*	ಅಂದೇಶ *andésha,*	Suspicion.
ಅಸಂಗತ *asangata,*	ತೊಂದರೆ *tondare,*	Inconvenience.
ಅನುಕೂಲ *anukúla,*	ಅನುಕೂಲ *anukúla,*	Convenience.
ಅವಘುತ *avaghata,*	ಅರಿಚೆರುವದು *arichiruvadu,*	Information.
ಅಭಾವ *abháva,*	ರೂಪಲ್ಲತೆ *rúpallate,*	Shapeless.
ಅನಂಗೀಕಾರ *anangíkára,*	ಒತ್ತವತದು *ottavatadu,*	Unacceptable.
ಅನ್ಯಾಯ *anyáya,*	ಅಂಞಾಯ *anyáya,*	Injustice.
ಅವಶ್ಯ *avasya,*	ಬೊಂಡಿಚಾಯಿತು *bonḍichá-yitu,*	Necessary.
ಅಡ್ಢಿ *aḍḍhi,*	ಅಡ್ಡಿ *aḍḍi,*	Hinderance.
ಅತಿಶಯ *atishaya,*	ಕಲಿಜಿಯ *kalijiya,*	Wonderful.
ಅಜ್ಞಾನ *agnána,*	ಅಜ್ಞಾನ *agnána,*	Spiritual-ignorance.
ಅದ್ಭುತ *adbhuta,*	ಕಲಿಜಿಯ *kalijiya,*	Astonishment.
ಅಸಂಖ್ಯಾತ *asankhyáta,*	ಎಂಣೊಕ್ಕೈಯತದಯ *eṇno-keiyatada,*	Incalculable.
ಅದಂರುವಾರು *aundaruváru,*	ಒಳುಲು *oḷulu,*	Inside.
ಅವಧಿ *avadhi,*	ಕಾಲ *kála,*	Period.
ಅವಿವೇಕ *avivéka,*	ಬುದ್ಧಿ ಇಲ್ಲತು *buddi-illatu,*	Ignorance.
ಅಕ್ರಮ *akrama,*	ಸಮ ಇಲ್ಲತೆ *sama-illate,*	Improper.
ಅಂತ್ಯ *antya,*	ತುದಿ *tudi,* ತಲೆ *tale,*	End.
ಅಪ್ರಮಾಣೀಕತೆ *apramáṇi-kate,*	ಅಂಞಾಯತು *anyáyatu,*	Dishonest.

Canarese.	*Coorg.*	*English.*
ಅರ್ಜೀದಾರ *arjidára,*	ಅರ್ಜೀಕಾರು *arjikáru,*	Petitioner.
ಅಸಂಹ್ಯ *asanhya,*	ಹೇಸಿಗೆ *hésige,*	Disgust.
ಅದೃಷ್ಟ *adrushṭa,*	ಅದೃಷ್ಟ *adrushṭa,*	Fortune, luck.
ಅಭ್ಯಾಸ *abhyasa,*	ನೇಮ *néma,*	Practice.
ಅವಸಾನ *avasána,*	ಚಾವಕ *chávaka,*	Period of dissolution.
ಅಪವಾದ *apaváda,*	ಬದ್ಲಾಮೆ *badláme,*	Blame.
ಅಭಿಲಾಷೆ *abhiláshe,*	ಆಸೆ *áse,*	Desire, wish.
ಅಂತರಂಗ *antaranga.*	ಗುಟ್ಟು *guṭṭu,*	Secrecy.
ಅಲಹಿದ *alahida,*	ಬೋರೆ *bóre,*	Separate.
ಅಜಾಗ್ರತೆ *ajágrate,*	ಅಜಾಗ್ರತೆ *ajágrate,*	Carelessness.
ಅಕಾಲ *akála,*	ನೇರ ಅಲ್ಲತು *néra-allatu,*	Untimely.
ಅಕಾರಣ *akáraṇa,*	ಮೊಳಿ ಇಲ್ಲತು *moḷi-illatu,*	Causeless.
ಅದ್ಯಾಪಿ *adyápi,*	ಇಕ್ಕಲು *ikkalu,*	Till now.
ಅಪ್ರಯೋಜನ *aprayójana,*	ಪ್ರಯೊಜನಕ್ಕಾಗತು *prayója nakkágatu,*	Useless.
ಅಪರಾದಿ *aparádi,*	ತಪ್ಪುಗಾರು *tappugáru,*	Offender.
ಅನಂತರ *anantara,*	ಪಿಂಞೆ *pinye,*	Afterwards.
ಅತಿಕ್ರಮ *atikrama,*	ಬೈಂಬು *baimbu,*	Transgression.
ಅನುಮಾನ *anumána,*	ತಮುಜ *tamuja,*	Suspicion.
ಅನಾಥ *anátha,*	ದಿಕ್ಕಿಲ್ಲತವು *dikkillatavu,*	Destitute.
ಅಣಗಿಸು *aṇagisu,*	ಅಡಕು *aḍaku,*	To take refuge.
ಅದಾವತು *adávatu,*	ಪಗೆ *page,*	Enmity.
ಅಯುಕ್ತ *ayukta,*	ಸರಿ ಇಲ್ಲತು *sari-illatu,*	Improper.
ಅಭಿಮಾನ *abhimána,*	ಮರಿಯಾದಿ *mariyádi,*	Regard, honor.
ಅಬಲಸ್ಥ *abalasta,*	ಬಲ ಇಲ್ಲತವು *bala-illatavu,*	An unable man.
ಅಂತಃಪುರ *antahapura,*	ಒಳು *oḷu,*	In, within.
ಅನಾಜು *anáju,*	ದವಸ *davasa,*	Grain.
ಅಸಾಧ್ಯ *asádya,*	ಆಗತದು *ágatadu,*	Impossible.
ಅಡವು *aḍavu,*	ಪೊಣೆ, ಅಡು *poṇe, aḍu,*	Mortgage.
ಅರ್ಜೀ *arji,*	ಅರ್ಜೀ *arji,*	Petition.
ಅಸಲು *asalu,*	ನಲ್ಲು, ಅಸಲು *nallu, asalu,*	Fair, principal.
ಆಧಾರ *ádhára,*	ಅದಾರ *adára,*	A basis, security.
ಅಟಂಕ *aṭanka,*	ಹರಕತು *harakatu,*	Objection.
ಆಜ್ಞಾಧಾರಕ *agnádháraka,*	ಸೇವಕು *sévaku,*	Obedient servant.
ಅತಂಕ *atanka,*	ಅಡ್ಡಿ *aḍḍi,*	Obstruction.

Judicial Words.

Canarese.	*Coorg.*	*English.*
ಆಖೈರು *ákheiru,*	ಅಕ್ಕೈರು *ákeiru,*	The end.
ಆರಂಭ *árambha,*	ಷುರು *ṣhuru,*	Beginning.
ಆಸಾಮಿ *ásámi,*	ಮನುಸು *manusu,*	Individual.
ಆಜ್ಞಾಪಿಸು *ágnápisu,*	ಅರಿಚಿರು *arichiru,*	To command.
ಆತ್ಮಹತ್ಯ *átma-hatya,*	ತಾಂಗುತಾನೆ ಚಾವು *tángutá-ne-chávu,*	Suicide.
ಆರಭ್ಯ *árabhya,*	ಅಕ್ಕಿಂಜಿ *akklnji,*	Since, thence.
ಆಕ್ಷೇಪಣೆ *ákshépaṇe,*	ಐಬು *eibu,*	Objection.
ಆನಂದ *ánanda,*	ಆನಂದ *ánanda,* [*yi,*	Happiness.
ಆರಿಸು *árisu,*	ಆರಿಚಿರು, ಆಯಿ *árichiru, á-*	To choose, to select.
ಇನ್ಕಾರು *inkáru,*	ಒತ್ತುವತು *ottuvatu,*	Rejection.
ಇತ್ತಿಲ್ಲೆ *ittille,*	ಅರಿಚಿರು *arichiru,*	To report.
ಇಸ್ತಿಹಾರು *istiháru,*	ಇಸ್ತಿಹಾರು *istiháru,*	Proclamation.
ಇಲಾಖಾ *ilákhá,*	ಇಲಾಖ *ilákha,*	Department.
ಇನ್ಸಾಪು *insápu,*	ವಿಚಾರಣೆ *vicháraṇe,*	Inquiry.
ಇಂತ್ಯಾನು *intyánu,*	ಜಡ್ತಿ *jaḍti,*	Examination.
ಉಡುವೆ *uḍuve,*	ಕಾಡು *káḍu,*	Jungle.
ಉಂಬಳಿ *umbaḷi,*	ಉಂಬುಳಿ *umbuḷi,*	Land given to Ryots with favourable rent.
ಉದ್ರು *udṛu,*	ವಲಿ *vali,*	To fall down.
ಉರುಳುಹಾಕು *uruḷuháku,*	ನೇಂದ *nénda,*	To hang one's self.
ಉಭಯಂ *ubhayam,*	ಎಲ್ಲ *ella,*	Total.
ಉಪಯೋಗ *upayóga,*	ಉಪಯೊಗ *upayoga,*	Useful.
ಉಲ್ಲಂಘನೆ *ullanghane,*	ದಿಕ್ಕರ *dikkara,*	Disobedience.
ಉದ್ಯುಕ್ತ *udyukta,*	ಪ್ರಯತ್ನ *prayatna,*	Attempt.
ಉಪಚಾರ *upachára,*	ಮರಿಯಾದಿ *mariyádi,*	Obliging conduct.
ಉಭಯತ್ರ *ubhayatra,*	ದಂಡಾಳು *dandáḷu,*	Both persons.
ಉನ್ನತ *unnata,*	ಒದರ *odara,*	High.
ಉದ್ಭವ *udbhava,*	ಪುಟ್ಟುವದು *puṭṭuvadu,*	Birth.
ಊಹಿಸು *úhisu,*	ನಿರೀಚಿರು *niríchiru,*	To guess.
ಎಚ್ಚರಿಕೆ *echcharike,*	ಎಚ್ಚರ *echchara,*	Warning.
ಎಣಿಸು *eṇisu,*	ಬೇರಿಚಿರು *bérichiru,*	To think.
ಎಥೇಷ್ಟ *etheṣhṭa,*	ದೂತ, ಪೆರ್ತ *dúta, perta,*	Much.
ಏಕಾಂಗಿ *ékángi,*	ಏಕಾಂಗಿ *ékángi,* [*chengú,*	A solitary life.
ಏವಂಚ *évancha,*	ಎನ್ನನೆ ಆಚೆಂಗೂ *ennane-á-*	However.

Canarese.	*Coorg.*	*English.*
ಏಕಪಕ್ಷ *ékapakṣha,*	ಒರುಕಡೆ *orukaḍe,*	One side.
ಏಕೀಭವಿಸು *ékíbhavisu,*	ಒಂದೇ ನೆನಪು *ondé-nenapu,*	To be unanimous.
ಐಜನ್ *eijan,*	ಅದೆ *ade,*	Same.
ಐಂದಾ *eindá,*	ಇಂನು ಮಿಂಞೆ *innu-minye,*	In future.
ಒಕ್ಕಲು *okkalu,*	ಒಕ್ಕ *okka,*	A tenancy.
ಓಣಿ *óṇi,*	ಓಣಿ *óṇi,*	A lane.
ಕಕ್ಷಿಗಾರ *kakṣhigára,*	ವೇಜ್ಯಗಾರ *véjyagára,*	Parties.
ಕ್ರಮ *krama,*	ಕಟ್ಲೆ *kaṭle,*	Rule.
ಕರಾರು *karáru,*	ಕರಾರು *karáru,*	Bond.
ಕಬೂಲಾತಿ *kabúláti,*	ಒತಂಡದು *otanḍadu,*	Consultation.
ಕರುಣ *karuṇa,*	ಪಿರಿತ *pirita,*	Favour.
ಕ್ರಯಸಾದನ *krayasáḍana,*	ಕ್ರಯಸಾದನ *krayasádana,*	Deed of sale.
ಕಚರ *kachara,*	ಕಸ *kasa,*	Sweepings.
ಕತ್ತುಕಿವಿಚು *kattukivichu,*	ಬೋಳೆನೆಕ್ಕು *bólenekku,*	To squeeze one's neck.
ಕರ್ತವ್ಯ *kartavya,*	ಸರಿಆನದು *sariánadu,*	Suitable.
ಕಲಹ *kalaha,*	ಜಗಳ *jagaḷa,*	Quarrel.
ಕಪಟ *kapaṭa,*	ಕಪಟ *kapaṭa,*	Fraud.
ಕಾಲಕ್ಷೇಪ *kálakṣhépa,*	ದಿನಕೈಪು *dinakeipu,*	Passing away time.
ಕಾಪಾಡು *kápáḍu,*	ಚಾಕು *cháku,*	To nourish,
ಕಿರುಕುಳ *kirukuḷa,*	ಕಿರುಕುಳ *kirukuḷa,*	Trifling trouble.
ಕುರಿತು *kuritu,*	ಗೊಂಡು *gonḍu,*	Regarding.
ಕುಯುಕ್ತಿ *kuyukti,*	ಕುಯುಕ್ತಿ *kuyukti,*	Craft, device.
ಕುಂಬೆಕಂಡಿ *kumbekanḍi,*	ಕುಂಬೆಗಂಡಿ *kumbeganḍi,*	Gate of the water-course of a paddy field.
ಕೈಪಿಯತು *keipiyatu,*	ಕೈಪಿಯತು *keipiyatu,*	Deposition.
ಕೈದಿ *keidi,*	ಕೈದಿ *keidi,*	Prisoner.
ಕೊಚ್ಚೆಕಾಡು *kochchekáḍu,*	ಕೊಚ್ಚೆಕಾಡು *kochchekáḍu,*	Shrubs.
ಕೊಪ್ಲು *koplu,*	ಕೊಪ್ಪ *koppa,*	Suburbs of a village.
ಕೋಪೋದ್ರೇಕ *kópodréka,*	ಚೊಡಿಬಂದು *choḍibandu,*	Provocation.
ಕೋಳ *kóḷa,*	ಕೋಳ *kóḷa,*	Handcuff.
ಕೋರುವಿಕೆ *kóruvike,*	ಕೋರುವದು *kóruvadu,*	Hope, desire.
ಕೋರಿ *kóri,*	ಕೋರಿ *kóri,*	Worn out.
ಮೊರ *mora,*	ಮೊರ *mora,*	Fan.
ಕೊಲೆ *kole,*	ಕೊಲೆ *kole,*	Murder.
ಕೊಲ್ಲು *kollu,*	ಕೊಲ್ಲು *kollu*	To kill.

Judicial Words.

Canarese.	*Coorg.*	*English.*
ಖರಾರುವಾಕ *kharáruváka,*	ಕರಾರು ಅನೆಕೆ *karáru-aneke,*	According to agreement.
ಖರಾರು *kharáru,*	ಕರಾರು *karáru,*	Document.
ಖುಲ್ಲಾ *khullá*	ತೊರಂದಿತು *toranditu,*	Open, unsealed.
ಖುಲಾಸು *khulásu,*	ಬುಡುಗಡೆ *buḍugaḍe,*	Release.
ಗಣಿತ *gaṇita,*	ಲೆಖ್ಖ *lekkha,*	Computation.
ಗತ *gata,*	ಕಯಿಂಜದು *kayinjadu,*	Past.
ಗರ್ಭವಿಚ್ಛಿಂನೆ *garbhavi-chchínne,*	ಕುಳಿಯಮೆಕರಕುವು *kuḷiya-mekarakuvu,*	Abortion.
ಗರ್ಭೀಕರಿಸು *garbhikarisu,*	ಕೂಡ ಇಡು *kúḍa-iḍu,*	To enclose.
ಗುಜರಾಯಿಸು *gujaráyisu,*	ಒಪ್ಪಿಚೆರು *oppichiru,*	To deliver.
ಗುಮಾನಿ *gumáni,*	ಗುಮಾನಿ *gumáni,*	Suspicion.
ಗುತ್ತಿಗೆ *guttige,*	ಗುತ್ತಿಗೆ *guttige,*	Contract.
ಗುದಸ್ತಾ *gudastá,*	ಕಯಿಂಜದು *kayinjadu,*	A year or month past.
ಗುಮಾಸ್ತೆ *gumáste,*	ಗುಮಸ್ತು *gumastu*	A clerk.
ಗೈರುವಾಜಬಿ *geiruvájibi,*	ಬರಾಬರಿ ಅಲ್ಲತು *bárabari-allatu,*	Unlawful.
ಗೈರುಸಾಬೀತು *geirusábítu,*	ರುಜು ಆತದು *ruju,-átadu,*	Unproved.
ಗೈರುಹಾಜರು *geiruhájaru,*	ಹಾಜರು ಇಲ್ಲತು *hájaru-illa-tu,*	Absence.
ಗೋಪ್ಯ *gópya,*	ಗುಟ್ಟು *guṭṭu,*	Secret.
ಘನವುಳ್ಳ *ghanavuḷḷa,*	ಮರಿಯಾದಿವುಳ್ಳು *mariyá-divuḷḷu,*	Honorable.
ಚತುರ್ಗಡಿ *chaturgaḍi,*	ಅರ್ದಿ *ardi,*	Boundary.
ಚಂಚಲ *chanchala,*	ಚಂಚಲ *chanchala,*	Fickle.
ಚಪಳತ್ವ *chapaḷatva,*	ಚಪಳ *chapaḷa.*	Fickleness.
ಚ್ಛಾತ್ವರ್ಯ *chchátvarya,*	ಚಾಲಕು *chaláku,*	Skilful, cleverness.
ಚಾಲು *chálu,*	ನಡತೆ *naḍate,*	Conduct.
ಚಿಕಟಾಯಿಸು *chikaṭáyisu,*	ಪತ್ತಿಚೆರು *pattichiru,*	To affix.
ಚಿತಾವಣೆ *chitáváṇe,*	ಪಡಿಪಿಚೆರುವು *paḍipichiru-vu,*	Persuasion.
ಛಪಾವಣೆ *chhpávaṇe,*	ಒಳಿಪಿಚೆರುವು *oḷipichiruvu,*	Concealment.
ಛರಸ್ಥಿತಿ *chharasthiti,*	ನಗ, ಸಾಮಾನ *naga, sámá-na,*	Moveable property.
ಛಾಪಕಾಗದ *chápakágada,*	ಮುದ್ರೆಕಾಗದ *mudre-kága-da,*	Stamp paper.

Canarese.	*Coorg.*	*English.*
ಜಮೀನು ***jamínu,***	ಭೂಮಿ ***búmi,***	Land.
ಜಂಗಮರು ***jangamaru,***	ಜಂಗಮಂಗ ***jangamanga,***	Linga priests.
ಜಪ್ತಿ ***japti,***	ಜಫ್ತಿ ***japhti,***	Attachment.
ಜವಾಬು ***javábu,***	ಉತ್ತರ ***uttara,***	Answer.
ಜಂಗಮಸ್ಥಿತಿ ***jangamasthiti,***	ನಗ ನಾಣ್ಯ ***naga-nánṇya,***	Personal property.
ಜವಾಬುದಾರಿ ***javábuddári,***	ಜವಾಬುದಾರಿಕೆ ***javábuddári-ke,***	Responsibility.
ಜಕಂ ***jakam,***	ಗಾಯ ***gáya,***	Wound.
ಜಹಗೀರು ***jahagíru,***	ಜಾಗೀರು ***jágíru,***	Land granted free of rent.
ಜಮ್ಮ ***jamma,***	ಜಂಮ ***jamma,***	Land given with favorable rent, on feudal tenure.
ಜಾಮೀನು ***jáminu,***	ತೊಣೆ ***toṇe,*** [*na,*	Bail.
ಜಾರತ್ವ ***járatva,***	ಪುಲಿಯಾಡಿತನ ***puliyaḍita-***	Adultery.
ಜೀವನಾಂಶ ***jívanánsha,***	ಬದಕುವ ಬಟ್ಟೆ ***badakuva-baṭṭe,***	Maintenance.
ಜಿಂದಗಿ ***jindgi,***	ಸಾಮಾನ, ನಗ ***sámána, na-ga,***	Property.
ಜುರುಮಾನ ***jurumána,***	ದಂಡ ***daṇḍa,***	Fine.
ಜ್ಞಾನ ***gnyána,***	ಬುದ್ಧಿ ***buddi,***	Wisdom.
ಜಗಳ ***jagaḷa,***	ಜಗಳ ***jagaḷa.***	Quarrel.
ಜಡ್ತಿ ***jaḍti,***	ಜಡ್ತಿ ***jaḍti,***	Examination.
ಝಾಡಿಸು ***jháḍisu,***	ಕೊಡಕು ***koḍaku,***	Shake.
ಟಕಾರಿ ***ṭakári,***	ಮೋಸ ***mósa,***	Deceit.
ಡಾಮೇಜು ***ḍáméju,***	ಲುಕ್ಸಾನು ***luksánu,***	Damage.
ಡಿಸುಮಿಸು ***ḍisumisu,***	ತಳ್ಳುವು ***taḷḷuvu,***	Dismiss.
ಡಿಕ್ರಿ ***ḍikri,***	ಪೈಸಲು ***peisalu,***	Decree.
ತೈಯಾರು ***teiyáru,***	ತೈಯಾರು ***teiyaru,***	Readiness.
ತಪ್ಪುಹೊರಿಸು ***tappuhorisu,***	ತಪ್ಪು ಪೊರಿಪಿಚಿರು ***tappu-poripichiru,***	To accuse.
ತನಿಕಿ ***taniki,***	ತನಿಕಿ ***taniki,***	Investigation.
ತಪಸೀಲು ***tapasílu,***	ತಪಸೀಲು ***tapasílu,***	Detail.
ತಗ್ಗೈರು ***tageiru,***	ಯಡುತಿರುವು ***yaḍutiruvu,***	Dismissal.
ತಕರಾರು ***takaráru,***	ತಕರಾರು ***takaráru,***	Dispute.

Judicial Words.

Canarese.	*Coorg.*	*English.*
ತರದೂಡು *taradúdu,*	ಪ್ರಯತ್ನ *prayatna,*	Attempt.
ತಮಾಮು *tamámu,*	ಯೆಲ್ಲಾ *yellá,*	All.
ತೃಪ್ತಿ *tṛupti,*	ಕುಶಿ *kushi,*	Satisfactory.
ತ್ವರ್ಯ *tvarya,*	ಬೆರಿಯ *beriya,*	Quickness.
ತ್ಯಜಿಸು *tyajisu,*	ಬುಟ್ಟುರು *buṭṭuru,*	To leave.
ತರ್ಜಿಮ *tarjima,*	ತರ್ಜಿಮ *tarjima,*	Translation.
ತರುವಾಯ *taruváya,*	ಪಿಂಞೆ *pinye,*	Afterwards.
ತದನಂತ *tadanantara,*	ಪಿಂಞೆ *pinye,*	Subsequently.
ತರಾತರ *tarátara,*	ತರಾತರ *tarátara,*	Different sor t.
ತಾಮಸ *támasa,*	ನಿದಾನ *nidána,*	Delay.
ತಾತ್ಸಾರ *tátsára,*	ನಿದಾನ *nidána,*	Dolay.
ತಾಬೆ *tábe,*	ಪಕ್ಕ *pakka,*	Possession.
ತಾತ್ಪರ್ಯ *tátparya,*	ಅರ್ಥ *artha,*	Purport.
ತ್ರಾಣ *tráṇa,*	ಬಲ *bala,*	Able.
ತೀರ್ಪು *tírpu,*	ತೀರ್ಪು *tírpu,*	Decree.
ತಿರಸ್ಕಾರ *tiraskára,*	ದಿಕ್ಕರ *dikkara,*	Contempt.
ತೀರ್ಮಾನ *tírmána,*	ತೀಪದು *típadu,*	Settlement.
ತಿವಿಯು *tviyu,*	ಕುತ್ತು *kuttu,*	To poke.
ತುರಿತು *tiuritu,*	ಬೆರಿಯ *beriya,*	Soon.
ತೆರಿ *teri,*	ನಡೆ *naḍe,*	A passage.
ಕೈಬಳ್ಳಿ *keibaḷḷi,*	ಪಾಲು ಬಳ್ಳಿ *pálu-baḷḷi,*	A wild sort of creeper.
ದಗಾ *dagá,*	ಮೋಸ *mósa,*	Cheating.
ದರ್ಯಾಪ್ತಿ *dayarphti,*	ವಿಚಾರಣೆ *vichárаṇe,*	Investigation.
ದಸ್ತಗಿರಿ *dastagiri,*	ಪುಡಿಪದು *puḍipadu,*	Apprehension.
ದಂಡನೆ *danḍane,*	ಸಜ *saja,*	Punishment.
ದಫನ್ *dapan,*	ವಪ್ಪ *vappa,* [*vuḷḷavu,*	Burial.
ದಯಾಳು *dayáḷu,*	ಕಿರುಬಿಯವುಳ್ಳವು *kirubiya-*	A kind man.
ದ್ರವ್ಯ *drarya,*	ಪಣ *paṇa,*	Wealth.
ದರ್ಕಾರು *darkáru,*	ದರಕಾರು *darakáru,*	Necessity.
ದರ್ಕಾಸ್ತು *darkástu,*	ಕೇಪದು *képadu,*	Application.
ದಾರಿ *dári,*	ಬಟ್ಟೆ *baṭṭe,*	Road.
ದಿಗರು *digaru,*	ಬದಲು *badalu,*	Separate.
ದರ್ಶನ *darshana,*	ಬೇಟೆ *béṭe,*	Visitation.
ದಾಖಲೆ *dákhale,*	ದಾಕ್ಲೆ *ḍákle,*	Reference.
ದಿನಚರಿ *dinachari,*	ಎಕ್ಕಲು *ekkalu,*	Every day, always.

Canarese.	*Coorg.*	*English.*
ದಿವಾಳಿ *divâḷi,*	ದಿವಾಳಿ *divâḷi,*	Bankruptcy.
ದೀರ್ಘ *dírgha,*	ಉದ್ದ *udda,*	Long.
ದುರಾಲೋಚನೆ *durálóchane,*	ಕೆಟ್ಟ ಯೋಚನೆ *keṭṭa-yóchane,*	Bad consideration.
ದುರ್ಮಾರ್ಗ *durmárga,*	ಕೆಟ್ಟ ಬುದ್ಧಿ *keṭṭa-buddi,*	Wickedness.
ದುಸ್ಸಂಗ *dussanga,*	ಕೆಟ್ಟ ಸಂಗ *keṭṭa-sanga,*	An improper connexion.
ದುರ್ನಡತೆ *durnaḍate,*	ದುರ್ನಡತೆ *durnaḍate,*	Bad conduct.
ದುರ್ಮರಣ - *durmaraṇa,*	ದುರ್ಮರಣ *durmaraṇa,*	Untimely death.
ದುರ್ವ್ಯಾಪಾರ *durvyapára,*	ಕೆಟ್ಟ ಬೆಪಾರ *keṭṭa-bepára,*	Bad practice.
ದುಷ್ಟ *dushṭa,*	ದುಶ್ಟು *dushṭu,*	Wicked.
ದೇಖತ್ *dekhat,*	ನೋಡುನವಡನೆ *nóḍunavaḍane,*	Immediately seen.
ದ್ವೇಷ *dvésha,*	ದೇಶ್ಯ *déshya,*	Enmity.
ದುರ್ಬೋದನೆ *durbódane,*	ದುರ್ಬೋದನೆ *durbódane,*	Bad advice.
ದೊಂಬಿ *dombi,*	ಗುಲ್ಲು *gullu,*	Confused noise.
ಧನಾಢ್ಯ *dhanádya,*	ಪಣಗಾರು *paṇagáru,*	Wealthy man.
ನಕಲು *nakalu,*	ನಕಲು *nakalu,*	Duplicate copy.
ನಮೂದು *namúdu,*	ಕಾಂಬದು *kámbadu,*	Appearance.
ನಮೂನೆ *namúne,*	ಮಾದ್ರಿ *mádri,*	Sample.
ನಗದು *nagadu,*	ನಗದು *nagadu,*	Cash or ready money.
ನಪಾವತಿ *napávati,*	ನಪೆ *nape,*	Profit.
ನವಾಶಿರ್ಷೆ *naváshirṣhe,*	ಪುದಿಜಾಯಿತು *pudijáyitu,*	Recently.
ನಷ್ಟ *nashṭa,*	ಲುಕ್ಸಾನು *luksánu,*	Loss.
ನಂಬು *nambu,*	ನಂಬು *numbu,*	To trust.
ನ್ಯಾಯ *nyaya,*	ಞಾಯ *nyáya,*	Justice.
ನಾಡು *náḍu,*	ನಾಡು *náḍu,*	A small district.
ನಿಶಿ *nishi,*	ನಡಪಾದ್ರ *naḍapádra,*	Midnight.
ನಿರಾಕರಿಸು *nirákarisu,*	ದಿಕ್ಕಾರ ಮಾಡು *dikkára-máḍu,*	To disgrace.
ನಿರ್ನಿಮಿತ್ಯ *nirnimitya,*	ಮುಂಡತೆ *munḍata,*	Causeless.
ನಿರ್ಮಾಣ *nirmáṇa,*	ಉಂಡಾಕುವದು *undákuvadu,*	Creation.
ನಿಂದ್ಯ *nindya,*	ಪಳಿ *paḷi,*	Blameable.
ನಿರ್ಜೀವಿ *nirjívi,*	ಜೀವ ಇಲ್ಲತದು *jíva-illata-* [*du,*	Inanimate.

Judicial Words.

Canarese.	*Coorg.*	*English.*
ನಿಬಂಧನೆ *nibandhane,*	ನಿಬಂದನೆ *nibandane,*	Rule.
ನಿರೀಕ್ಷಿಸು *niríkṣhisu,*	ನೋಟಿಯಂಡಿರು *nóṭiyanḍi-ru,*	To expect.
ನಿರಾಧಾರಿ *nirádhárì,*	ಬಡವು *baḍavu,*	An unsupported man.
ನಿರಾಪರಾಧಿ *niráparádhi,*	ತಪ್ಪು ಇಲ್ಲತು *tappu-illatu,*	Not guilty.
ನಿಪುಣ *nipuṇa,*	ನಿಪಣು *nipaṇu,*	A clever man.
ನಿರ್ದೋಷಿ *nirdóṣhi,*	ಪಾಪ ಮಾಡತವು *pápa-má-ḍatavu,*	An innocent man.
ನಿಷ್ಠೂರ *niṣhṭúra,*	ನಿಟ್ಟೂರ *niṭṭúra,*	Harsh, cruel.
ನಿರ್ಗತಿ *nirgati,*	ಗತಿಯಿಲ್ಲತು *gati-illatu,*	Insolvent.
ನಿತ್ರಾಣ *nitraṇa,*	ನಿತ್ರಾಣ *nitráṇa,*	Powerless.
ನಿರ್ವ್ಯಾಜ್ಯ *nirvyájya,*	ಕೆಟ್ಟವೇಜ್ಯ *keṭṭavéjya,*	Not litigious.
ನೂನ್ಯತೆ *núnyate,*	ಕೊರಉ *koravu,*	Deficience.
ಪಂಚಾಯಿತಿ *pancháyiti,*	ಪಂಚಾತಿ *panchâti,*	Arbitration.
ಪದ್ಧತಿ *paddati,*	ಮರುವಾದಿ *maruvádi,*	Custom.
ಪರಬಾರೆ *parabáre,*	ಬೋರೆ *bóre,*	Separate.
ಪೌತಿ *pouti,*	ಸತ್ತದು *sattadu,*	Deceased.
ಪಕ್ಷಪಾತ *pakṣhapáta,*	ಪಕ್ಷಪಾತ *pakṣhapáta,*	Partial.
ಪರಿಶೀಲನೆ *parishílane,*	ಸೋಡ್ನೆ *sódne,*	Examination.
ಪಸಂದು *pasandu,*	ನಲ್ಲದು *nalladu,*	Good.
ಪರನಿಂದ್ಯ *paranindya,*	ವಭನಪಳಿಯೊ *vabhana-pa-ḷiyo,*	Abusing others.
ಪರೋಪಕಾರ *parópakára,*	ಪರಉಪಕಾರ *paraupakára,*	Patriotism.
ಪರವರ್ಶಿ *paravarshi,*	ಸಾಕುವದು *sákuvadu,*	Protection.
ಪರಿಕ್ಷೆ *parikṣhe,*	ಜಡ್ತಿ *jadti,*	Examination.
ಪರಂತು *parantu.*	ಪಿಂಞೆ *pinye,*	Afterwards.
ಪ್ರತಿವಾದಿ *prativádi,*	ಪ್ರತಿವಾದಿ *prativádi,*	Defendant.
ಪ್ರಮಾಣ *pramáṇa,*	ಸತ್ಯ *satya,*	Oath.
ಪ್ರಕಾರ *prakára.*	ಅಂನನೆ *annane,*	According to.
ಪ್ರಾರಂಭ *prárambha,*	ಸುರು *suru,*	Commencement.
ಪ್ರಾರ್ಥಿಸು *prárthisu,*	ನೆನೆ *nene,*	To praise.
ಪರಿಶೋಧನೆ *parishódhane,*	ಸೋದನೆ *sódane,*	Examination.
ಪ್ರವೇಶ *pravésha,*	ಕೂಡುವು *kúḍuvu,*	Entering.
ಪ್ರಪಂಚ *prapancha,*	ಪ್ರಪಂಚ *prapancha,*	World.
ಪಾಲ *pála,*	ಪಾಲ *pála,*	Wooden bridge.

Canarese.	*Coorg.*	*English.*
ಪಾಂಡಿ *pánḍi,*	ಪಾಂಡಿ *pánḍi,*	A kind of bamboo boat.
ಪಿರ್ಯಾದು *piryádu,*	ಪ್ರಿಯಾದಿ *priyádi,*	Complaint.
ಪರಿಣಾಮ *pariṇáma,*	ನಲ್ಲೋಣೆ *nallóṇe,*	Welfare.
ಪ್ರವೀಣ *pravíṇa,*	ಗಟ್ಟಿಗು *gaṭṭigu,*	A prudent man.
ಪ್ರಕಟಣೆ *prakaṭaṇe,*	ಸುದ್ದಿ *suddi,*	Promulgation.
ಪಿತೂರಿ *pitúri,*	ಪಿತೂರಿ *pitúri,*	Plot.
ಪಾಪರು *páparu,*	ಪಾಪರು *páparu,*	Pauper.
ಪುನರ್ವಿಮರ್ಶೆ *punarvi-marshe,*	ಬದ್ಲಾಯಿತು ವಿಚಾರ *badlá-yitu-vichára*	Review.
ಪೈಸಲು *peisalu,*	ಪೈಸಲು *peisalu,*	Decree.
ಪರಾಂಬರಿಸು *parámbarisu,*	ನೋಡು *nóḍu,*	To see.
ಪತ್ತೆ *patte,*	ಪುಡಿಪದು *puḍipadu,*	To catch, apprehension.
ಪರಾರಿ *parári,*	ಓಡಿಪೋಪು *óḍipópu,*	Absconding.
ಪರಸ್ಪರ *parasvara,*	ಪರಬಾರೆ *parabáre,*	Mutual.
ಪ್ರತ್ಯೇಕ *pratyéka,*	ಬೋರೆ *bóre,*	Separate.
ಪ್ರತಿ ಕಕ್ಷಿಗಾರ *prati-kakṣhi-gára,*	ಒರೊರು ವೆಜ್ಯಗಾರು *ororu-vejyagáru,*	Each party.
ಪರಾಕ್ರಮ *parákrama,*	ಪರಾಕ್ರಮ *parákrama,*	Power.
ಪರಿಷ್ಕಾರ *parishkára,*	ನಲ್ಲೋಣೆ *nallóṇe,*	Decoration.
ಪ್ರಬುದ್ಧ *prabudda,*	ಬುದ್ಧಿಕಾರು *buddikáru,*	A wise or learned man.
ಪ್ರೌಡ *prauḍa,*	ಗಟ್ಟಿಗು *gaṭṭigu,*	Clever man.
ಪ್ರೇಮ *préma,*	ಕೊಡಿ *kodi,*	Affection, kindness.
ಪೇರಿಸ್ತು *péristu,*	ಪೇರಿಸ್ತು *péristu,*	Abstract.
ಬಡ್ಡಿ *baḍḍi,*	ಚುಂಗಡಿ *chungaḍi,*	Interest.
ಬರೀ *barí,*	ಬೊರಿ *bori,*	Empty.
ಬಮೋಜಿಬು *bamójibu,*	ಅಂನನೆ *annane,*	According to.
ಬರೆ ಹಾಕು *bare-háku,*	ಬರೆಬೆಯಿ *bare-beyi,*	To fire cattle.
ಬಲಿ *bali,*	ಬೆಲಿ *beli,*	To offer a sacrifice.
ಬಲಿ *bali,*	ಬೊಳ್ಳೆ *boḷe,*	To grow.
ಬಗೆಯು *bageyu,*	ನಿರಿಚಿಡು *nirichiḍu,*	To suppose.
ಬರತರ್ಫ *baratarpa,*	ಯೆಡತು ಬುಡುವದು *yeḍatu-buḍuvadu,*	Dismissal.
ಬದಸ್ತೂರು *badastúru,*	ಅಂನನೆ *annane,*	According to.
ಬಟ್ಟುವಾಡೆ *baṭṭuváḍe,*	ವೋದಿ *vódi,*	Distribution.
ಬಲಾತ್ಕಾರ *balátkára,*	ಬೈಂಬು *beimbu,*	Force.

Judicial Words.

Canarese.	*Coorg.*	*English.*
ಬಂದುತ್ವ *bandutva,*	ಬೆಂದೂರ್ತ *bendúrta,*	Relationship.
ಬಲಿಷ್ಟ *baliṣhṭa,*	ಬಲ ಉಳ್ಳವು *bala-uḷḷavu,*	A strong man.
ಬಾಧ್ಯತೆ *bádhyate,*	ಸಮಂದ *samanda,*	Claim.
ಬೆದರಿಕೆ *bedarike,*	ಪೋಡಿ *póḍi,*	Fright.
ಬೇವಾರ್ಸು *bévársu,*	ದಿಕ್ಕಿಲ್ಲತವು *dikkillatavu,*	A destitute.
ಬೇದಸ್ತೂರಿ *bédastúri,*	ನಡಪು ಅಲ್ಲತು *naḍapu-alla-tu,*	Uncustomary.
ಭೂತ *bhúta,*	ಕೂಳಿ *kúḷi,*	A goblin.
ಭಾಗಾಂಶ *bhágámsha,*	ಪಾಲು *pálu,*	A share.
ಮಲಪೂಪು *malapúpu,*	ಕೂಡೆ ಇಡುವದು *kúḍe-iḍu-vadu,*	Enclosure.
ಮರೆ ಪಡಿಸು *mare paḍisu,*	ಮರೆ ಮಾಡು *mare-máḍu,*	To hide.
ಮಜ್ಕುರು *majkuru,*	ಅದೇ *adé,*	Same.
ಮಜಮೂನು *majamúnu,*	ಅರ್ಥ *artha,*	Purport.
ಮದ್ದು ಹಾಕು *maddu-háku,*	ಮದ್ದು ಇಡು *maddu-iḍu,*	To poison.
ಮತಲಬು *matalabu,*	ಅರ್ಥ *artha,*	Meaning.
ಮಾಲು ಜಾಮೀನು *málu-jáminu,*	ಮಾಲು ಜಾಮೀನು *málu-jáminu,*	Security for things.
ಮಾನ *mána,*	ಮಾನ *mána,*	Respectability.
ಮಾಮೂಲ್ *mámúlu,*	ನಡಪು *naḍapu,*	Usage.
ಮಾನ ನಷ್ಟ *mána-naṣṭa,*	ಮಾನಕೇಡು *mánakéḍu,*	Defamation of character.
ಮಾರಿಪತ್ತು *máripattu,*	ಮಾರಿಪತ್ತು *máripattu,*	Through.
ಮಾತುಬಾರಿ *mátu-bári,*	ನಂಬಿಗೆವುಳ್ಳು *nambigevuḷḷu,*	Trust worthy.
ಮಾಟ ಮಾಡುನು *máṭa-máḍunu,*	ಮಾಟ ಮಾಡುನು *máṭamáḍunu,*	Bewitched.
ಮಾಹೆಯಾನ *máheyána,*	ತಿಂಗವಾರು *tingaváru,*	Monthly.
ಮೀರು *míru,*	ಮೀರು *míru,*	To transgress.
ಮಿಳಿತ *miḷita,*	ಸೇರುವದು *séruvadu,*	Connection.
ಮಿಶ್ರ *mishra,*	ಕೂಟುವದು *kúṭuvadu,*	Mixture.
ಮುಖಾಂತ್ರ *mukhantra,*	ಮುಖಾಂತ್ರ *mukhántra,*	Through.
ಮುಶ್ಕಿಲು *mushkilu,*	ಮುಶ್ಕಿಲು *mushkilu,*	Difficult.
ಮೂಢಾತ್ಮ *múḍátma,*	ಮೂಡು *múḍu,*	Idiot.
ಮೋದಂಡ *móḍanḍa,*	ಮೋದಂಡ *móḍanḍa,*	Underminded.
ಮೋಸ *mósa,*	ಮೋಸ *mósa,*	Cheating.
ಮೋಹಸಂ *móhasam,*	ಕಾಲ *kála,*	Season.

Canarese.	*Coorg.*	*English.*
ಮೋಹಸಲೆ *móhasale,*	ಕೂಡೆ ಕೂಟಿತು *kúḍe-kúṭitu,*	Custody.
ಮೊಯತಬಾರು *moyatabáru,*	ನಂಬಿಗೆಯುಳ್ಳ *nambigeyuḷḷu,*	Trustworthy.
ಮೊಖದ್ದಮೆ *mokhaddame,*	ಸಂಗ್ತಿ *sangti,*	Case.
ಮೊಖ್ತ್ಯಾರು *mokhtyáru,*	ಮೊಖ್ತ್ಯಾರು *mokthyáru,*	Self master.
ಯಾದಾಸ್ತು *yádástu,*	ಯಾದಾಸ್ತು *yádástu,*	Memorandum.
ಯಾಲ *yála,*	ಯಾಲ *yála,*	Cardamom.
ಯಥಾರ್ಥ *yathártha,*	ನೇರು *néru,*	Fact, true.
ಯೋಗ್ಯ *yógya,*	ಯೋಗ್ಯು *yógyu,*	A worthy man.
ಯುಕ್ತ *yukta,*	ಬರಾಬರಿ *barábari,*	Proper.
ರವಾನೆ *raváne,*	ಅಯೆ *aye,*	To send.
ರದ್ದು *raddu,*	ಪಾಳು *páḷu,*	Waste.
ರಜಾ *rajá,*	ರಜ *raja,*	Leave.
ರಫ್ತು *raptu,*	ಸಾಗುವದು *ságuvadu,*	Exportation.
ರಗಳೆ *ragaḷa,*	ರಗಳೆ *ragaḷe,*	Incoherent talk.
ರಿವಾಜು *rivája,*	ನಡಪು *naḍapu,*	Usage.
ರುಜುವಾತು *rujuvátu,*	ರುಜುವಾತಿ *rujuváti,*	Proof.
ರಸ್ತೆ *raste,*	ಬಟ್ಟೆ *baṭṭe,*	Road.
ಲಕ್ಷಣ *lakṣhaṇa,*	ಚಾಯಿ *cháyi,*	Beauty.
ಲಾಗುವಡು *láguváḍu,*	ಆನಕರ್ಚಿ *ánakarchi,*	Compensation.
ಲಾಭ *lábha,*	ಲಾಭ *lábha,*	Profit.
ಲುಬ್ಧ *lubdha,*	ನಾಸಲು *násalu,*	A miser.
ಲೂಟಿ *lúṭi,*	ಲೂಟಿ *lúṭi,*	Plundering.
ಲೇವಾದೇವಿ *lévádévi,*	ಲೇವಾದೇವಿ *lévádévi,*	Dealings.
ಲೋಭಿ *lóbhi,*	ನಾಸಲು *násalu,*	A stingy man.
ವದಂತಿ *vadanti,*	ಸುದ್ದಿ *suddi,*	News.
ವರ್ತಮಾನ *vartamána,*	ವರ್ತಮಾನ *vartamána,*	Rumour.
ವ್ಯವಸಾಯ *vyavasáya,*	ಬೆಸಾಯ *besáya,*	Cultivation.
ವ್ಯಭಿಚಾರ *vyabhichára,*	ಪುಲಿಯಾಡಿತನ *puliyáḍitana,*	Adultery.
ವಾಕ್ಯ *vákya,*	ತಕ್ಕು *takku,*	Sentence.
ವಾಯಿದೆ *váyide,*	ಗಡುಬ *gaḍuba,*	Term.
ವಾಗ್ದಂಡನೆ *vágdanḍane,*	ವಾಕ್ದಂಡನೆ *vákdanḍane,*	Reprimand.
ವ್ಯಾಜ್ಯ *vyájya,*	ವೇಜ್ಯ *véjya,*	Suit.

Judicial Words.

Canarese.	*Coorg.*	*English.*
ವಾದಿ *vádi,*	ವಾದಿ *vádi,*	Plaintiff.
ವಾರಿಸುದಾರ *várisudára,*	ಸಮಂದಗಾರು *samandagá-ru,*	Relationer.
ವಿಚಾರಣೆ *vicháraṇe,*	ವಿಚಾರಣೆ *vicháraṇe,*	Inquiry.
ವಿಭಾಗ *vibhága,*	ಪಾಲು *pálu,*	Share.
ವಾರ್ತೆ *várte,*	ಸುದ್ದಿ *suddi,*	News.
ವದೆಯು *vadeyu,*	ಚಉಟು *chauṭu,*	To kick.
ವಾಗ್ದಾನ *vágdána,*	ಭಾಷೆ *bháṣhe,*	Promise.
ವಶ *vasha,*	ಪಕ್ಕ *pakka,*	Possession.
ವರ್ಗ *varga,*	ಬದಲು *badalu,*	Exchange.
ವಿಶ್ವಾಸ ಘಾತಕ *vishvása-ghátaka,*	ನಂಬಿತುಚದಿಪು *nambitucha-dipu,*	Criminal breach of trust.
ವಾಸ್ತವ್ಯ *vástavya,*	ನೇರು *néru,*	Fact.
ವಿಷಾ ಹಾಕು *viṣhá-háku,*	ವಿಷ ಇಡು *viṣhaiḍu,*	To poison.
ಶರಹಾ *sharahá,*	ಶರಹಾ *sharahá,*	Remarks.
ಶಾಹಿದಿ *sháhidi,*	ಸಾಕ್ಷಿ *sákṣhi,*	Witness.
ಶ್ರಮ *shrama,*	ಸಂಗಟ *sangaṭa,*	Pain.
ಶೀಕ್ಷೆ *shíkṣhe,*	ಸಜ *saja,*	Punishment.
ಶುದ್ಧಿ *shuddi,*	ಸುದ್ದಿ *suddi,*	News.
ಶುಭ *shubha,*	ನಲ್ಲದು *nalladu,*	Auspicious.
ಶೃಂಗಾರ *shṛungára,*	ಚಿಂಗಾರ *chingára,*	Ornament.
ಶ್ರೀನಾಮೆ *shrináme,*	ಶ್ರೀನಾಮೆ *shrináme,*	Heading.
ಶೇಕಡ *shékaḍa,*	ಶೇಕಡ *shékaḍa.*	Per 100.
ಸಹಾಯ *saháya,*	ಕುಮ್ಮಕು *kummaku,*	Assistance.
ಸಹಿತ *sahita,*	ಕೂಡ *kúḍa,*	Also.
ಸನ್ನಿಧಾನ *sannidána,*	ಸನ್ನಿದಾನ *sannidána,*	Presence.
ಸಮಕ್ಷಮ *samakṣhama,*	ಮಿನ್ಯೆಲು *minyelu,*	Front.
ಸಹವಾಸ *sahavása,*	ಜೊತೆ *jote,*	Company.
ಸರಕು *saraku,*	ಸಾಮಾನ *sámána,*	Goods.
ಸರಂಜಾಮು *saranjámu,*	ಸಾಮಾನ *sámána,*	Furniture.
ಸಮೂಹ *samúha,*	ಸಭೆ *sabhe,*	Association.
ಸಂತುಷ್ಟ *santuṣhṭa,*	ಸಂತೋಷಾನವು *santóṣhá-navu,*	Delighted man.
ಸಂಶಯ *samshaya,*	ಸಂಶಯ *samshaya,*	} Doubt.
ಸಂದೇಹ *sandéha,*	ತಮಜ *tamaja,*	

Canarese.	*Coorg.*	*English.*
ಸಮರ್ಥ ***samartha,***	ಗಟ್ಟಿಗು ***gaṭṭigu,***	An able man.
ಸಂಭಾಷಣೆ ***sambháṣhaṇe,***	ತಕ್ಕುಬಾಕು ***takkubáku,***	Conversation.
ಸಲೀಸು ***salísu,***	ಸುಲುಭ ***sulubha,***	Easy.
ಸಂಖ್ಯೆ ***sankhye,***	ಲೆಖ್ಖ ***lekhkha,***	Number in general.
ಸಂಕ್ಷೇಪ ***sankṣhépa,***	ಚೆಂನಂಗುಲು ***chennangulu,***	Abridgement.
ಸ್ಪಷ್ಟ ***spaṣhṭa,***	ನಲ್ಲೋಣೆ ***nallóṇe,***	Clear, plain.
ಸೃಷ್ಟನೆ ***srushṭane,***	ನಿರ್ಮಾಣ ***nirmáṇa,***	Forgery.
ಸಾಗಿಸು ***ságisu,***	ಅಯೆ ***aye,***	To send.
ಸಾದರು ***sádaru,***	ಅಯೆತು ***ayetu,***	Issued.
ಸಾವಕಾಶ ***sávakásha,***	ನಿದಾನ ***nidána,***	Delay.
ಸಾಮರ್ಥ್ಯ ***sámarthya,***	ಬಲ ***bala,***	Able.
ಸವಾಲು ***saválu,***	ಸವಾಲು ***saválu,***	Question.
ಸರಹದ್ದು ***sarahaddu,***	ಅರ್ದಿ ***ardi,***	Boundary.
ಸಬಬು ***sababu,***	ಮೊಳಿ ***moḷi,***	Excuse.
ಸಜಾ ***sajá,***	ಸಜ ***saja,***	Punishment.
ಸಾಗುವಳಿ ***ságuvaḷi,***	ಸಾಗುವಳಿ ***ságuvaḷi,***	Cultivation.
ಸಾಲ ***sála,***	ಸಾಲ ***sála,***	Debt.
ಸಾಲಗಾರ ***sálagára,***	ಸಾಲಗಾರು ***sálagáru,***	Debtor.
ಸಾಬೀತು ***sábítu,***	ರುಜು ***ruju,***	Proof.
ಸಾಕ್ಷಿ ***sákṣhi,***	ಸಾಕ್ಷಿ ***sákṣhi,***	Witness.
ಸುಪರ್ದು ***supardu,***	ಸುಪರ್ದು ***supardu,***	Assumption.
ಸುಗುಣ ***suguṇa,***	ನಲ್ಲಗುಣ ***nallaguṇa,***	Morality.
ಸೂಚನೆ ***súchane,***	ಸೂಚನೆ ***súchane,***	Intimation.
ಸ್ಥಾವರ ***sthávara,***	ಅಳ್ಳಾಡತು ***aḷḷáḍatu,***	} Immoveable.
ಸ್ಥಿರ ***sthira,***	ಸ್ಥಿರ ***sthira,***	
ಸ್ಥೂಲ ***sthúla,***	ಬಂಣ ***banṇa,***	Big, large.
ಸೂಕ್ಷ್ಮ ***súkṣhma,***	ಸೂಕ್ಷಮ ***súkṣhama,***	Minute.
ಸ್ವರೂಪ ***swarúpa,***	ಸ್ವರೂಪು ***smarúpa,***	One's own proper figure.
ಸಂಕಟ ***sankaṭa,***	ಸಂಗಟ ***sangaṭa,***	Pain.
ಸೋಡಿ ***sóḍi,***	ಸೋಡಿ ***sóḍi,***	Remission of a debt.
ಸೊತ್ತು ***sottu,***	ಸೊತ್ತು ***sottu,***	Property.
ಸೋಕು ***sóku,***	ಸೋಕು ***sóku,***	To affect, to touch.
ಸುದಾ ***sudá,***	ಕೂಡ ***kúḍa,***	Also.
ಸುಲಭ ***sulabha,***	ಸುಲುಭ ***sulabha,***	Easy.
ಸೇವಕ ***sévaka,***	ಆಳು ***áḷu,***	Servant.

Judicial Words.

Canarese.	*Coorg.*	*English.*
ಹಸ್ತ *hasta,*	ಕೈ *kei,*	Hand.
ಹಣ *haṇa,*	ಪಣ *paṇa,*	Money.
ಹರಕತ್ತು *harakattu,*	ಹರಕತ್ತು *harakattu,*	Prohibition.
ಹವಾಲೆ *havále,*	ತಾಬೆ *tábe,*	Possession.
ಹಮರಹ *hamaraha,*	ಕೂಡೆ *kúḍe,*	Alongwith.
ಹಂಚಿ ಕೊಳ್ಳುವದು *hanchi-koḷḷuvadu,*	ಓದಿಇಟ್ಟುವದು *ódi-iṭṭavadu,*	Distributing.
ಹಂಗಾಂ *hangám,*	ಕಾಲ *kála,*	Season.
ಹಕ್ಕುದಾರಿ *hakkudári,*	ಒಡೆಕಾರಿಕೆ *oḍekárike,*	A holder of any thing.
ಹರಯೇಕು *harayéku,*	ಯೆಲ್ಲ *ella,*	Every body or thing.
ಹಕ್ಕು *hakku,*	ಹಕ್ಕು *hakku,*	Claim.
ಹವಾಲ್ತೆ *haválte,*	ತಾಬೆ *tábe,*	Surety, possession.
ಹರಾಮ *haráma,*	ಹರಾಮು *harámu,*	A wicked man.
ಹಾಜರು ಜಾಮೀನು *hájaru-jáminu,*	ಜಾಮೀನು *jáminu,*	Bail.
ಹಾಲಿ *háli,*	ಇಕ್ಕಲತು *ikkalatu,*	Present.
ಹಾಜ್ರು *hájru,*	ಹಾಜರು *hájaru,*	Present, ready.
ಹಾರೈಸು *háreisu,*	ಅಪೇಕ್ಷೆ ಮಾಡು *apékṣhe-máḍu,*	To desire, to wish.
ಹುಕ್ಕುಂ *hukkum,*	ಅಪ್ಪಣೆ *appaṇe,*	Order.
ಹಿಂಸೆ *himse,*	ಹಿಂಸೆ *himse,*	Hurt.
ಹುಟ್ಟುವಳಿ *huṭṭuvaḷi,*	ಪುಟ್ಟುವಳಿ *puṭṭuvaḷi,*	Production.
ಹಿಸ್ಸೆ *hisse,*	ಪಾಲು *pálu,*	Share.
ಹೊಸಾಗಮೆ *hoságame,*	ಪುದಿಜಾಯಿತು ಸಾಗು ಮಾಡುನು *pudijáitu-ságumá-ḍunu,*	Recently cultivated.
ಹೋಲಿಕೆ *hólike,*	ಪೋಲೆ *póle,*	Resemblance.
ಹಿಂಗಟುಮುರಿ *hingaṭumuri,*	ಬೆಂಗೈಕಟ್ಟು *benge-ikaṭṭu,*	Pinioning.
ಕ್ಷಾಮ *kṣháma,*	ಬರ *bara,*	Famine.
ಕ್ಷಿಪ್ರ *kṣhipra,*	ಬೆರಿಯ *beriya,*	Soon.
ಕ್ಷೇಮ *kṣhém,*	ನಲ್ಲೋಣೆ *nallóṇe,*	Good health.

LIST OF NAMES OF THE FRUITS GROWN IN THE GARDENS, &c.

Canarese.	*English.*	*Coorg.*
ಅತ್ತಿ *atti,*	A country fig,	ಅತ್ತಿಪಣ್ಣು *atti-panṇu.*
ಅನಾನಾಸು *anánásu,*	Pine apple,	ಪರಂಗಿಚಕ್ಕೆ *parangi-chakke.*
ಈಚಲು *íchalu,*	Wild date,	ಈಚಿಪಣ್ಣು *íchipanṇu.*
ಕರ್ಬೂಜ *karbuja,*	Melon,	ಬತ್ತೆಂಗೆ *battenge.*
ಕಲ್ಲಂಗಡಿ *kallangadi,*	Water melon,	ಕಲ್ಲಂಗಡಿ *kallangaḍi.*
ಕಾರೆ *káre,*	A fruit of thorny bush,	ಕಾರೆ *káre.*
ಕಿತ್ತಲೆ *kittale,*	Orange,	ಕಿತ್ತುಳಿಪಣ್ಣು *kittuḷi-panṇu.*
ಕುಂಬಳ *kumbaḷa,*	Gourd,	ಕುಂಬಳ *kumbaḷa.*
ಚಕೋತರ *chakó-tara,*	Pumple nose,	ಚಕ್ಕೋತು *chakkótu.*
ಜಂಬನೆರಳೆ *jamba-néraḷe,*	Rose apple,	ಜಂನೇರುಪಣ್ಣು *jumnéru-panṇu.*
ದಾಳೆಂಬಿ *dáḷembi,*	Pomegranate,	ದಾಳಿಂಬಿ *dáḷambi.*
ನೇರಳೆ *néraḷe,*	Nevel fruit,	ನೇರುಪಣ್ಣು *nérupanṇu.*
ನಿಂಬೆ *nimbe,*	Lime,	ಚೊರಂಗಿಪುಳಿ *chorangipuḷi.*
ಪರಂಗಿ *parangi,*	Papaya,	ಅಕ್ಕತಂಗೆಕಾಯಿ *akkatange-káyi.*
ಬಸರಿ *basari,*	Waved leaf fruit,	ಕೊಳಿಪಣ್ಣು *koḷipanṇu.*
ಬಾಳೆ *báḷe,*	Plantain,	ಬಾಳೆ *báḷe.*
ಮಾದಳ *mádaḷa,*	Citron,	ಮಾದೂಳಿ *mádúḷi.*
ಮಾವು *mávu,*	Mango,	ಮಾಂಗೆ *mánge.*
ಶೀಬಿ *shíbi,*	Gauva,	ಕಲಂದಿಕಾಯಿ *kalandikáyi.*
ಶೀತಾಫಲ *shítá-phala,*	Custard apple,	ಶೀತೀಪಣ್ಣು *shitápanṇu.*
ಹಲಸು *halasu,*	Jack,	ಚಕ್ಕೆ *chakke.*

M

Names of Fruits.

Canarese.	*English.*	*Coorg.*
ಹಿಪ್ಪಲಿನೆರಳೆ *hippali-néruḷe,*	Mulbery,	ಚಿಪ್ಪಿಲಿಪಂಣು *chippilipaṇṇu.*
ಹೆರಳೆ *heraḷe,*	A kind of bitter orange,	ಕೈಪುಳಿ *keipuḷi.*
	Fruits of Wild Forest Trees, the Botanical names of which are unknown.	ಅಮ್ಮೆಪಂಣು *ammepaṇṇu.*
		ಬಿಕ್ಕಿಪಂಣು *bikkipaṇṇu.*
		ಪುಂಗಿಪಂಣು *pungipaṇṇu.*
		ಕೊಟ್ಟೆಪಂಣು *koṭṭepaṇṇu.*
		ಯೆಲಂದೆಪಂಣು *yalandepaṇṇu.*
		ಹಡಗಿನಕಿತ್ತೂಳಿ *haḍaginakittúḷi.*
		ಚೀನಿಂಬೆ *chínimbe.*
		ಪೊಳೆಬಂಡೂಳಿ *póḷebanḍúḷi.*
		ಕೂಮೆಪಂಣು *kúmepaṇṇu.*
		ಉಪ್ಪಲಿಪಂಣು *uppalipaṇṇu.*
		ಕರ್ಮುಂದಿಪಂಣು *karmundi-paṇṇu.*
		ಪಾಲೆಪಂಣು *pálepaṇṇu.*
		ಗೋತ್ರಿಪಂಣು *gótripaṇṇu.*
		ಪಡಚಿಪಂಣು *paḍachipaṇṇu.*
		ಕಕ್ಕಡೆಪಂಣು *kakkaḍepaṇṇu.*
		ಪೂಮತ್ತಿಪಂಣು *púmattipaṇṇu.*

COORG CARDINAL NUMBERS.

ಒಂದು *ondu,*	೧	1
ದಂಡು *danḍu,*	೨	2
ಮೂಂದು *múndu,*	೩	3
ನಾಲು *nálu,*	೪	4
ಅಂಜಿ *anji,*	೫	5
ಆರು *áru,*	೬	6
ಏಳು *éḷu,*	೭	7
ಎಟ್ಟು *eṭṭu,*	೮	8
ಒಯಿಂಬದು *oyimbadu,*	೯	9
ಪತ್ತು *pattu,*	೧೦	10
ಪನ್ನೊಂದು *pannondu,*	೧೧	11
ಪನ್ನೆರಂಡು *pannerandu,*	೧೨	12
ಪದಿಮೂಂಡು *padimúnḍu,*	೧೩	13
ಪದಿನಾಲು *padinálu,*	೧೪	14
ಪದಿನಂಜಿ *padinanji,*	೧೫	15
ಪದಿನಾರು *padináru,*	೧೬	16
ಪದಿನೇಳು *padinéḷu,*	೧೭	17
ಪದಿನೆಟ್ಟು *padineṭṭu,*	೧೮	18
ಪತ್ತೊಯಿಂಬದು *pattoyimbadu,*	೧೯	19
ಇರುವದು *iruvadu,*	೨೦	20
ಇರುವತ್ತೊಂದು *iruvattondu,*	೨೧	21
ಇರುವತ್ತೆರಂಡು *iruvatterandu,*	೨೨	22
ನುಪ್ಪದು *nuppadu,*	೩೦	30
ನಾಪದು *nápadu,*	೪೦	40
ಐಂಬದು *imbadu,*	೫೦	50
ಅರುವದು *aruvadu,*	೬೦	60
ಎಳುವದು *eḷuvadu,*	೭೦	70
ಎಂಬದು *embabu,*	೮೦	80
ತೊಂನೂರು *tonnúru,*	೯೦	90
ನೂರು *núru,*	೧೦೦	100

Cardinal Numbers.

ನೂಯಿತ್ತೊಂದು *núyittondu*, . .	೧೦೧	**101**
ಇಂನೂರು *innúru*, . .	೨೦೦	**200**
ಇಂನೂಯಿತ್ತೊಂದು *innúyittondu*, . .	೨೦೧	**201**
ಮುಂನೂರು *munnúru*, . .	೩೦೦	**300**
ಮುಂನೂಯಿತ್ತೊಂದು *munúyittondu*, .	೩೦೧	**301**
ನಾನೂರು *nánúru*, . .	೪೦೦	**400**
ನಾನೂಯಿತ್ತೊಂದು *nánúyittondu*, . .	೪೦೧	**401**
ಅಂಞೂರು *anynúru*, . .	೫೦೦	**500**
ಅಂಞೂಯಿತ್ತೊಂದು *anynúyittondu*, .	೫೦೧	**501**
ಆರುನೂರು *árunúru*, . .	೬೦೦	**600**
ಆರುನೂಯಿತ್ತೊಂದು *árunúyittondu*, .	೬೦೧	**601**
ಏಳುನೂರು *éḷunúru*, . .	೭೦೦	**700**
ಏಳುನೂಯಿತ್ತೊಂದು *éḷunúyittondu*, .	೭೦೧	**701**
ಎಟ್ಟುನೂರು *eṭṭunúru*, . .	೮೦೦	**800**
ಒಂಬಯಿನೂರು *ombayinúru*, . .	೯೦೦	**900**
ಆಯಿರ *áyira*, . .	೧,೦೦೦	**1,000**
ಆಯಿರತನೂರು *áyiratanúru*, . .	೧,೦೦೧	**1,001**
ಆಯಿರತನೂಯಿತ್ತೊಂದು *áyiratanúyittondu*,	೧,೧೦೧	**1,101**
ದಂಡಾಯಿರ *danḍáyira*, . .	೨,೦೦೦	**2,000**
ಮೂಂದಾಯಿರ *múndáyira*, . .	೩,೦೦೦	**3,000**
ನಾಲು ಆಯಿರ *náluáyira*, . .	೪,೦೦೦	**4,000**
ಅಂಜಾಯಿರ *anjáyira*, . .	೫,೦೦೦	**5,000**
ಆರಾಯಿರ *áráyira*, . . .	೬,೦೦೦	**6,000**
ಏಳಾಯಿರ *éḷáyira*, . . .	೭,೦೦೦	**7,000**
ಎಟ್ಟಾಯಿರ *eṭṭáyira*, . . .	೮,೦೦೦	**8,000**
ಒಯಿಂಬದಾಯಿರ *oyimbadáyira*, . .	೯,೦೦೦	**9,000**
ಪತ್ತಾಯಿರ *pattáyira*, . . .	೧೦,೦೦೦	**10,000**
ಲಕ್ಷ *lakṣha*, . . .	೧೦೦,೦೦೦	**100,000**
ಕೋಟಿ *kóṭi*, . . .	೧,೦೦೦,೦೦೦	**10,000,000**

THE FOLLOWING ARE THE COORG FRACTIONS.

೧	ಒಂದು	*ondu,*	1
[illegible]	ಮುಕ್ಕಾಲು	*muk-kálu,*	$\frac{3}{4}$
[illegible]	ಅರೆ	*are,*	$\frac{1}{2}$
[illegible]	ಕಾಲು	*kálu,*	$\frac{1}{4}$

MEASURES OF CAPACITY.

ಮಣ	*maṇa,*	maund.	
ಮುಕ್ಕಾಲುಮಣ	*mukkálumaṇa,*	$\frac{3}{4}$	of a maund.
ಅರೆ ,,	*aremaṇa,*	$\frac{1}{2}$	of a Do.
ಕಾಲು ,,	*kálumaṇa,*	$\frac{1}{4}$	Do.
ಸೇರು ,,	*séru,*	$\frac{1}{40}$	Do.

MEASURES OF PROVISIONS.

ಬಟ್ಟಿ	*baṭṭi,*	1 *baṭṭi,* (contains 80 seers)	
ಮುಕ್ಕಾಲು ಬಟ್ಟಿ	*mukkálu-baṭṭi,*	$\frac{3}{4}$	of a *baṭṭi,*
ಅರೆ ಬಟ್ಟಿ	*are,* ,,	$\frac{1}{2}$	Do.
ಕಾಲು ,,	*kálu,* ,,	$\frac{1}{4}$	Do.
ಪಾನಿ	*páni,*	$\frac{1}{40}$	Do.
ಸೇರು	*séru,*	$\frac{1}{80}$	Do.
ಮಾನ	*mána,*	$\frac{1}{160}$	Do.

FRACTIONS OF A RUPEE.

ಮುಕ್ಕಾಲು ಉರುಪಿ	*mukkálu-urupi,*	$\frac{3}{4}$	of a Rupee.
ಅರೆ ಉರುಪಿ	*are-urupi,*	$\frac{1}{2}$	Do.
ಪಾಉಲಿ	*páuli,*	$\frac{1}{4}$	Do.
ಬೋಳ್ಳಿ ಪಣ	*bóḷḷi-paṇa,*	$\frac{1}{5}$	Do.
ದುಡ್ಡು	*duḍḍu,*	$\frac{1}{48}$	Do.
ಕಾಸು	*kásu,*	$\frac{1}{192}$	Do.

GOLD SOVEREIGN.

ಪತ್ತಾಕು	*pattáku,*	A Sovereign of 20 Rupees value.
ಕಾಜಿಪೊಂನು or ಆಮಡೆ	*kájiponnu or* *ámaḍe,*	Do. of 5 Rupees Do.
ಬಿರಾನು	*biránu,*	Do. of 4 Do.
ಪಣ	*paṇa,*	Do. of 14 Duddu's value.

MEASURES OF LENGTH.

ಗಾವದ	*gávada,*	four leagues.
ಹರದಾರಿ	*haradári,*	one league.
ಮಾರು	*máru,*	fathom.
ಮೊಳ	*moḷa,*	cubit.
ಗೇಣು	*géṇu,*	span.
ಮೊಟ್ಟು	*moṭṭu,*	foot.

SPECIMENS OF TRAVEL TALK FOR PURPOSES OF COMPARISON WITH THE OTHER PRINCIPAL LANGUAGES OF SOUTHERN INDIA.

ENGLISH.	CANARESE.	TELUGU.	TAMIL.	COORG.
What is the name of this village?	*í úrina hesaru énu?*	*í úri péru émi?*	*inda úrin pér enná?*	*í úruda peda ennu?*
Are you the Police officer here?	*nínu í úrige kotwálanó?*	*míru í úriki kotwáludá?*	*ní inda úrukku kotwálaná?*	*nínu í úruda kotwálana?*
Is their any sickness in it?	*illi énádaru róga untó?*	*ichchaṭa rógum émainá kaladá?*	*inge vyádhi edávadu undó?*	*illi ennáchengi róga undu?*
Are there any cases of cholera?	*vánti bhédi róga énádaru tagali ideyó?*	*vánti bhédi rógam émaina koladá?*	*vánti bhédi vyádhi edávadu paṭṭu irukkiradá?*	*sanni róga ennáchengi ániyaṭa?*
Is the water good?	*níru voḷḷédó?*	*níḷḷu manchivá?*	*taṇṇi nalladá?*	*níru nallada?*
Is there a maistry who could repair my coach?	*nanna bhanḍiyannu sarimáḍalu vobba méstriyu shikyánó?*	*náaokka baḍini chakka peṭṭaḍánaku voga méstrí chikkuna?*	*ennuḍaya vanḍiyai shoppaniḍa voru méstri agappaḍuváná?*	*éda gádina cháikútu wakku oru méstri kittuwa?*

English.	Canarese.	Telugu.	Tamil.	Coorg.
Can I procure fresh bearers or fresh bullocks?	*hosa bestarágali ettugaḷágali shkiyavó ?*	*kotta bóyilugáni eddulu gáni dorakuná ?*	*pudu bóyigaḷávavdu mádugaḷávadu agappaḍuma?*	*pudiya bóiya ádu eṭṭu ádu kittuwa?*
My servant requirs firewood, milk, eggs, two fowls, rice, gram and straw,	*nanna áḷige soude, hálu, moṭṭe, eraḍu kóḷiguḷu akki, huruḷi mattu hullu békanté ?*	*náyokka banṭrótuku kaṭṭelu, pálu gudlu, renḍu kóḍlu bíyu vuluvalu kasuvu, kávalenaṭa.*	*ennuḍaya shévaganuku veragu, pál, muṭṭe kóḷi, arisi, koḷḷu, pil, véṇumám.*	*éda áluku puḷḷi, pálu, mutte, ḍandu kóḷi, akki-mudre, pillu bónduólo?*
I should like fresh cocoanuts,	*nanage eḷaníru béku,*	*náku eḷaníḷḷu kávalenu ?*	*enakku eḷanír véṇum,*	*nángu eḷaníru bóndu?*
Is there a washerman who could wash my clothes?	*nanna baṭṭegaḷannu ogeyalu obba agasa shikyánó ?*	*náyokka baṭṭalanu udakaḍánaku vokka chákalaváḍu dorakuná ?*	*enudaya tuṇigaḷai tókkiradarku voru vaṇṇán agappaḍuváná ?*	*éda kuppiya-tuni olipukku, oru madioḷu kittuwa?*
I must have them back before the evening,	*nanage avugaḷannu sáyenkálakke muncheyé tandu koḍa béku ?*	*náku váṭlanu sáyenkálamunaku mundugáné techchi ivavalenu ?*	*enakku adugaḷai iraḷukku munbágavé konḍuvandu koḍukkavénum.*	*adana baitápángu minya kondaraṇdu.*
Where can I get some good bread?	*nanage swalpa oḷḷe roṭṭi elli shikkitu ?*	*náku koncham munchi roṭṭa echchuṭa dorakunu ?*	*enakku konjam nalla roṭṭi enge agappaḍum ?*	*nángu chennángu nallu oṭṭi ellikittu?*
Are plantains to be had here?	*illi báḷe haṇṇugaḷu shikyávó ?*	*ichchaṭa araṭi pandlu dorakuná ?*	*inge váḷapaḷangaḷ agappaḍumá ?*	*illi báḷe paṇṇu kittuwa?*

Are there no other fruits except these that you have brought?	*nínu tandu iruva í haṇṇugaḷu hortu inyávadú illavó ?*	*míru techchina pandlu káka vérévilévá ?*	*ní koṇḍu vanda paḷangoḷ tavira véronrum kiḍeyáḍó ?*	*nínu kondu bandu í paṇṇu allate innu édú illeya?*
Are not these the names of them, mango, orange, jack, lime, apple, pomegranate, &c.	*avugaḷa hesaru mávina haṇṇu, kittale haṇṇu, halasina honṇu, nimbé haṇṇu, shévu haṇṇu, dáḷimbari haṇṇu, embadági allavó ?*	*váṭla péru mámiḍi panḍu, kichchali panḍu, panasa panḍu, nimma panḍu, sébu panḍu, dálimba panḍu. ani kádá.*	*adugaḷ pér, mám paḷam, kichchili paḷam, peḷá paḷam, elumicham paḷam, appils paḷam, mádalam paḷam, enru allavá.*	*adanda peda mánge paṇṇu, kittuli paṇṇu, chakke paṇṇu, chórange paṇṇu, shébu paṇṇu, dálambi paṇṇu índu alla?*
What vegetables are to be had here?	*illi káyi palyagaḷu yávadu shikutté,*	*ichchaṭa kúrakáyalu évi dorakunu ?*	*inge káyi kari enna agappaḍum ?*	*illi panje ennu kittuwa?*
Do they grow them here plentifully?	*avugaḷannu illi mastági beḷeyuttáró ?*	*ichchaṭa váṭlanu tarchugá panḍistunnárá ?*	*inge adugaḷai rombú viḷaivaikkurárgaḷá ?*	*adana illi perta boḷatuwa?*
Have you ever seen the Bangalore vegetables?	*nínu bengaḷúrina káyi palyagaḷannu endádaru nóḍi iddiya ?*	*míru ennaṭikainá bengaḷúruyokka kúrakáyalanu zúchi unnává ?*	*ní eppóvávadu bengaḷúrin káyi karigaḷai párttu irupiyá ?*	*nínu bengaḷúr punje ekkáchengi nóḍiṭu uḷḷiya?*
Do they bring the seeds from that place?	*bíjagaḷannu allindulé taruttáró ?*	*vittulannu achchaṭanunḍi testárá ?*	*veregaḷai avaḍattil irundu konḍuvarugurárgaḷá ?*	*kottena allinjé kondu bappa?*

ENGLISH.	CANARESE.	TELUGU.	TAMIL.	COORG.
If so, can you get me some nice Beans, Cabbages, Peas, Potatoes, Cucumbers, &c.	*hágúdaré swalpa voḷḷe hurali káyi, kósu gaḍḍe, baṭáṇi, uruḷugaḍḍe saute káyi, muntáddannu nanage tandu koḍuviyá ?*	*álágaịté náku koddi manchi ulava káyalu, kósa gaḍḍalu, baṭáṇi káyilu urla gaḍḍalu, dósa káyilu, víṭni techchi ichchévá ?*	*appaḍiyáṇál enakku sila koḷḷu káyi, kósu kiḷangu, baṭaṇi uraḷa kiḷangu, veḷḷeri káyi idugaḷai konḍuvandu koḍuppiyá ?*	*annaneáchengi chennungu mudre, gósu-geḍḍe, batáni, vilaiti geḍḍe, chaute innatánella nángu kondu bandu tappiya?*
I hear the same people also grow different sort of greens: can you get me some greens?	*adé janagaḷé hala bage soppugaḷannu beḷeyuttárendu kéḷuttene ; kelavu soppugaḷannu nanage tandu koṭṭiyá ?*	*várlé shánd kúráku lanu panḍistunárani vinnánu : koddi kúrákulanu náku techchi echchévá ?*	*avargaḷtán kíregaḷeyum viḷaivaikkurárgaḷ enru nán kéṭṭu irukkirén , sila kíregaḷai enakku konḍu vandu koḍuppịyá ?*	*adé jana tará tara ṭoppu boḷatuwa indu kétiye, chennangu toppu nángu kondu bandu tappiga?*
As I see these are very nice, I wish to have some more to take with me to B.—	*ivu bahaḷa channági iruvaddarinda nana sangaḍa B—ge innaṣḥṭu hechchági tegadukonḍu hógabékendu apékṣhisuténe,*	*ivi chálá chakkaga unḍuṭavalla B—ki nátó kúḍá koncham hechchugá konipóvalenani enchutánu,*	*iduga! nanrá yirukkirapaḍiyál ennuḍan kudá B—ki innnm konjam konḍu pógavéṇum enru eṇṇugurén.*	*idu perta nallone uḷḷánagondu nánu B—ku innu chennangu kondu póndu indu manasu máduvi.*
If my friends there require some more, I will write to you.	*á úralli iruva nanna snéhitaru innaṣḥṭu békandaré, ninage bariyutténe,*	*achchaṭa unḍé náyokka snéhitalu inká kávalenani cheppinaṭṭaité, níku vráyuchunnánu.*	*ange irukkura ennuḍaya snéhitáḷ innum véṇum enru sounál unakku yeḷudugurén.*	*á úrulu uḷḷu éda jóstigára innu chennangu bonduindu eṇṇichengi níngu eladuvi.*

You had better send for a smith to nail the box, so that the vegetables may not be spoilt on the road.	*í káyi palya soppu saha keḍada húge vondu pettigeyalli háki, moḷegaḷannu maḍáyisalu vobba kammáranna karesu.*	*í kúrakáyalu, kúráku modalainavi cheḍakuṇḍá vokka peṭṭeló peṭṭi, moḷalanu koṭṭaḍamunuku gánu vokka inamu panivánni rappinchu.*	*inda káyi kari, kíre mudalánadai keḍímal voru poṭṭiyili vaitu áṇigaḷai aḍikka voru korimánai aḷeppi.*	*i punje kettu póvataneke oru pottilu ittiṭu áni badipaku oru tachana kákchiru.*
Here is the hire of the man for doing it.	*igó uvonige á kelasa máḍiddakke kúlí.*	*idó váṇiki á pani chésinanduku kúlí.*	*idó avanukku anda vélaikkága kúlí.*	*idá avangu á pani kejjángu kúli.*
Get me some good sugar.	*nanage swalpa voḷḷe sakkareyannu tandu koḍu.*	*náka kyncham manchi chakkeranu teohchi immu.*	*enakku kónjam nella shekkareyai konḍu vandu koḍu.*	*nángu chennangu nallu chakkere kondandutá.*
Do they mix it with jaggory?	*adarondige bellavannu berisutáró ?*	*dánitó bellamunu chéristárá ?*	*adarku vellattai shérkurárgaḷá ?*	*ánda kúda bella kútuwa?*
Have you ever seen the English or Aṣhṭagrám sugar?	*aṣhṭagrám sakkare yannágali shímé sakkare yannágali endúdaru nóḍi idhiya ?*	*ennaḍaina shíma chakkaragáni aṣhṭagrámpu chakkerenngáni zúchi unnává ?*	*eppovávadu shime shekkareyai alludu aṣhṭagrámattin shekkareyai partu iruppiyá ?*	*ashtagráma chakkeri ádu síme chakkeri ádu ekkáchengi nótiṭuḷḷiya?*
As the horse-keeper says that the bridle requires some repair, can you bring me a saddler?	*lagámannu swalpa sari máḍa békendu nanna kudareyavanu héḷuttánági, vobba jínagáranannu karataruviyá ?*	*kaḷyamunu koncham chekka peṭṭavalenani ná gurrnpuváḍu cheppntúḍuganuka, okka jínagar váṇṇi pilavan ampévá ?*	*kaḍuváḷattat konjam sari paḍuttavéṇum enru en kuduraikkaran sholugurán ágaiyál, oru jín vélekkáranai aḷai.*	*lagámuna chennangu chéyi mádandúndu éda kudrekáru eṇṇuẁa, ánagondu oru jínugárana kákiendu bappiya?*

ENGLISH.	CANARESE.	TELUGU.	TAMIL.	COORG.
Get my horse properly shod by some skilfull farrier.	*vobba buddhivanta nalbandi kaili nanna kudarege laḷá kaṭṭisu.*	*okka gaṭṭiváḍaina nálbandi chéta ná gurrániki nál kaṭṭinchu.*	*oru gaṭṭikkárandna láḍakkárannálé en kuduraikki láḍam kaṭṭivai.*	*oru buḍḍiontu nálabandira kailu éda kudreku láḷa kattichiru.*
What does he want for it?	*adakke avanige énu koḍu békú ?*	*anduku vániki émi ivvavalenu ?*	*adarkúga avanukku enna koḍukkavéṇum ?*	*adangu avangu ennu kodukondu?*
As I have now done my breakfast, I should like to go a hunting; is there any jungle in the vicinity of this village?	*nanage íga beḷagina úṭá áyitu, áddarinda nánu byáṭe aḍalu hógabéku í úrina hatra aḍavi éndaru unṭó ?*	*náku ippuḍu televári bhójanam áyanu ganuka véṭa áḍa póvalenu, í úri dagg͓ira édina aḍivi unnadá ?*	*enakku kálaime sháp páḍu áchchidu ágayál nán véṭṭai áda póga véṇum ; inda urukku kiṭṭa edávadu kád irakkuradá.*	*nángu ikka palákuṭuna úṇu ánánagondu nángu, bóte aduwaku póndu; i úruda pukka kádu ennachangi unda?*
What game does it abound in?	*alli enthá byáṭe unṭu ?*	*achchaṭa éḍláṭi véṭa unnadi ?*	*engé eppaḍippaṭṭa véṭṭai undu ?*	*alli ennaṭu bóṭe undu?*
Do you know if there are any hunters here?	*illi yáraduru byáṭegárru íródu balliyá ?*	*ichchaṭa véṭagáḍlu evarainá unḍédánni míru eraguduvá ?*	*inge véṭṭaikkárar yárávadu irahknraṭṭai ariviya ?*	*illi árdchengi botekára uḷḷaḍu goṭunda?*
What must I give them were I to engage half a dozen of them to follow me the whole day?	*avaroḷage áru mandi voppattu nannondige bandare, avarigé nánu énu koḍa békú ?*	*vánḍlaló áru mandi nátó vokka náḍ anṭá vasté, nénu vánḍlaku émi ivvavalenu ?*	*avargaḷukkuḷḷé áru pér ennóḍe oru náḷ ellám vanḍirundál, nán avargaḷukku enna kuḍukkavéṇum ?*	*ayenda kútulu áráḷu oru poṭṭu éda kúda bútengi, ayengu nánu ennu kodukandu?*

There are two roads to B—; which is the safer?	*B—ge eraḍu hádi idhe; yávadu voḷḷédu?*	*B—ki renḍu dóvalu unnavi; édi manchidi?*	*B—ku irenḍu veḷi irakkuradu edu nalladú?*	*B—ku erandu batte undu; édu nalladu?*
Tell me will there be any scarcity in procuring fresh Bullocks or fresh Bearers in the next stages.	*mundina majalugaḷalli bestarágali ettugaḷágali shikkuvadillavó énu héḷu.*	*mundari majaluló bóyilugáni eddulugáni chikkuvó émi cheppu.*	*mun majalgaḷil bóyigaḷávadu máḍugaḷávadu agappaḍumaṭṭádó énna shollu.*	*minyelaṭu mokámulu bóyealádu eṭṭádu kittuwa killeyu ennu eṇṇu?*
If so, what do these of your village ask for carrying me the whole way?	*hágádare, nimma úrinavaru kaḍigú baralu énu kéḷuttáré?*	*álágaite miyokka úruvánḍlu aḍviki vachchéṭanduku émi aḍugutáru?*	*appaḍikki ánál, ungaḷ úruváḷ kaḍashikum vara enna kéḷkurárgaḷ?*	*annane áchengi ningada úrukára kadekitta bappaku ennu képa?*
Tell them, I'll reward them handsomely, provided they behave well on the road?	*avaru dárili tunṭa tana máḍadé iddaré, avarige voḷḷé inám koḍutténe endu avarige hélu.*	*vánḍlu dóvuló tondarachúyaka unṭé nénu vanḍlaku manchi inám ittunani vánḍlaku cheppu.*	*avargaḷ veḷil tondiravusheyyámal irundál, avargaḷukku nella inám koḍuppén enru shollu.*	*avu battelu tante mádaṭe injatengi ayangu nallu inám kodupíndu ayangu eṇṇu.*
Are you sure that there is no fear of thieves on the road?	*dárili kaḷḷara káṭa énu illá endu channági balliyá?*	*dóvaló dongalu upadravam émi lédani nívu búga eruguduvá?*	*yaḷiyil tiraḍar bhayam oṇrum ille enru nín naṇráyi ariviyá?*	*battelu kaḷḷada káta édu illéndu nallóṇe goṭṭundu?*
Have any robberies been committed of late?	*kelavu divasakke munché kaḷḷatana énnádaru naḍaitó?*	*koddi rózulaku munapu dongatanam émainanaḍichi unnadá?*	*sila náḷaikki munne tiraṭṭu edávadu naḍarndadá?*	*chennangu náḷuku minye kaḷḷatana ennáchengi nadandaṭa?*

English.	Canarese.	Telugu.	Tamil.	Coorg.
Is there no cause for fear in crossing over that hill at night?	*rátri hottinalli á beṭṭada mélakke hóguvagá bhaya énú illavó ?*	*chígaṭiló á koṇḍaku paina póyéṭappuḍu bhayam émi lédá ?*	*iraṭṭil anda maleyin méle pógumpódu bhayam édávadu unḍó ?*	*baitu néraṭu ú kondu-da kodiya pópaku pódi édu illoya ?*
Is there a proper place on the top of it, where I may have my tent pitched?	*nanna guḍáravannu hodiyuvadakke adara kumbhiya mélé tavu idheyó ?*	*ná ḍéránu koṭṭaḍamunaku gánu dáni paina chóṭa unnadá ?*	*en ḍérávai aḍikka udin méle eḍam irukkiradá ?*	*éda tambuna poyuwakku ánda kodilu jága unda ?*
Get me some torches (made of a kind of wild sticks,)	*kelavu goravi kaḍḍigaḷannu nanage tandu koḍu.*	*koddi velturu kaḍlanu náku techchi immu.*	*sila kórán kattaigalai enakku konḍuvandu koḍu.*	*chennangu túdú nangu kodandu tá.*
Bring a memo of how much I am indebted to you for all these things.	*ivakkelládakkú nánu énu koḍabékó á bagye vondu paṭṭiyannu tegadukonḍu bá.*	*víṭlaku gána nénu ém ívvavalenó dániki okka jábitánu tísukó rá.*	*idugaḷ ellátukkum nán enna koḍukka véṇumó adarkága oru shíṭṭai konḍu vá.*	*iḍangelángu nánu ennu ṭarandu adangu oru potti kondandu tá.*
Here is the money as per your memorandum.	*ninno paṭṭí mérige igó haṇa.*	*míyokka jábitá myáraku idó rúkalu.*	*unnoḍayu shíṭṭin paḍikki idó paṇam.*	*nída patti paragára idá paṇa.*
Do you find them all right?	*avu sariyági idheyó ?*	*avi sarígá unnádá ?*	*adugaḷ sariyáy irukkiradá ?*	*adu barábari unda ?*
Is the river beyond that village fordable?	*á úráché hoḷeyannu háyu bahudó ?*	*á úriki ágaṭa unḍéṭi nadini dáṭa kúḍunó ?*	*anda úrukku appaṛam irukkira árai dánḍalámá ?*	*á úrudapparaṭiya poḷe kadakaluwa ?*

Is there no danger whatever?	*alli bhaya énu illavó?*	*achchaṭa marémi bhayam léddá?*	*ange pinnei oṇrum buayam kiḍeiyáḍó?*	*aḷḷi pódi édu illeya?*
Are boats always ready there?	*alli harigólu yávágyú hájar idheyó?*	*achchṭa váḍalu eppuḍunnu hajar unnavá?*	*ange parishil eppódum ájar irukkumá?*	*aḷḷi dóni ekkálu ippa?*
Do they know how to manage boats well?	*ambigaru harigóla channági naḍesa balla-ró?*	*váḍagánḍlu váḍalanu naḍipinchaḍam telishiyunnárá?*	*parishilkárar parishilai naḍaitta arivâḷá?*	*dónikarakudóni nallóne nadatuwaku goṭṭunda?*
Have all my luggage sent out to the other side of the river before I reach the ford.	*nánu kaḍavige baruva hottige nanna sámán elilánu áché daḍakke kaḷuhisu.*	*nénu révuku vachchéṭi vyáḷaku ná sámánalantá ágaṭ a gaṭṭuku pampu.*	*nán dánḍum iḍattukku vara munné en sámánei ellâttayum akkureikki anuppu.*	*nánu kadavku bakkeneke éda sámána eḷḷu apparaṭṭu kareku ayé.*
Very well, police man, I give you these few rupees for your ready and punctual attention.	*oḷḷédu, nínu máḍida kashṭakke kelavu rúpáyigaḷannu ninage koḍutténe.*	*manchidi, nívu chésina mehanattu zuchi koddi rúpáyilanu níku istunánu,*	*nelladu, nín sheida kashṭattei pártu inda rúpáyigaḷei unakku koḍnkkurén.*	*naḷḷadu nínu mádunu kashṭaku cheṇṇangu urupeya ningu tappi.*
Place my Pálankín in the Boat together with the bearers.	*nanna palakiyannu bestarondige harigólalli maḍagisu.*	*ná pálakini bóyilató kúḍa váḍaló peṭṭinchu.*	*en pallakkei bóyigaḷóḍe parishṭlil veikkashollu.*	*éda pálakina bóyiada kailu dónilu beppichiru.*
Take care, boatmen, you do not upset us all.	*ambigará. jópáná, nammam ellá illiyádaru mulugisírí.*	*vaḍagánḍlárá, bhadram, mammulanantá echchaṭeiná munchéru.*	*parishilkárargaḷé, badram, nammei yellám engeyávadu muḷugaḍippírgaḷ.*	*dónikuré jopána engala eḷḷa eḷḷiyachengi marchiruviru.*

English.	Canarese.	Telugu.	Tamil.	Coorg.
If you find it too heavily loaded, tell me, that I may send out some men and things in order to lessen the burthen.	*bahaḷa bháravági iddaré héḷi, bháravannu kaḍime máḍulu kelavarannu sámán ondige horakke kaḷuhisuvenu.*	*chánà baruvugánunṭé chepyanḍi, baruvunu takkuva chaynau koddi janamunu sámánutó kúḍá baiṭa pampénu.*	*irombá baḷuváy irundál shollangal, baḷuveḳoreikkavum sila pérei sámánéde veḷḷle anuppuvén.*	*perta pore áitendengi eṇṇi pore kummi máduwaku cheṇṇanga áluna sámánatira kúḍa porame ayapi.*
Is the river fordable in other seasons too?	*kaḍime kálagaḷallú holeyannu dáṭa bahudó?*	*takkina kálamulónú nadini dáṭa kúḍunó?*	*meitta kálangaḷilum árei dánḍalámé?*	*báre kálaṭṭulu pole kadakaluwa?*
Where does it take its rise, and were discharge itself into a sea or a lake?	*adu elli huṭṭi samudrakke ágali kerege ágali yátáva shérutté?*	*adi echchaṭa puṭṭi samudramuuu gáni cheruvunu gáni yáda chérutunnadi?*	*adu enge porandu kúḍaleiyávadhu ériyeiyávadhu enge shérugiradu?*	*adu eḷḷi puṭṭitu samuḍrakádu kerekádu eḷḷi kúduwa?*
Well boatman, I am very well satisfied with your skill in landing us in safety?	*ambigará, nívu namellánnu jópánavági daḍada méle iḷisiddakkági nánu bahaḷa mechidenu.*	*óyi váḍagánḍlárá, mammu bhadramugá gaṭṭuló dimpinadukei chána triptini pondinánu?*	*parishilkárargaḷé, nammei yellam badramáyi kare yéttinadharku nán rombavum santóṣham adainden.*	*dónikaré ninge engaleḷḷá jopánatulu kareku ulupunángu nánu perta mechchiné.*
Here is a present for your labour.	*igó nimmu kashṭakkági koḍuva inámu.*	*idó miyokka mehanattukugánu ichéṭi inámu.*	*idó ungaḷoḍaya kashṭattei patti koḍukkum inám.*	*idú ningada kuṭṭakáitu kodupu inám.*

I want something to eat.	*nanage tinnuvadakke énádaru béku.*	*náku tinuṭaku émainá kávalenu.*	*enakku sháppaḍu edúvadu véṇum.*	*nángu timbaku enná chengi bóndu.*
Give me a chair.	*nanage ondu kurchiyannu koḍu.*	*náku okka kurchin immu.*	*enakku oru nárkályi koḍu.*	*nángu oru kurchi tá.*
Boil some water for tea.	*té nírige níru kásu.*	*té nílluku níḷḷanu uḍaka peṭṭu.*	*té taṇṇikkága taṇṇiyai káchchu.*	*té níru káchu.*
Bring the tea-urn.	*té nírina baṭlannu tegadukonḍu bá*	*té níḷḷuyokka ginnenu temmu.*	*té taṇṇiyin kiṇṇiyai konḍuvá.*	*ti níruda baṭṭala edutandu bá.*
Have you made the tea?	*té níranna máḍi áyitó?*	*té níḷḷu cháyabudinadá.*	*té taṇṇiyai shaidhu áchchudá?*	*ti níru máḍiṭṭu ácha?*
I want coffee.	*nanage kápi níru béku.*	*náku kápi níḷḷu kávalenu.*	*enakku kápi taṇṇi véṇum.*	*nánga kápi níru bóndu.*
I wish to have the milk cold.	*nanage hálu taṇṇageira béku.*	*náku pálu challagáṇunḍavalenu.*	*enakku pál kuḷund irukkavéṇum.*	*nangu pálu tanin jiṭu irandu.*
There are not enough cups.	*baṭlugaḷu sáladu.*	*ginnelu chálavu.*	*kiṇṇigaḷ porádu.*	*baṭṭala teiya.*
I should like some bread and butter.	*nanage swalpa roṭṭi beṇṇé saha béku.*	*náku koncham roṭṭa venna kúḍa kávalenu.*	*enakku konjam roṭṭiyum veṇṇeym véṇum.*	*nángu chennangu aṭṭi boṇṇe nei bóndu.*
Give me a sharp knife.	*nanage haratavádachúriyannu koḍu.*	*náku monaina chúrini immu.*	*enakku shúrikattiyai koḍu.*	*nángu parivala kaṭṭi konda.*
The coffee is not strong.	*í kápí níru kháravági illá.*	*í kápí níḷḷu khháramuga lédu.*	*inda kápi taṇṇi káramáy illai.*	*í kápí níru káravaiṭṭu ille.*

English.	Canarese.	Telugu.	Tamil.	Coorg.
Let the Potatoes be well boiled.	*uraḷa geḍḍegaḷu chennági béyali.*	*urala gaḍḍalu bága uḍukaní.*	*uraḷa kiḷungu naṉráyi végaṭṭum.*	*viláiti geḍḍe nallóne béyadu.*
Let the Peas be well fried.	*í baṭáṇeyannu chennági huriya béku.*	*í baṭáṇenu bága vépavalenu.*	*inda baṭáṇiyai nanráyi porikkavéṇum.*	*í battanina nallone porikandu.*
Hand me that plate.	*á taṭṭeyannu nanage koḍu.*	*á taṭṭanu náku immu.*	*anda taṭṭai enakku koḍu.*	*á taṭṭena nángu tá.*
Is wine to be had here.	*illi vayin sáráyi shikkuttó?*	*ichchaṭa vayin sáráyi dorukuná?*	*inge vayin shárayam agappaḍumá?*	*illi wine kíttuwa?*
Push the dish nearer.	*taṭṭeyannu innú hatrakke taḷḷu.*	*taṭṭenu inka daggariki tóyi.*	*taṭṭai innamum kiṭṭa taḷḷu.*	*taliyatuna inyu pakka teraku.*
Have you any pudding?	*ninnalli kaḍabu untó?*	*ní vadda kuḍumu unnadá?*	*unniḍattil iḍḍaḷi irukkiradá?*	*nída pakka kadumbuṭṭu unda?*
I don't want supper.	*nánu rátriya úṭá vollé.*	*nénu rátri bhojanam volla.*	*nán rátri sháppaḍa máṭṭén.*	*nángu baiteku kúlu bónda.*
I must go to bed.	*nánu malaguvadakke hóga béku.*	*nénu panḍukonédániki póvalenu.*	*nán paḍukka póga véṇum.*	*nángu buḍḍavaku póndu.*
Snuff the candles.	*dípada kuḍiyannu kattarisu.*	*dípam vattiyokka konanu kattarinchu.*	*veḷakkin koḍiyai kattarí.*	*bolaku keḍutu.*

Who are you?	*nínu yáru ?*	*nívu evvaḍu.*	*ní yár ?*	*ninu áru ?*
How far is Yelahankam from Bangalore?	*bengaḷúrindá yalahanka eshṭu dúrá ?*	*bengaḷúriki yalahankam entu dúram ?*	*benguḷúrukku yalavankam evvaḷavu dúram?*	*bengalúrinji yalahanka echchaku dúra ?*
Is there any travellers Bungalow?	*alli musáfir bangalé untó ?*	*achchaṭa musáfir bangalá unnadá ?*	*ange musáfir bangaḷá irukkiradá ?*	*alli musápari bungili unda ?*
What is the name of the Kotwall of that village?	*á úru kotwálana hesaru énú ?*	*achchaṭi kotwáluṇi pér émí ?*	*avaḍattiya kotwalan pér enná ?*	*á úru kotwalanda peda eṇṇu ?*
Is water good in that village?	*á úru níru voḷḷédó ?*	*achchaṭi níḷḷu manchivá ?*	*avaḍattiya taṇṇi nalladá ?*	*á úru níru nallada ?*
Of these two tanks, which water is good to drink?	*á eraḍu kereyaḷoḷage yávadara níru kuḍiyuvadakke voḷḷédu ?*	*á renḍu cheruvulaló déni níḷḷu táguṭaku manchidí ?*	*anda irenḍu érigaḷil edinoḍaya taṇṇi kuḍikka nalladu ?*	*í ḍandu kerelu édanda níru kudipakku nalladu ?*
Is the road thither good?	*allige dári chennági idheyó ?*	*achchaṭiki dóva bágá unnadá ?*	*avaḍattukku vaḷi nandráy irukkiradá ?*	*alliku baṭṭe cháyile unda ?*
Well peon, go and call the Kotwall.	*eló vóḷékárá, kotwálanannu kare.*	*oré javánuḍá, kotwáluṇṇi pilavu.*	*aḍá shévagané, kotwálanai aḷai.*	*é kólkára kotwalana káku.*
For how many years have you held this situation?	*í chákariyalli nínu eshṭu divasadinda idhíyé ?*	*í chákariló nívu enni dinamulugá unnávú ?*	*inda shévagattil nín ettinai náḷáy irukkurdy?*	*í chákrilu nínu echchaku nálinji ulliya ?*
What is your pay?	*ninage sambaḷa eshṭu ?*	*níyokka jítam émí ?*	*unnoḍaya shambaḷam enná ?*	*níngu sambala echchaku ?*

ENGLISH.	CANARESE.	TELUGU.	TAMIL.	COORG.
What district does this village belong to?	*í haḷḷiyu yáva tálúkige shériddu?*	*í palla é tálúkáku chérinadí?*	*inda úr enda tálúkávukku shérndadu?*	*í úru édu tálókku kúdanadu?*
Get me gram and straw.	*nanage hullannu huruḷiyannu saha tundu koḍu.*	*náku kusuvunú ulavalanú techchi immu.*	*enakku pillaiyum koḷḷaiyum konḍu vandu koḍu.*	*nángu pillu mudre kondandu tá.*
What is the price of them?	*avagaḷa bele énú?*	*váṭlayokka vela émí?*	*adugaḷoḍaya velai enná?*	*adanda bele ennu?*
Can they be had here?	*avu illi shikkgávó?*	*avi ichchaṭa dorukuná?*	*adu inge agappaḍumá?*	*adu illi kittuwa?*
How large is the rope with which you tie up the bundle of straw?	*hullina horeyannu kaṭṭuva hagga eshṭu uddá?*	*kasuvuyokka mópunu kaṭṭéti paggam enta peddadí?*	*pil shamayai kaṭṭum kair ettinai níḷam?*	*pillu pore kettuwu kéru echchaku údda?*
How many seers of raw rice can we get for a rupee?	*vondu rúpáyige akki eshṭu shéru shikkutté?*	*okka rúpáyiki bíyam enni shérulu chikkunu?*	*oru rupágikki arishi ettinai shér agappaḍum?*	*oru urupiyaku akki echchaku séru kittuwa?*
By the time I leave this early in the morning, you must have here ready two carriage Bullocks, five common carts, eight coolies, and a set of Palankin bearers.	*nánu náḷe beḷigge horaḍuva hottige, eraḍu horé yettugaḷu, eidu chápé bandigaḷu, enṭu mandi kuliyavaru, ondu páḍi bestaru, ivagaḷannu hájar mádi irabéku.*	*nénu tellaváriki veḷḷéṭi prodduku rendu móshéṭi yaddulu, eidu chápa bandlu, enimidi mandi kúlivánḍlu, pannenḍu mandi bóyilu, viṭlanu hájar chéshi unḍavalenu.*	*nán náḷai kálaimé porappaḍum véḷaikki, irenḍu shomaimáḍugaḷ, anji páyi venḍigaḷ, eṭṭu pér kúlikkárurgaḷ, panirenḍu pér bóyigaḷ, idugaḷai tayár shaidu vaikkavéṇum.*	*nánu nále poraduwu néraku erandu páru ettua, anji palambu gádi, ettu kúli álu, oru paleke baiya iḍaneḷa kútendu irandu.*

Tell me what will be the cost for all these from this to Devanhaḷḷi?	*illinda dévanahaḷḷiya variye avakke kúli énu águttê?*	*ichchaṭanundi dévana palle varku kúli émi autunnddí?*	*ivaḍattil irunḍu déva-nakaḷḷi varaikki kúli en-nam águm?*	*illivjí devanallikitta udangella ennáku?*
What is the price of cocoanut and castor oils?	*koppari mattu karaḷe eṇṇegaḷige bele énu?*	*tenkáyi núna, ámi-dam éṭládu ammutunna ví?*	*téngáy eṇṇai, viḷakeṇ-ṇai ennamáyi virukkira-du?*	*koppariku avanaken-neku bele ennu?*
What produce is abundant here?	*illi yáva beḷe mastági águtte?*	*ichchaṭa éṭi pairu ta-rchuyá panḍutunnadi?*	*inge enda pair rom-baváyi viḷaigirdu?*	*illi édu bole dúta ápa?*
How is grain selling here now?	*íga illi dhányagaḷu hyáge máruttavé?*	*íppuḍu ichchaṭa dhá-nyamulu élagu ammutu-nnavví?*	*ippo ivaḍattil dhány-angaḷ eppaḍi virukkira-du?*	*ikka illi davasa en-nane maruwa?*
It is getting rather late, and I shall therefore be off immediately.	*íga bahuḷa hottu agu-ttú bantu; nánu í kṣha-ṇu horaḍa béku.*	*ippuḍu chánú proddu ainadi ganuka í kṣhaṇam nénu veḷḷa valenu.*	*ippo rombavum poḷud achchidu, áyaiyál, nán inda nimiṣham proappa-ḍa véṇum.*	*ikká dúta néra áya-ndu báttu, nánu ikkalé porandandu.*
Kotwál, go to your business, as I must prepare myself for my journey.	*eló kotwálané, nínu ninna kelasakke hógu; nánu nanna prayaṇakke sidhavága béku.*	*oré kotwáluḍá, nívu níyokka paniki pommu, nénu prayáṇamunaku ta-yár kávalenu.*	*aḍá kotwalané, ni un vélaikki pó, nán payaṇ-attukku tayár ágavéṇum.*	*é kotwala, ninn nída chakriku pova nánu éda payanaku tuiyarumúda-ndu.*
How many houses are there in this village?	*í úralli eṣhṭu manega-ḷavé?*	*í palleló enni inḍlu unavi?*	*inda úril evvaḷavu ví-ḍugaḷ irukkiradu?*	*i úrulu echchuku ma-ne undu?*

ENGLISH.	CANARESE.	TELUGU.	TAMIL.	COORG.
What is that large upstair house that lies there?	*alli káṇisuva doḍḍa mahaḍi yávadu.*	*achchaṭu agupaḍéṭi pedda midda émí.*	*ange teṉbaḍugira periya middai enná ?*	*alli kámbu balliyu up pirike édu ?*
Tell the bearers to carry my Palankín there.	*nanna pállakkiyannu allige konḍu hóga heḷi bestarige héḷu.*	*ná pálakini achchaṭiki tísukoni pommani boyílaku cheppu.*	*en paḷḷakkai araḍattukku konḍu pogachcholli bóyigaḷukku shollu.*	*éda pálekina alliku kondupóndundu boyaku eṇṇu.*
Will you follow me?	*nínu nannonḍige baruviyá ?*	*nívu nátó kúḍá vachévá ?*	*ní ennóde kúḍá varuviyá ?*	*nínu éda kúda bappiá?*
Can I alight here?	*nánu illi iḷiya bahudó ?*	*nénu ichchaṭu diga kúḍunó.*	*nán inge erengalámó ?*	*nánu illi iḷiyaluwa ?*
Give me a clever servant to bring me the things I require.	*nanage békáda sámánu taruvadakke obba ghaṭṭigannáda áḷannu koḍu.*	*náku kávaleṣhina sámán techchéṭanduku okka ghaṭṭiváḍaina maniṣhini immu.*	*enakku vénḍiya sámánai konḍuvara oru geṭṭikáranán shévaganai koḍu.*	*enaku bóndiya sámana kondapaku oru gettiánu áḷu tá.*
What cooly is to be given to him for a day?	*avanige ondu dinakke kúli énu ?*	*váṇiki okka náṭiki kúli émi.*	*avanukku oru náḷaikki kúli enná ?*	*avangu oṇándeku kúli eṇṇu.*
Go to the Post Office and see if there are any letters for me.	*ancheya manege hógi, nanage kágadu énádaru bandu idheyé nóḍi bá.*	*tapál intiki, póyi, naku káyidál émainá vachchi unnadá zúchi rá.*	*tappál chávaḍikki póyi enakku kaḍádáshigaḷ edúvadu vand irukkiradá párttu vá.*	*anche maneku poitui enaku káyada ennéng banietándu nótitu bá.*

If there be any, bring.	*énddaru iddare tegadukoṇḍu bá.*	*émaina unṭé tísukonirá.*	*edúvad irandál kondu vá.*	*eṇṇégi badietenngi edutaṇḍu bá.*
My name is—.	*nannu hasáru—.*	*ná péru—.*	*en pér—.*	*éda peda.—*
The butter you got me was very bad?	*nínu nanage tandu koṭṭa beṇṇé voḷḷédalla.*	*nívu náku techchi ichchina venna manchidi kádu.*	*níy enakku konḍuvandu koḍuttu veṇṇai nalad alla.*	*nínu enaku kondandu tandu boṇṇenai naḷḷa daḷḷa.*
Bring me some more milk.	*nanage hálannu swalpa hechági tandu koḍu.*	*náku pálu koncham hechchugá techchi immu.*	*enakku pál konjam adikamáyi kondu vandu koḍu.*	*enaku pálu cheṇṇanga dúta kondandu tá.*
Who is the Transit Clerk here?	*illi tapálu banḍi mutsaddi yárú?*	*ichchaṭa tapál banḍi mutsaddi evvaḍu?*	*inge tappál vanḍi mutsaddi yár?*	*illi tapálu gádi mutsaddi áru?*
As I don't like to be bothered with the noise of the bearers, I intend travelling by your Transit.	*bestara kúgu nanage súkáyitu, áddarinda ninna banḍiyalli hóga békendu yóchisutténe.*	*bóyila kúta náku cháaindi ganuka, níyokka banḍiló póvalenani yóchistunnánu.*	*bóyigaḷoḍaya kúchchel anakku pórumáy irukiradu, úgaiyal unnoḍaiya vanḍiyil pógavéṇum enru yóchikkurén.*	*bóyada kútu enaku madiáchi ánagondu nída yadilu póndúndu mánasu unḍu.*
What do you want from this to the next stage?	*illinda mandina majallge ènu kéḷuttíyé?*	*ichchatanunḍi munupaṭi majaluku émi aḍugutunnávu?*	*viaḍattil irandu min majalukku enna kéḷkuráyi?*	*illingi minyslatu jágaku ennu kepiya?*
How far is it from hence?	*illige adu eṣhṭu dúra idhé?*	*ichohaṭiki adi enṭdúram unnadí?*	*ivaḍattukku aḍu ettinai dúram irukkirdu?*	*illiku adu echchaku dúra undu?*

ENGLISH.	CANARESE.	TELUGU.	TAMIL.	CROOG.
How is the road ?	*dáriyu hyágé idhé ?*	*dóva élág unnadí ?*	*vaḷia eppaḍui irukkiradu ?*	*butte eṇnane undu ?*
Get a coach and two horses ready here about 6 o'clock tomorrow morning.	*náḷé beḷigge áru ghanṭeya hottige illi ondu sawári banḍiyannu, eraḍu kudaregaḷannu sahá hájar máḍu.*	*répu telavári áru ghanṭala prodduku ichchaṭa okka savári banḍiné renḍu gurramulanú hájar cháyavalenu.*	*náḷai kálaimé áru maṇi vlaikki inge oru savári vanḍiyaiyum, irenḍu kuduregaḷaigum ájar sheyya véṇum.*	*nále palaka áru mani néraku illi oru savári gádi dandu kudreyu hajar mádu.*
Take out all the luggage from my palankín, and place them in the carriage.	*nanna pallakiya sámán ellánu horage tegadu bhanḍiyali iḍu.*	*ná pallakkiyokka sáman baiṭatíshi banḍiló unchu.*	*en pallakkin sámánai veḷiḷe vángi vanḍiyil vai.*	*éda paḷeki sámana ella porame kondanditu gadilu idu.*
Well coachman, why don't you drive as fast as you can ?	*eló bhanḍiyavané, béga bóga yáke hoḍiyaláré ?*	*oré banḍiváḍá, végira végira yála tólavu ?*	*aḍá vanḍikárá, shuru shrukkáy én óṭṭa máṭṭáy?*	*ó bandikára beri beriya ennangu átulé ?*
Avoid ruts and rough parts.	*haḷḷa koḷḷa nóḍi hoḍi.*	*pallam miṭṭanu zúchi tólu.*	*paḷḷam méḍu párttu óṭṭu.*	*gundu moṭṭe not ita áttu.*
Take care, you don't upset us.	*elládaru keḍavi biṭṭiyé, jópáná.*	*ehchaṭaina porlinchevu bhadram.*	*engeyávadu koḍe kavuttu póḍuváyi, badram.*	*elliáchengi búkiruwa jópana.*
If you drive on faster, I will give you a good present.	*nínu béga hoḍadare ninage voḷḷé inám koḍuvenu.*	*níru végira télité, níku munchi inám istunánu .*	*ní shurukkay óṭṭinál unakku nalla inám koḍukkurén.*	*nínu beriya átichengi níngu nalla inam tapé.*

There are many stones before the village gate: don't drive against them.	*á úru bágala hatra kallugaḷu sháne ave, nóḍi hoḍi.*	*á úri rákali daggira ráḷḷu shánú unnavi ; zúchi tólu.*	*anda úr váshil minne kallugaḷ rombu irukkiradugal, pártta vóṭṭu.*	*í úru gandira pakka kallu pertu undu, nótitu útu.*
Stop, driver.	*nillisu.*	*nilapu.*	*niruttu.*	*nippichiru.*
As it seems that I cannot reach the next stage before dusk, you must give me a torch-bearer with light and sufficient quantity of oil.	*nánu mundina majalige shéruvadara oḷage kattale yáyuvahúge káṇutte áddarinda maṣhál, eṇṇe, maṣhálchiyannu sahá nanage nínu koḍa béku.*	*nénu mundari mojaluku chérélóga chígaṭi ayéṭaṭṭu agvpaḍutunnadi ganuka mashál, núna, maṣhálchitó kúḍa náku níru ivvavalenu.*	*nán min majalukku poguradarkuḷḷé iraṭṭi pógum polé irukkiradu, ágaiyál dívaṭṭi, eṇṇai, dívaṭṭi káranóḍe kúḍa enakku ní koḍukka véṇum.*	*nánu minyelatu jágaku muttuwánda olúlu beitu ápaneke kúmba ánagondu poṭṭe poṭṭekarankúde nangu ninu tarandu.*
Driver, open all the glass windows as the heat is very oppressive.	*bahaḷa shekhey águtte, áddarinda kannaḍi bágalugaḷannu teri.*	*chálá sheka autu unnadi ganuka addála talapulanu timmu.*	*rombavum irakkum águradu, ágeiyál kannáḍi kadavugaḷei tiravu.*	*bandikára dúta seke ápu ánugondu kannadi padi tora.*
Awake me about 5 o' Clock in the morning.	*beḷagina eidu ghanṭege nannannu ebbisu.*	*vékuva jhámamuló eidu ghanṭalaku nannu lépu.*	*vediya anju maṇikkennei eḷuppu.*	*polanjati anji maniku enna oppu.*
Place the paper, pen and inkstand in the Coachman's box.	*í kágada, lékhaṇi, mashiyannu sahá mundina peṭṭigeyalli maḍagu.*	*í kágadam, shyáyi buḍḍi, lékhaṇi, víṭlanu, mundari peṭṭuló peṭṭu.*	*inda káyidam, sháyibuḍḍi pénávei min poṭṭiyil vei.*	*í kágada, lukkanike, kappuna ella minyelata poṭṭilu beiyi.*
Be careful, driver, that the horse does not take fright in the dark.	*kattaleyalli kudaregaḷu elli ádaru bedaryávu, jópáná.*	*chígatilo gurrálu bhayapuḍéni, bhadram.*	*iraṭṭil kuduregaḷ enigeyávadu meraḷum, badram.*	*iruṭaṭulu kudre elliáchengi boṭṭu, jopanu.*

P

ENGLISH.	CANARESE.	TELUGU.	TAMIL.	COORG.
Why is my luggage thrown down at the gate?	*nanna sámán úru bágalalli yáke biddu idhé?*	*nayokka sámán úru vakililo yála paḍi unnadi?*	*en sámán úruváshalil én kiḍakkiradu?*	*éda sámána úru gandilu ennangu budditullu?*
Am I to pay any tax?	*nánu sunkava énádaru koḍa békó.*	*nénu ásal émainá ivavalenó?*	*nán tírvaiy edávadu koḍukka véṇumó?*	*nánu sunka ennáchengu kodukanduwa?*
As there is nothing taxable in it, let it be carried away.	*adaralli sunkada sámán énu illá áddarinda sámán mundakke hógali.*	*dániyandu hásal sámán emí lédu ganuka sámán mundariki póni.*	*adil tírvei, sámán oṇrum illei ágaiyál sámán minnukku pógaṭṭum.*	*adaṭulu sunkatu sámána édu illatanagondu sámána minyeku pódu.*
Get me an umbrella or two for my servants.	*nanna chákararige onderaḍu kai chhatrigaḷannu tarisi koḍu.*	*ná sévaklanu okkaṭi renḍu chéti goḍugulanu techchi immu.*	*en shévagarukku oru renḍu kei koḍegaḷei konḍu vandu koḍu.*	*éda chákrikáraku onderanda kode kondarachi tá.*
The rain seems very heavy.	*maḷé bahaḷa balavu embadági káṇutte.*	*vána chána balam ani agupaḍutunnadi.*	*maḷei rombá balam eṇru tenbaḍugiradu.*	*male dúta jorúndu kúmba.*
Will it not cease soon?	*maḷé íga nilluvad illavó?*	*vána végira nilavadó?*	*maḷei shurukkáyi nikka máṭṭádó?*	*male ikka nippadilliya?*
Is this good for the Tanks and roads?	*idu keregaḷigú márgakkú voḷḷédó?*	*idi cheruvulakunnú dóvulakunnú manchidá?*	*idu érigaḷukkum vaḷigaḷukum nalladó?*	*idu kereku baṭṭeku nallada?*
I think both must suffer if the rain continues long.	*averuḍakkú maḷé hechchádaré voḷḷédallá vendu nánu éṇisutténe.*	*avi renṭikinní váná jástiyeite, manchidikádani nénu talustunánu.*	*adugaḷ irenḍukkum maḷei rombavánál, nalladallavenru nineikkurén.*	*aderandangú male dútáchengi naḷḷadalla indu nánu nenepi.*

Do you keep the water course open when it rains?	*maḷé huyyuvága kóḍi sovaruttiró?*	*vána kurichéṭappuḍu maravanu terichiyunṭunnárá?*	*maḷei péyum pódu kalingallei tirandu viḍuvírgaḷá?*	*male poyuwaka ṭóduna torandu beppira.*
How deep is the water of this Tank.	*í kereyalli níru eṣhṭu udda idhé?*	*í cheruvuló níḷḷu yanta lótugá unnadí?*	*inda ériyil taṇṇi ettinei áḷum irukkiradu?*	*í kerelu niru echchaku ála undu?*
Does it irrigate any land?	*adara keḷage bhúmi yénádaru ságuvaḷi águttó?*	*dáni venakajamín émaina panḍutunnadá?*	*adin pinne nelam edávadu viḷeiguradá.*	*adanda kédalu bhúmi ennáchengi ságu ápa?*
Does any river discharge itself into this Tank?	*í kerege yávadádaru hólé bandu shéruttó?*	*í cheruvuku édaina nadi vchchi chérutunnadá?*	*inda érikki edávaduáru vandu shérugiradá?*	*í kereku édéngi pole bandu kúduvu?*

THE END. Samápti. Sampúrṇam. Muḍivu. Akairu.

FRAGMENT

OF AN ENGLISH AND COORG DICTIONARY.

A.

Abandon, *v. a.* *ಬುಟು ಬುಡು, ಬುಟ್ಟುರು *buṭu buḍu, buṭṭuru,* ಕೈ ಬುಡು, ಕೈ ಬುಟ್ಟುರು, *kei buḍu, kei buṭṭuru,* ಕೈ ಬೂಡೋದು, *kei búḍódu.*

Abandonment, *s.* ಬುಟ್ರೋದು *buṭródu.*

Abase, *v. a.* ತಗ್ಗಿಚಿರು *taggichiru.*

Abasement, *s.* ತಗ್ಗಿಚಿರುವದು *taggichiruvadu.*

Abash, *v. a.* ಙ್ಞಾಣ, ಪಡಿಚಿಡು *ynáṇa, paḍichiḍu.*

Abate, *v. a.* ಕಮ್ಮಿ ಮಾಡು *kammi máḍu.*

Abatement, *s.* ಕಮ್ಮಿ *kammi.*

Abbreviate, *v. a.* ಚೆಂನಂಗಲೆ ಮಾಡು *chennangalé máḍu.*

Abbreviation, *s.* ಚೆಂನಂಗು *chennangu.*

Abdicate, *v. a.* ಬುಟ್ಟು ಬುಡು, ಬುಟ್ಟುರು *buṭṭu buḍu, buṭṭuru.*

Abdication, *s.* ಬುಟ್ಟು ಬುಡುವದು *buṭṭu buḍuvadu.*

Abet, *v. a.* ಗುಣ ಮಾಡು, ಸಾಯ ಮಾಡು *guṇa máḍu, sáya máḍu.*

Abhor, *v. a.* ಹೇಸಿಗೆ ಪಡು, ಗೊಜೆ ಪಡು *hésige paḍu, goje paḍu.*

Abhorrence, *s.* ಗೊಜೆ, ಹೇಸಿಗೆ *goje, hésige.*

Abide, *v. n.* ನೆಲೆಯಾಯಿತಿರು *neleyáyitiru.*

Abject, *s.* ಕೆಟ್ಟವು, ನೀಚು, ಕೆಟ್ಟದಾನು *keṭṭavu, níchu, keṭṭadánu.*

Ability, *s.* ಪೊದ *poda.*

Abjure, *v. a.* ಬುಟ್ಟು ಬುಡುವಿಂದು, ಆಣೆ ಇಡು *buṭṭu buḍuvindu, áṇe iḍu.*

Able, *a.* ಪೊದವುಳು *pódavuḷu.*

Ablution, *s.* ಕುಳಿ *kuḷi.*

Abode, *s.* ಭಾವೊ ಜಾಗ, ಇಪ್ಪ ಜಾಗ *bhávo jága, ippa jaga.*

Abolish, *v. a.* ಎಡಿತಿತಿಡು, ಎಡತು ಬುಡು *eḍitititiḍu, eḍatu buḍu.*

Abolition, *s.* ಎಡಿತಿಡುವದು, ಎಡಿತಿ ಬುಡುವದು *eḍitiḍuvadu, eḍiti buḍuvudu.*

Abominable, *a.* ಪರಿಕಡು ಆನು, ಹೇಸಿಗೆ ಆನು *parikaḍu ánu, hésige ánu.*

Abominate, *v. a.* ಪರಿಕಡು ಪಡುವ, ಹೇಸಿಗೆ ಪಡುವ *parikaḍu paḍuva, hésige paḍuva.*

---

* N. B. Short u as oo in foot— ಡ ḍ ದ d

Abo.

Abortion, *s.* ಕುಳಿಚಿ, ಪೋಪು ***kuḷichi, pópu.***

Above, *prep.* ಮೇಕೆ, ಕೊಡಿ ***méke, koḍi.***

Abound, *v. n.* ದೂತಹಾಯಿತಿರು, ಪೆರ್ತಹಾಯಿತಿರು ***dútaháyitiru, pertahdyitiru***

About, *prep.* ಸುತ್ತೂಲ ಆಯಿತು ***suttúla áyitu.***

Abreast, *ad.* ಸಾಲೋಡೆ ***sálóḍe.***

Abridge, *v a.* ಚೆನ್ನಂಗಲೆ ಮಾಡು ***chennangale máḍu.***

Abridgement, *s.* ಚೆನ್ನಂಗು ***chennangu.***

Abroad, *ad.* ಪೊರಮೆ ***porame.***

Abrogate, *v. a.* ಎಡಿತಿತಿಡು, ಎಡತುಬುಡು ***eḍititiḍu, eḍatubuḍu.***

Abrogation, *s.* ಎಡಿತಿತಿಡವದು, ಎಡತುಬುಡುವದು ***eḍititiḍavadu, eḍatubuḍuvadu.***

Abruptly, *ad.* ಬಲ್ಲಾದೆ, ಅರಿಯತೆ ***balláde, ariyate.***

Abscess, *s.* ಪಣ್ಣು, ಬಾಪು ***paṇṇu, bápu.***

Abscond, *v. n.* ಮೂಡು ತಪ್ಪಿಚಿರು ***múḍu tappichiru.***

Absence, *s.* ಇಲ್ಲೆ ***ille.***

Absent, *a.* ಇಲ್ಲತದು ***illatadu.***

Absolve, *v. a.* ತೀತೊ ***títo.***

Absolute, *a.* ಬೊಂಡಿ ಅಚ್ಚಕು, ನೇರಾಯಿತ್ತು ***bonḍi achchaku, nérâyittu.***

Absolution, *s.* ತೀತವದು ***títavadu.***

Absorb, *v. a* ಊತಿಯ ***útiya,***

Absorption, *s.* ಊತಿಯವದು ***útiyavadu.***

Abstain, *v. a.* ಮಾಡತಿರು, ಬಾಯಿ ಕಟ್ಟು ***máḍatiru, báyi kaṭṭu.***

Abstemious, *a.* ಬೊಂಡಿ ಅಚ್ಚಕು ಉಂಬದಾನ, ಬೊಂಡಿ ಅಚ್ಚಕು ಕುಡಿಪದಾನ ***bonḍ achchaku umbaddna, bonḍi achchaku kuḍipadána.*** In eating, In drinking.

Abstinence, *s.* ಮಾಡತಿಪ್ಪದು, ಬಾಯಿ ಕಟ್ಟುವದು ***máḍatippadu, báyi kaṭṭuvadu.***

Abstract, *s.* ಚೆನ್ನಂಗು ***chennungu.***

Abstract, *adj.* ಮರ್ಮ ಉಳ್ಳ ***marma uḷḷa.***

Abstract, *v. a.* ಚೆನ್ನಂಗು ಮಾಡು ***chennange máḍu.***

Abstraction, *s.* ಬೋರೆ ಮಾಡುವದು, ಬೋರೆ ಆವದು ***bóre máḍuvadu, bóre ápadu.***

Abstruse, *a.* ಮರ್ಮವಾನು ***marmavánu.***

Absurd, *a.* ಬುದ್ಧಿ ಇಲ್ಲತು, ಅರಿಯತು ತೆಳಿಪಿಚಿರುವು ***buddhi illatu, ariyatu teḷipichiruvu.***

Abundance, *s.*
Aboundant, *a.* } ಪೆರ್ತ ***perta.***

Abuse *s.* ಪಳಿವು, ಬೈಲು ***paḷivu, beilu.***

Abuse, *v. a.* ಪಳಿಂಜಿರು, ಬೈಯಿ ***paḷinjiru, beiyı.***

Abut, *v. n* ಪಕ್ಕಲು ಆಯು, ಪಕ್ಕಲು ಮಾಡು, ಪಕ್ಕಲು ಅಡಿಪಿಚಿರು ***pakkalu áya, pakkalu máḍu, pakkalu aḍipichiru.***

Abyss, *s.* ಬುಲ್ಯದು ***bulyadu.***

Academy, *s.* ಮಠ, ಎಳತು ಪಡಿಪು ಜಾಗ ***matha, eḷatu paḍipu jága.***

Accede, *v. n.* ವೊತ್ತವು ***vottavu.***

Accelerate, *v. a.* ಬೆರಿಯ, ಮಾಡಿಚಿರು ***beriya, máḍichiru.***

Acceleration, *s.* ಬೆರಿಯ ಮಾಡಿಚಿರುವದು ***beriya máḍichiruvadu.***

Accent, *s.* ಕೂತು, ದನಿ ***kútu, dani.***

Accent, *v. a.* ದನಿಯಾಯಿತೆಣ್ಣು ***duniyáyiteṇṇu.***

Accept, *v. a.* ಕೊಡಿಯಾಯಿತು ಎಡುತಾ ***kodiyáyitu eḍutá.***

Acceptable, *a.* ಕೊಡಿ ಅನದು, ನೆನಪಂತದು ***kodiánadu, nenapantadu.***

Acceptance, Acceptation, *s.* ವೊತ್ತವದು ***vottavadu.***

Access, *s.* ಕೂಡುವದು ***kuḍuvadu.***

Accessary, *a.* ಗುಣವಾಯಿತು ಉಳ್ಳ, ಸಾಯವಾಯಿತು ಉಳ್ಳ ***guṇaváyitu uḷḷu, sáyaváyitu uḷḷa.***

Accessory, *s.* ಗುಣ ಮಾಡುವವು, ಸಾಯ ಮಾಡುವವು ***guṇa máḍuvavu, sáya máḍuvavu.***

Accessible, *a.* ಕೂಡುವಂತದು ಕೂಡುವರು ***kuḍuvantadu kuḍuvaru***

Accession, *s.* ಪೊಳ್ಳೆಪಡು ***poḷepaḍu.***

Accident, *s.* ಕಾಲಕೇಡು ***kálakéḍu.***

Acclamation, *s.* ಕುದಿಚಿತು ಎಣ್ಣುವ ಕೂತು ***kudichitu eṇṇuva kútu.***

Accommodate, *v. n.* ಕಣಕು ಆಪಂನೆಕೆ ಮಾಡು, ಬುದ್ದವ ಜಾಗ ಕೊಡು ***kaṇaku ápanneke máḍu, buddava jága koḍu.***

Accompany, *v. a.* ಕೂಡೆ ಪೋಪು ***kuḍe pópu.***

Accomplice, *s.* ಸಾಯ ಮಾಡುವವು, ಗುಣ ಮಾಡುವವು ***sáya máḍuvavu guṇa máḍuvavu.***

Accomplish, *v. a.* ತೀತಿರು ***títiru.***

Accomplishment, *s.* ತೀರ ***tíra.***

Accord, *v. a.* ವಪ್ಪಿಚಿಡು, ಕೂಡಿಚಿಡು, ಕೂಡು ***vappichiḍu, kúḍichiḍu, kúḍu.***

Accordance, *s.* ಕೂಡುವದು ***kúḍuvadu.***

According, *prep.* ಅಂನನೆ, ಅಂನಂಕೆ ***annane, annanke.***

Accost, *v. a.* ಕಾಕು ***káku.***

Account, *s.* ಲೆಕ್ಕಾ, ಕಣಕು ***lekká, kaṇaku.***

Account, *v. a.* ಲೆಕ್ಕ ವಪ್ಪಿಚಿರು, ಲೆಕ್ಕ ಕೂಟು *lekka vappichiru, lekka kúṭu.*

Accountable, *a.* ಲೆಕ್ಕ ವಪ್ಪಿಚಿರುವಂತು *lekka vappichiruvantu.*

Accounter, *v. a.* ಆಯಿದ ತೆಕು *áyida teku.*

Accrue, *v. a.* ಉಂಡಾದು *unḍáḍu.*

Accountate, *v. a.* ಪೆರ್ಪಿಚಿರು, ಕೂಡಿಚಿರು *perpichiru, kuḍichiru.*

Accurate, *a.* ಸರಿ, ತಪ್ಪಿಲ್ಲತು *sari, tappillatu.*

Accurse, *v. a.* ಚಾಪ್ಲಿ ಚೆರು *chápli cheru.*

Accursed, *a.* ಚಾಪ್ಲಿ ಚಿಟ್ಟು *chipli chiṭṭu.*

Accusation, *s.* ತಪ್ಪು ಪೊರ್ಪಿಚಿರುವದು *tappu porpichiruvadu.*

Accuse, *v a.* ತಪ್ಪು ಪೊರ್ಪಿಚಿರು *tappu porpichiru.*

Accuser, *s.* ತಪ್ಪು ಪೊರ್ಪಿಚಿರುವವು *tappu porpichiruvavu.*

Accustom, *v. a.* ಅಭೆಸ ಮಾಡು, ಅಭ್ಯಾಸ ಮಾಡು *abhesa máḍu, abhyasu máḍu.*

Ache, *s.* ನೊಂಬಲ, *nombala, v. n.* ನೊಂಬಲ ಆಪು *nombala ápu.*

Achieve, *v. a.* ಸಾಧಿಚಿರು *sádhichiru.*

Achievement, *s.* ಸಾಧಿಚಿರುವದು *sádichiruvadu.*

Acid, *a.* ಪುಳಿಯಾನುನು *puḷiyánanu.*

Acknowledge, *v. a.* ಅರಿಕೆ ಮಾಡಿಯಾ, ಉಂಡುಂದು ಎಂಣು *arike mádiyá, undundu yeṇṇu.*

Acquaint, *v. a.* ಅರಿಚಿರು *arichiru.*

Acquaintance, *s.* ಗೊತ್ತು, ಗೊತ್ತು ಉಳ್ಳವು *gottu, gottu ullavu.*

Acquiesce, *v. n.* ಒತ್ತ, ವೊಪ್ಪಿಯ *wotta, woppiya.*

Acquire, *v. a.* ನೇಡು *néḍu.*

Acquisition, *s.* ನೇಡುವದು *neḍuvadu.*

Acquit, *v. a.* ತಪ್ಪಿಲ್ಲೆಂಡೆಣಿತು ತೀತಿರು *tuppillendeṇitu títiru.* The *tu* in *tutiru* to have pronounciation of *eu.*

Acquittal, *s.* ತಪ್ಪಿಲ್ಲೆಂಡೆಂಣಿತು ತಿರುವರು *tappillendenṇitu tiruvaru.*

Acrid, *a.* ಎರಿಪದು ಕೈಯಿ *eripadu keiyi.*

Acrimony, *s.* ಎರಿ ಬೇದನೆ *eri bédane.*

Accross, *ad.* ಬೆಲಕವಾಂಯಿತ್ತು *belakaváyittu.*

Act, *s.* ನಡಪು ಮಾಡುವದು, *naḍapu máḍuvadu, v. a.* ನಡತು ಮಾಡು *naḍatu máḍu.*

Action, *s.* ನಡಪು, ಬತ್ಲೆ ಪಡೆ *naḍapu, batle, paḍe.*

Active, *a.* ಚುರುಕು ಉಳ್ಳು, ಬೆರಿಯ *churuku uḷḷu, beriya.*

Activity, *s.* ಚುರುಕು *churuku.*

Actor *s.* ಮಾಡುವವು *máḍuvavu.*

Actual, *a.* ನೇರಾನು *néránu.*

Actuate, *v. a.* ಪಡಿಪಿಚೆರು *paḍipichiru.*

Acute, *a.* ಮರ್ಮ ಉಳ್ಳು, ಚುರುಕುಬುದ್ಧಿ ಆನು *marma uḷḷu, churuku buddhi ánu.*

Adage, *s.* ಗಾದಿ *gádi.*

Adamant, *s.* ವಜಿರುತು ಕಲು *vajirutu kaḷu.*

Adapt, *v. a.* ಕೂಡಿಚೆರು ಸರಿ ಆಪನೆಕೆ ಮಾಡು *kúḍichiru, sari ápaneke máḍu.*

Adaptation, *s.* ಕೂಡುವದು, ಸರಿ ಆಪದು *kúḍuvadu, sari ápadu.*

Add, *v. a.* ಇನ್ನು ಇಡು, ಪೆರ್ಪಿಚೆರು, ತರಕೂಟ್ಟು *innu iḍu, perpichiru, tarakúṭṭu.*

Adder, *s.* ನಲ್ಲಪಾಂಬು, ಪಾಂಬು *nallapámbu, pámbu.*

Addict, *v. a.* ಸಾದಗ ಮಾಡು, ಅಭೆಸ ಮಾಡಿಯು *sádaga máḍu, abhesa máḍiyu.*

Addition, *s.* ಕೂಡುವದು *kúḍuvadu.*

Address, *s.* ಪಳ್ಮೆ, ಲಕೊಟುಡಮೆಕೆ ಎಳ್ದುವದು ಚಾಲಾಕು *paḷme, lakoṭuḍameke eḷuduvadu chálákú.*

Address, *v. a.* ಅರ್ಜಿ ಎಳ್ದಿಯು, ಪಳ್ಮೆಯೆಂಣು ಲಕೊಟುಡ ಮೇಕೆ ಎಳ್ದು *arji eḷudiya, paḷmeyeṇṇu lakoṭuḍa méke eḷadu.*

Adept, *s.* ಚಾಲಾಕುಕಾರು *chálákukáru.*

Adequate, *a.* ಸರಿ ಆನು, ಬೊಂಡಿಯದಾನು *sari ánu, bonḍiyadánu.*

Adhere, *v. n.* ಪತ್ತಿಯ *pattiya.*

Adherent, *s.* ಬೋರೆ ಒಬ್ಬನ ನಂಬುವು, ಬೊರೆ ಒಬ್ಬನ ಕೂಡುವು *bóre obbana nambuvu, bore obbana kúḍuvu.*

Adhesion, *s.* ಪತ್ತಿಯವರು *pattiyavaru.*

Adjacent, Adjoining, *a.* ಪಕ್ಕಲಾನು ಅಡಿತಿತುಳ್ಳು *pakkalánu aḍitituḷḷu.*

Adjective, *a.* ಗುಣವಾಚಕ *guṇavāchaka.*

Adjourn, *v. a.* ನಿಪ್ಪಚೆರು *nippachiru.*

Adjudge, *v. n.* ತಿತುರು, ಕಂಡಿತ ಮಾಡು *tituru, kanḍita máḍu.*

Adjudication, *s.* ನಾಯತಿಪರು *náyatiparu.*

Adjunct, *s.* ಸಮಾರ ಸೆರುವರು *samára seruvaru.*

Adjure, *v. a.* ಸೇರುಕೆಯಿಚೆರು *sérukeyichiru.*

Adjust, *v. a.* ಬರೊಬರು ಮಾಡು, ಸರಿಮಾಡು *barobaru máḍu, sari máḍu.*

Adjutant, *s.* ಸಾಯ ಮಾಡುವವು *sáya máḍuvavu.*

Administer, *v. a.* ಕೊಡು, ನಾಯ ಕೇಳು, ನೇರುಕೆಯಿಚೆರು *koḍu, náya kéḷu, nérukeyichiru.*

Administration, *s.* ನ್ಯಾಯ ಕೇಪರು, ರಾಜ್ಯತುಭಾರ, ಧೊರೆತನ *nyáya képaru, rájyatubhára, dhoretana.*

Admirable, *a.* ಚಾಯಿ, ಆನು ಎಲಂಗುವದಾನು *cháyi, ánu elanguvadánu.*

Admiral, *s.* ಪಡೆ ಕಪ್ಪಕು ಕೊರವುಕಾರು *paḍe kappaku koravukáru.*

Admire, *v. a. & n.* ಚಾಯಿ ಆಯಿತಿರು, ಕೂಟು, ನೆನೆ *chάyi áyitiru, kúṭu, nene.*

Admissible, *a.* ವತ್ತವದಾನು *vattavadánu.*

Admission, *s.* ವತ್ತವದು, ಒಪ್ಪಿಯವದು *vattavadu, oppiyavadu.*

Admit, *v. a.* ವತ್ತಾ, ವಪ್ಪಿಯ, ಕೂಡುವನೆಕೆ ಮಾಡು, ಕೂಡಿಚಿರು *vattá, vappiya, kúḍuvaneke máḍu, kuḍichiru.*

Admonish, *v a.* ಬುದ್ಧಿ ಯೆಂಣು *buddhi yeṇṇu.*

Adopt, *v. a.* ಯೆಡುತಾ, ಸಮುಂದಕು ಯೆಡುತಾ, ಸಮುಂದ ಮಾಡಿಯಾ *yeḍutá, samandaku yeḍutá, samanda máḍiyá.*

Adoption, *s.* ಸಮುಂದ *samanda.*

Adorable, *a.* ತುದಿಪನತ್ತು *tudipanattu.*

Adoration, *s.* ತುದಿ, ತುದಿಪು *tudi, tudipu.*

Adore, *v. a.* ತುದಿ *tudi.*

Adorn, *v. a.* ಅಣಿಚಿರು, ಅಣಿ *aṇichiru, aṇi.*

Adrift, *v. n.* ಬಡಿಚಂಡುಪೊವು *baḍichanḍupovu.*

Adroit, *a.* ಚುರುಕಾನು, ಚಾಲಾಕು ಆನು *churukánu, cháláku ánu.*

Adroitness, *s.* ಚುರುಕು, ಚಾಲಾಕು *churuku, cháláku.*

Advance, *s.* ದೂತ ಮುಂಗಡ *dtúa mungaḍa.*

Advance, *v. a.* ಮಿಂಞೆಕು ಕೊಂಡ, ದೂತ ಮಾಡು, ಬೆರಿಯ ಮಾಡು, ಮುಂಗಡ ಕೊಡು *minyeku konḍa, dúta máḍu, beriya máḍu, mungaḍa koḍu.*

Advance, *v. n.* ಮಿಂಞೆಕುನಡ, ದೂತ, ಪೆರ್ತ *minnyakunaḍa dúta, perta.*

Advancement, *s.* ಮಿಂಞೆಕುನಡಪದು *minnyakunaḍapadu.*

Advantage, *s.* ಲಾಬ, ಆದೆಯ *lába, ádeya.*

Advantageous, *a.* ಲಾಬವುಳ್ಳು, ಆದೆಯವುಳ್ಳು *lábavuḷḷu, ádeyavuḷḷu.*

Advent, *s.* ಬಿಪ್ಪದು *bippadu.*

Adventure, *s.* ಕಾಲಕೇಡು, ಸಾಯ *kálakéḍu, sáya,*

Adventurer, *s.* ದೈರಿಯಕಾರು *deiriyakáru.*

Adventurous, *a.* ದೈರಿಯವುಳ್ಳು, ಮೋಸ ಆನು *deiriyavuḷḷu, mósa ánu.*

Adverb, *s.* ಕ್ರಿಯಾ ವಿಶೇಷಣ *kriyá vishéshaṇa.*

Adversary, *s.* ಪಗೆಯ, ಚತ್ರು *pageya, chatru.*

Adverse, *a.* ಪಗೆ ಆನು, ಚತ್ರುವಾನು *page ánu, chatruvánu.*

Adversity, *s.* ಕಟ್ಟು, ಕಪ್ಪ, ಚಿಕು *kaṭṭu, kappa, chiku.*

Advert, *v n.* ಮನಸು ಮಾಡು, ಮನ ಮಾಡು *manasu máḍu, mana máḍu.*

Advertise. *v. a.* ಅರ್ಪ, ಅರಿಚಿರು *arpa, arichiru.*

Advertisement, *s.* ಅರ್ಪಿಚಿರುವುಕಾಗದ, ಅರಿಚಿರುವುಕಾಗದ *arpichiruvukágada, arichiruvukágada.*

Advice, *s.* ಬುದ್ಧಿ, ಬೇರ ***buddhi, béra.***

Advisable, *a.* ಸರಿ ಆನು, ನ್ಯಾಯ ಆನು ***sari ánu, nyaya ánu.***

Advise, *v. a.* ಬುದ್ಧಿ ಎಣ್ಣು, ಬೇರ ಯೆಣ್ಣು, ಬೇರ ಕೇಳು ***buddhi eṇṇu, béra yeṇṇu, béra kéḷu.***

Adulation, *s.* ತುರಿವರು ನೋಣಿ ***turivaru noṇi.***

Adult, *s.* ಪೆರಿಯವು, ಪೆರಿಯರಾನು ***periyavu, periyaránu.***

Adulterate, *v. a.* ಬೆರಕೆ ಮಾಡು, ಕೆಡ್ತು ***berake máḍu, keḍtu.***

Adulteration, ಬೆರಕೆ ಕೆಡುಕುವರು ***berake keḍukuvaru.***

Adulterer, *s.* ಮವಿಯಾಡಿಆಣು ***maviyáḍi áṇu.***

Adultery, *s.* ಪುಲಿಯಾಡಿ ಪುಲಿಯಾಡಿ ಕಳಿ ***puliyáḍi puliyáḍi kaḷi.***

Advocate, *s.* ಅರಿಕೆಮಾಡುವವು, ವರುಕಡೆಕು ತಕ್ಕಪರೆವವು ***árike máḍuvavu, varukaḍeku takkaparevavu.***

Advocate, *v. a.* ಅರಿಕೆ ಮಾಡು, ವರುಕಡೆಕುಕತಪರೆ ***arike máḍu, varukaḍekukatapare.***

Aerial, *a.* ಬಾನತಿರ ಆವಿಜತುರ ***bánatira ávijatura.***

Afar, *ad.* ದೂರಕಾಯಿತು ***dúrakáyitu.***

Affability, *s.* ಪೋತುವರು ಚಾಕುವದು ಮುಂದು ***pótuvaru chákuvadu mundu.***

Affable, *a.* ಪೋತುವದಾನ್ ***pótuvadán.***

Affair, *s.* ಚೋವಿ, ಜಾರಿಬಾರ, ಕಾರಿಯ ***chóvi járibára, káriya.***

Affect, *v. a.* to touch. ಮುಟ್ಟು ***muṭṭu*** to touch the mind. ಮನಸಕರೆಯಿಚಿರು, ಕೊಯಿಮೆಕಾಟ್ಟು, ***manasakareyichiru, koyimekáṭṭu,*** to pretend. ಬಡಾಯಿಕಾಟ್ಟು, ಕಳಿಪೊರಡು ***baḍáyikáṭṭu, kaḷiporaḍu*** to assume a disguise.

Affectation, *s.* ಡಬ್ಬು, ಬಡಾಯಿ, ಕಳಿ ***ḍabbu, baḍáyi, kaḷi.***

Affection, *s.* ಕೋಡಿ ***kóḍi.***

Affectionate, *a.* ಕೋಡಿಆನು ***kódiánu.***

Affidavit, *s.* ನೇರು ಆಣೆ ***néru áṇe.***

Affinity, *s.* ಸಮಂದ ***somanda.***

Affirm, *v. a.* ಉಂಡಂದು ಎಣ್ಣು, ನೇರಾಯಿತು ಎಣ್ಣು, ನೆಲೆಆಯಿತು ಎಣ್ಣು ***unḍandu eṇṇu, néráyitu eṇṇu, neleáyitu eṇṇu.***

Affirmation, *s.* ನೆಲೆ ***nele.***

Affirmative, *s.* ಉಂಡೆಂದು ಎಣ್ಣುವರವು ***unḍendu eṇṇuvaravu.***

Affix, *s.* ಸಮವು ***samavu.***

Affix, *v. a.* ಪತ್ತಿಚಿರು ***pattichiru.***

Afflict, *v. a.* ಕಟ್ಟ ಪಡಿಚಿರು, ಕಷ್ಟಪಡಿಚಿರು ***kaṭṭa paḍichiru, kashṭapaḍichiru.***

Agi.

Affliction, *s.* ಕಟ್ಟು, ಕಷ್ಟ *kaṭṭu, kashṭa.*

Affluence, *s.* ಪೆರ್ತ ಭಾಗ್ಯ, ಯಾರ ಭಾಗ್ಯ *perta bhágya, yára bhágya.*

Affluent, *a.* ಪೆರ್ತ ಭಾಗ್ಯ ಉಳ್ಳು, ಯಾರ ಭಾಗ್ಯ ಉಳ್ಳು *perta bhágya uḷḷu, yára bhágya uḷḷu.*

Afford, *v. a.* ಕೊಡು *koḍu.*

Affray, *s.* ಜಗಳ *jagaḷa.*

Affright, *v. a.* ಪೋಡಿಕಾಟು *póḍikáṭu.*

Affront, *v. a.* ಚೆಡಿಬಪ್ಪಿಚಿರು *cheḍibappichiru.*

Afloat, *ad.* ತೇವಿಯಾಡು, ನೀತಿಯಾಡು *téviyáḍu, nitiyáḍu.*

Afoot, *ad.* ಕಾಲುನಡ್ತೆಲು *kálunaḍtelu.*

Afraid, *v. n.* ಅಂಜು ಪೊಡಿಚಿರು *anju poḍichiru.*

Afresh, *ad.* ಪುದಿಯದಾಯಿತ್ತು, ಪಿಂಞೆ *pudiyadáyittu, pinye.*

After, *ad.* ಪಿಞೆ, ಪಿಂಞೆ *pinyi, pinnye,*

Afternoon, *s.* ಮಜಣ *majaṇa.*

Afterword, *ad.* ಪಿಂಞೆ *pinnye.*

Again, *ad.* ಇಂಞೊಂಮ, ಇಂನೊಂಮ *innyonme, innomma.*

Against, *prep.* ಯೆದಿರಾಯಿತು, ಇರೋದ ಆಯಿತು *yediráyitu, iródadyitu.*

Age, ಬಯತು ಕಾಲ, ಬಯತುಕಾಲ *bayatu, kála, bayatukála.*

Aged, *a.* ಮುದಿ *mudi.*

Agency, *s.* ಮಾಡುವದು, ವಸೀಲು, ವಕಾಲತ್ತು *máḍuvadu, vasílu, vakálattu.*

Agent, *s.* ಮಾಡುವವು, ವಕಿಲು, ವಸಿಲು, ಸಾಮಿಲು *máḍuvavu, vakilu, vasilu, sámilu.*

Aggrandize, *v. a.* ಬಲ್ಯದು ಮಾಡು, ಯಾರ ಮಾಡು, ಪಿರ್ತ ಮಾಡು *balyudu, máḍu, yára máḍu, pirta, máḍu.*

Aggregate, *v. a.* ಚೆಡಿಬರ್ತ, ದೂತ ಮಾಡು *cheḍibarta, dúta máḍu.*

Aggregate, *s.* ವಕ್ಕ, ಪೆರಂಗು, ಗುಂಪು *vakka, perangu, gumpu.*

Aggression, *s.* ಜಗಳಪುಟ್ಟಿಚಿರುವದು, ಮೇಲೆಬೂವದು *jagalapuṭṭichiruvadu, mélebúvadu.*

Aggressor, *s.* ಜಗಳಪುಟ್ಟಿಚಿರುವವು, ಬೆಲಕಬಪ್ಪವು *jagalapuṭṭichiruvavu, belakabappavu.*

Aggrieve, *v. a.* ದುಃಖ ಪಡಿಚಿರು, ಕರಕರೆಪಡಿಚಿರು *duahaka padichiru, karakarepaḍichiru.*

Aghast, *ad.* ಪೋಡಿ ಆಯಿತ್ತು *póḍiáyittu.*

Agile, *a.* ಬೆರ್ರಿಯ *berriya.*

Agility, *s.* ಬೆರಿಯ *beriya.*

Agitate, *v. a.* ಗಾಬ್ರಿ ಮಾಡು, ಅಲ್ಲಾಡಿಚಿರು *gábri máḍu, alláḍichiru.*

Agitator, *s.* ಬೋರಿಚಿರುವವು *bórichiruvavu.*

Ago, *ad.* ಮಿಂಞೆ *minnye.*

Agony, *s.* ಬೇದನೆ, ಸಂಗಟ *bédane, sangaṭa.*

Agree, *v a.* ವತ್ತಾ, ವಪ್ಪಿಯ *vattá, vappiya.*

Agreement, *s.* ವಡಂಬಡಿಕೆ. ವತ್ತಂತರು *vaḍambaḍike, vattanḍaru.*

Agreeable, *a.* ಮನತೋಡೆ ಆನು, ಸರಿಆನು *manetóḍe ánu, sariánu.*

Agriculture, *s.* ಮನೆತನ, ವಕ್ಕಲುತನ *manetana, vakkalutana.*

Agriculturer, *s.* ಗೆಯಿ ಆಮೆಗಾರು, ಬದುಕುಗಾರು *geyiámeyáru badakugáru.*

Aground, *ad.* ನೆಲಪತ್ತಿತು ಉಳ್ಳು ಆನಗೊಂಡು *nelapattitu uḷḷu ánagonḍu.*

Ague, *s.* ಕುಳುಲು ಪನಿ *kuḷulu pani.*

Ah! *int.* ಅಹ *aha.*

Ahead, *ad.* ಮಿಞೆ ಆಯಿತು *minnye áyitu.*

Aid, *s.* ವತಾಸು ಸಾಯ, ಸಾಯ ಮಾಡು *vatásu sáya, sáya máḍu.* [*tiru.*

Ail, *v. n.* ನೊಂಬಲ ಆಯಿತಿರು, ಕರಕರೆಆಯಿತಿರು *nombala áyitiru, kaaakare áyi-*

Ailment, *s.* ನೊಂಬಲ, ಕರಕರೆ *nombala karakare.*

Aim *s.* ಕುರಿ, ನೋಟ *kuri, nóṭa.*

Aim, *v. a.* ಕುರಿ ನೋಡು, ಯತ್ನ ಮಾಡು *kuri nóḍu, yatna máḍu.*

Air, *s.* ಬಾನ, ಕಾತ್ತು *bána, káttu.*

Airing, *s.* ಕಾತು ಸವಾರಿ, ಕಾತುಲು ತಿರುಗುವದು *kátu savári, kátulu tiruguvadu.*

Airy, *a.* ತೆಂಪಾನು *tempánu.*

Akin, *a.* ಸಮಂದವಾನು. ಸಮ ಆನು *samandavánu, sama ánu.*

Alacrity, *s.* ಬೆರಿಯ, ಸಂತೋಷ ಮಾಡುವದು *beriya, santósha máḍuvadu.*

Alarm, *s.* ಪೋಡಿ, *póḍi, v. a.* ಪೋಡಿಚಿರು ಬೊತ್ತಿಚಿರು *póḍichiru bottichiru.*

Alas! *int.* ಆಯ್ಯೋ *ayyó.*

Albeit, *ad.* ಆನಕ್ಕಲೂ, ಎಂದಕ್ಕಲೂ *ánakkalu, endakkalu.*

Alert, *a.* ಬೆರಿಯ ಆನು, ಕಡುಪು ಆನು *beriya ánu, kaḍupu ánu.*

Algebra, *s.* ಬೀಜಗಣಿತ *bíjayaṇita.*

Alien, *s.* ನಾಟುಂ, ಪರದೇಶಕಾರು, ಬದಲುದೇಶಕಾರು, ಪಿಂಞೊರುದೇಶಕಾರು *náṭum, paradéshakbru, baduludéshakáru, pinnyorudáshakbru.*

Alienate, *v. a.* ಚಾಞಾರಿಭೇದ ಮಾಡು. ಚಞಾರಿಭೇದ ಕಾಂಬು, ಪಿಂಞೊಬ್ಬಂಗು ವಪ್ಪಿಚಿರು *channyáribhéda máḍu, channyáribheda kámbu, pinnyobbangu, vappichiru*

Alienation, *s.* ಚಾಞಾರಿಭೇದ, ಪಿಞೆಬ್ಬಂಗು ಆವರು, ಪಿಂಞೊಬ್ಬಂಗು ಆವದು *channyáribhéda, pinyebbangu ávaru, pinnyobbangr ávadu.*

Alo.

Alight, *v. a.* ಇಳಿ *iḷi,*

Alike, *ad* ಸಮಾನಾಯಿತು *samanáyitu.*

Aliment, *s.* ಊಣು, ತೀನಿ *úṇu, tíni.*

Alive, *a.* ಜೀವ ಉಳ್ಳು *jíva uḷḷu.*

All, *ad.* ಎಲ್ಲಾ, ತೀರ *ellá, tíra.*

Allay, *v. a.* ಅಡೆತಿಯ ಆರಿಚಿರು *aḍetiya árichiru.*

Allege, *v. a.* ಎಂಣು, ನೆರಾಯಿತುಯೆಂಣು *eṇṇu, nerdyituyeṇṇu.*

Allegiance, *s.* ದೊರೆಯತು ಹಲಾಲು *doreyatu halálu.*

Allegory, *s.* ಗಾದಿ *gádi.*

Alleviate, *v. a.* ಲಘು ಮಾಡು, ಗುಣಮಾಡು, ಕಮ್ಮಿಮಾಡು *laghu máḍu. guṇa máḍu kammi máḍu.*

Alley, ಸಂದು, ಯೇಪು *sandu, yépu.*

Alliance, *s.* ಸಮಂದ *samauda.*

Alligator, *s.* ಮುಸಳೆ *mosaḷe.*

Allot, *v. a.* ಪಾಲುಯಿಡು, ಪಾಲುಮಾಡು, ವೋದಿಯಿಡು *páluyiḍu, pálumáḍu, vódi-yiḍu.*

Allotment, *s.* ವೋದಿ, ಪಾಲು *vódi, pálu.*

Allow, *v. a.* ಇಪ್ಪಕ್ಕುಬುಡು, ಮಾಡುಪಕ್ಕುಬುಡು *ippakkubuḍu, máḍupakkubuḍu.*

Allowance, *s.* ಅಪ್ಪಣೆ *appaṇe.*

Allude, *v. a.* ಅರಿಚಿರು, ಗೇನಮಾಡು *arichiru, génamáḍu.*

Allure, *v. a.* ಆಶೆಪಡಿಚಿರು ಆಸೆಪಡಿಚಿರು *áshepaḍichiru, ásepaḍichiru.*

Allusion, *s.* ಸೂಚನೆ, ಇಸಾರೆ *súchane, isáre.*

Ally, *s.* ಚಂನ್ಯಾರಿಸ್ನೇಹಿತು, ಕೂಟು, ಸೇರುಚಿರು *channyárisnéhitu, kúṭu, séruchi-ru.*

Almanac, *s.* ಪಂಚಾಂಗ *panchánga.*

Almighty, *s.* ಯುಲ್ಲಾಂಗು ಬಲ್ಯವು *yallángu balyavu.*

Almighty, *a.* ಯುಲ್ಲಾಂಗು ಬಲ್ಯವನಾನು *yellángu balyavanánu.*

Almond, *s.* ಬಾದಮ್ಮು *bádammu.*

Almost, *ad.* ಚೆಂನಂಗು ಕಮ್ಮಿ ಆಯಿತು *chennangu, kammi áyitu.*

Alms, *s.* ದಾನ *dána.*

Aloes, *s.* ಲೋಳಿಸರ *lóḷisara.*

Aloft, *ad.* ಮೇಕೆ, ಕೊಡಿಲು, ಮಿರಾರ *méke, koḍilu, míra.*

Alone, *a.* ವೊಂಟಿ ಆಯಿತು, ಪತ್ತೆ ಆಯಿತು *vonṭi áyitu, patte áyitu.*

Aloof, *ad.* ದೂರಕಾಯಿತು *durakáyitu.*

Aloud, *ad.* ಕೂತಾಯಿತು *kutáyitu.*

Alphabet, *s.* ಅಕ್ಷರ *aṣhkarı.*

Already, *ad.* ಇಕ್ಕಲೇ *ikkalé.*

Also, *ad.* ಕೂಡ *kúḍa.*

Altar, *s.* ಬೆಲಿಪೀಠ, ತಟ್ಟು *beliphíṭha, taṭṭu.*

Alter, *v. a.* ಬದ್ಲಾಯಿಚಿರು, ಬೋರೆ ಮಾಡು *badlayichiru, bóre máḍu.*

Alternation, *s.* ಭೇದ, ಬೋರೆ, ತರ *bhéda, bóre, tara.*

Alterative, *s.* ಬೋರೆ ಮಾಡುವದು *bóre máḍuvadu.*

Altercate, *v. n.* ಜಗಳ ಮಾಡು, ತರ್ಕ ಮಾಡು, ಕಯಚಲು ಮಾಡು *jagaḷa máḍu, tarka máḍu, kayachala máḍu.*

Altercation, *s.* ಜಗಳ, ತರ್ಕ, ಕಯಿಚಲು *jagaḷa, tarka kayichalu.*

Alternate, *v. a.* ತಿರುಕಿತಿರಿಕಿ ಮಾಡು *tiruki tiriki máḍu.*

Alternative, *s.* ದಂಡಾಲುವವರನ್ನ ಆರಿಚಿತು ಎಡುವ್ರದು *danḍáluvavaranna árichitu-eḍuvudu.*

Although, *a. d.* ಆನಕಲೂ, ಆಚೆಂಗ್ಯೂ *ánakalú, áchengyú.*

Altitude, *s.* ವೊದರ *vodara.*

Altogether, *a. d.* ಯೆಲ್ಲ, ತೀರ *ella, tíra.*

Alum, *s.* ಪಟಿಕ *patika.*

Always, *a. d.* ಯೆಕ್ಕಾಲು *ekkálu.*

Amalgam, *s.* ಪಾದರಸ ತಿರ ಬೆರಕೆ *pádarasa tira berake.*

Amalgamate, *v. a.* ಪಾದರಸ ಬೆರಸು *pádarasa berasu.*

Amanuensis, *s.* ಯೆಳೆದುವವು *yeḷaduvavu.*

Amass, *v. a.* ಕೂಟು, ಸೇರಿಚಿರು *kúṭu, sérichiru.*

Amaurosis, *s.* ವರುತರಕಣ್ಣು ನೊಂಬಲ *varutarakaṇṇu nombala.*

Amaze, *v. a.* ಭ್ರಮೆಪಡಿಚಿರು *bramepaḍichiru.*

Amazement, *s.* ಭ್ರಮೆ *brame.*

Amazon, *s.* ಆಣುಡ ಗುಣವುಳ್ಳ ಪೊಣ್ಣು *áṇuḍa guṇvuḷḷu poṇṇu.*

Ambassador, *s.* ಪರಧಾನಿ, ದಳಬಾಯಿ, ದೊರೆರಕಡೆ ವಕೀಲು *paradháni, daḷabáyi, dorerakaḍe vakílu.*

Amber, ಚೆಂಗನೆನರುವು *chenganenaruvu.*

Ambient, *a.* ಎಲ್ಲಲ್ಲಿಯು ಉಳ್ಳ *ellalliyu uḷḷu.*

Ambignity, *s* ಅನುಮಾನ, ಅಂದೇಶ *anumána andésha.*

Ambiguous, *a.* ಅಂದೇಶಾನು *andéshánu.*

Ambition, *s.* ಬಲ್ಯರಿಕೆರ ಮೇಲೆ ಆಸೆ *balyarikera méle áse.*

Ambitious, *a.* ಬಲ್ಯರಿಕೆರ ಮೇಲೆ ಆಸೆ ಉಳ್ಳ *balyarikera méle áse uḷḷu.*

Amble, *v. a* ನಡಿಗೆ ನಡ *naḍige naḍa.*

Amp.

Amazing, *a.* ಭ್ರಮೆಆನು *brameánu.*

Amazingly, *ad.* ಭ್ರಮೆ ಆಯ್ತು, ಆಚರಿ ಆಯ್ತು *brame áytu, áchari áytu.*

Ambrosia, *s.* ಅಮೃತ *amṛuta.*

Ambulation, *s.* ನಡಪದು *naḍapadu.*

Ambulatory, *a.* ನಡಪನತು *naḍapanatu.*

Ambuscade, Ambush, *s.* ಒಳಿಪೊಜಾಗ *oḷipojága.*

Ameliorate, *v. a.* ಗುಣ ಮಾಡು, ಗುಣಪಡುತು *guṇa máḍu, guṇapaḍutu.*

Amelioration, *s.* ಗುಣಆಪದು *guṇaápadu.*

Amen, *ad.* ಅಂನನೆಆಡು *annaneáḍu.*

Amenable, *a.* ಉತ್ತರ ಕೊಡುಪನತು *uttara koḍupanatu.*

Amend, *v. a. & n.* ತಿದ್ದು, ನೇರೆ ಮಾಡು, ಗುಣ ಆಡು *tiddu, nére máḍu, guṇa áḍu.*

Amendment, *s.* ಗುಣ ಆಪದು *guṇaápadu.*

Amends, *s.* ತಳ್ಳಿ *taḷḷi.*

Amerce, *v. a.* ಪೊಳ್ಳೆವಾಡು ಎಡುಪು, ಜುಲುಮಾನೆ ಎಡುಪು *poḷeváḍu eḍupu, julumáne eḍupu.*

Amethyst, *s.* ವರುತರ ರತ್ನ, ವೈಡೂರ್ಯ *narutara ratna, veidurya.*

Amiable, *a.* ಕೊರಿ ಆನು *kori ánu.*

Amicable, *a.* ಚಂಜೊದಿ ಆನು *chanjodi ánu.*

Amidst, *prep.* ನಡುಲು *naḍulu.*

Amiss, *ad.* ತಪ್ಪಾಯಿತು *tappáyitu.*

Amity, *s.* ಸ್ನೇಹ, ಕೂಡ್ಯಾಡುತು *snéha, kuḍyáḍutu.*

Ammunition, *s.* ರಸ್ತು, ಬೊಡಿಮದ್ದು ಉಂಡೆ ಮೊದಲಾನು ಸಾಮಾನ *rastu, boḍimaddu unḍe modalánu sámána.*

Amnesty, *s.* ತಪ್ಪು, ಮರಂದು ಪೋಪದ *tappu, marandu pópadu.*

Amenity, *a.* ಸಂತೋಷ ಉಳ್ಳು *santóṣha uḷḷu.*

Amongst, *prep.* ಬೆರಕೆ ಆಪು *berake ápu.*

Amorous, *a.* ಮರಉಳ್ಳು *marauḷḷu.*

Amount, *s.* ಎಲ್ಲ, ತೀರ, ತೀರಆಪು *ella, tíra, tíraápu.*

Amphibious, *a.* ಸೀರುಲೂ ಭೂಮಿರ ಮೇರುಲೆಯೂ ಬದುಕುವಂತ್ತು *sírulu bhumira méruleyú badukuvanttu.*

Ample, *a.* ದೂತುಆನು, ಪೆರ್ತಆನು, ಅಗಲವಾನು *dútuánu, pertaánu, agalavánu.*

Amplification, *s.* ದೂತಮಾಡುವರು, *dútumáḍuvaru.*

Amplitude, *s.* ದೂತ, ಪೆರ್ತ, ಅಗಲ *duta, perta, agala.*

Amputate, *v. a.* ಕೊಂಚಿತು ಇಡು, ಮುರಿಚಿತು ಇಡು *konchitu iḍu, murichitu iḍu.*

Amputation, *s.* ಕೊಯ್ಯುವದು, ಮುರಿವದು ***koyyuvadu, murivadu.***

Amulet, *s.* ಯಂತ್ರ ***yantra.***

Amuse, *v. a.* ತಕ್ಕನ ಗೊಂಡು ಸಂತೋಷ ಪಡಿಚಿರು, ನೇರಂಗಳೆ ***takkana gonḍu santósha paḍichiru, nerangaḷe.***

Amusement, *s.* ಸಂತೋಷವಾನು ತಕ್ಕು, ಸಂತೋಷ, ಕಾಲಕೈಪು ***santóshavánu takku, santósha, kálakeipu.***

Anachronism, *s.* ಕಾಲ ಏರ ಕೋರೆ ***kála éra kóre.***

Analogy, *s.* ವಂದನನೆಕೆ ಪಿಂಞೊಂದು ಉಂಡುಂದು ಎಣ್ಣುವರು ***vandananeke pinnyodu unḍundu eṇṇuvaru.***

Analogical, Analogous, *a.* ವಂದನನೆಕೆ ಪಿಂಞೊಂದು ಉಳ್ಳು ***vandananeke pinnyondu uḷḷu.***

Analysis, *s* ಬೊರೆ, ಚೆನ್ನಂಗು ***bore, chennangu.***

Analytical, *a.* ಪಾಲಾನು ***pálánu.***

Analyze, *v. a.* ಪಾಲು ಮಾಡು, ಚೆನ್ನಂಗು ಮಾಡು ***pálu máḍu, chennagu máḍu.***

Anarchy, *s.* ಅನ್ಯಾಯ, ಗಡುಬುಡಿ, ಗವಿಚಿರಿ ***annyáya, gaḍubuḍi, gavichiri.***

Anathema, *s.* ಸಾಪ ***sápa.***

Anathematize, *v. a.* ಸಾಪ ಕೊಡು ***sápa koḍu.***

Anatomize, *v. a.* ಚತ್ತವಂಡತಡಿನ ಮುರಿಚಿತು ಸೋದನೆ ಮಾಡು, ಚಾವು ಸೋದಿಚಿರು ***chattavanḍataḍina murichita sódane máḍu, chávu sódichiru.***

Anatomy, *s.* ಚತ್ತವಂಡತಡಿನ ಮುರಿಚಿತು ಸೋದನೆ ಮಾಡುವ ವಿದ್ಯ, ಚಾಟ ಸೋದನೆ ***chattavanḍataḍina murichitu sódane máḍuva vidya, cháṭa sódane.***

Anatomical, *a.* ಚಾವು ಸೋದನೆ ವಿದ್ಯತುರ ಹಿಸೆಯಾನು ***chávu sódane vidyatura hiseyánu.***

Anatomist, *s.* ಚಾವು ಸೋದನೆಕಾರು ***chávu sódanekáru.***

Ancestor, *s.* ಪೆರಿಯವು, ಪಳೆಯವು ***periyavu, paḷeyavu.***

Ancestry, *s.* ಸಂತಾನ, ಸಂತಾನಗಾರ ***santána santánagára.***

Anchor, *s.* ಕಪ್ಪ ನಿಪ್ಪಿಚಿರುವು ಚಂಗೊಲೆ ***kappa nippichiruvu changole.***

Anchorage, *s.* ಕಪ್ಪ ನಿಪ್ಪಿಚಿರುವಕು ಚಂಗೊಲೆ ಇಡುವ ಜಾಗ, ಕರೆ ***kappa nippichiruku changole iḍuva jága, kare.***

IDIOMATIC SENTENCES.

1. I HAD BEEN TO THE PADDY-FIELDS EARLY IN THIS MORNING.

Coorg.	ನಾನು	ಪಲಾಕ	ನೇರತೆ	ಬೇಲುಕು	ಪೋಯಿತು	ಇಂಜೆ.
Ro. Ch.	*nánu*	*paláka*	*nérate*	*béluku*	*póyitu*	*inje.*
	I	morning	early	to the paddy fields	had	been.
Telugu.	*nénu*	*poddunne*	*anta padduké*	*maḍiki*	*pói*	*unṭi.*
Sanscrit.	,,	,,	,,	,,	,,	,,
Canarese.	*nánu*	*beḷigye*	*aṣhṭottige*	*gaddege*	*hógi*	*idde.* 1
Tamil.	*nán*	*kátále*	*néram* 2	*keiṇiki*	*póyi*	*irunddne.*
Malayalum.	,,	,,	,,	,,	,,	,,

2. HE WENT TO THE RAGI-FIELDS AT NOON, AND RETURNED AFTER REAPING THE RAGI.

Coorg.	ಅಂವು	ಮಜ್ಜಣಾಕ	ಪೊಲಕು	ಪೋಯಿತು	ಯೆರಯಿ	ಕೊಜ್ಜಂಡು	ಬಾತು.
	anvu	*majjaṇaka*	*polaku*	*póyitu*	*yerayi*	*kojjanḍu*	*bátu.*
	He	noon	to the ragi fields	having been	ragi	plucking	came.
Tel.	*átaḍu*	*madhyanamu*	*polamuku*	*poyi*	*rágalu*	*perukoni*	*vachche.*
Sans.	,,	,,	,,	,,	,,	,,	,,
Can.	*avanu*	*madhyanna*	*holakke* 3	*pógi or hógi* 4	*rági*	*kuyudu konḍu*	*banda.*
Tamil.	*avan*	*madhyana*	*kolleku*	*póyi*	*kévaru*	*aratukonḍu*	*vandá.*
Mala.	,,	,,	,,	,,	,,	,,	,,

---

1. "Pogi idda" is old Canarese and in modern Canarese "Hogi idda." Words beginning with *p* in ancient Canarese change into *h* in modern words. This rule equally applies to a number of words that are borrowed from the Tamil and Telugu into the Canarese. As: "Peñù" female in Tamil is changed into "Heñù" in Canarese; "Puli" tiger to "Huli" in Canarese and "Pal" to "Hal." In Telugu from "Pùvvu" to "Hùvù" and "Pùdi" to "Hùdi."
2. Neram means in Tamil time, as explained in the other paper.
3. See note 1.
4. See note 1.

3. THIS MAN WENT TO A WEDDING AT ANANTANAD YESTERDAY AND CAME TO DAY.

Coorg.	ಇಂವು	ನಿಂನಾಂದು	ಅನಂತನಾಡುಕು	ಮಂಗಲಕು	ಪೋಯಿತು	ಇಂದು	ಬಾತ್ತು.
	invu	*ninnándu*	*anantanáḍuku*	*mangalaku*	*póyitu*	*indu*	*báttu.*
	He or this man.	yesterday	to anantanad*	to a wedding	having gone	to-day	came.
Tel.	*ítaḍu*	*nenna*	,,	*mangalumuku* 5	*poyi*	*indu* 6	*vachche.*
Sans.	,,	,,	,,	*mangalam* 5	,,	,,	,,
Can.	*ivanu*	*nenne*	,,	*maduvige* 5	*hógi*	*íhottu*	*banda.*
Tamil.	*ivvan*	*néttu*	,,	*mangalatirku* 5	*poi*	*inniki*	*vanda.*
Mala.	,,	,,	,,	,,	,,	,,	,,

---

4. SHE IS SITTING IN THE YARD STITCHING A JACKET.

Coorg.	ಅವ	ತೆತ್ತಿಲು	ಯೆಳತಂಡು	ಕುಪ್ಪಿಯು	ಪೊಲ್ಲುವಳ.
	ava	*tettilu*	*yeḷatanḍu*	*kuppiya* 7	*polluraḷa.* 9
	She	in the yard	sitting	a jacket	stitches.
Tel.	*adi*	*inṭánakaló*	*kúkoni*	*niluva choga*	*kúrustundi.*
Sans.	,,	,,	,,	,,	,,
Can.	*avaḷu*	*jagalili* 8	*kúttukonḍu*	*niluvangi*	*holliyutáḷe.* 10
Tamil.	*avval*	*poḷakaḍel*	*ukkáandu*	*sokkayi*	*tekkiraḷ.*
Mala.	,,	,,	,,	,,	,,

---

5. I AM WRITING A SONG IN THE ROOM.

Coorg.	ನಾನು	ಕೋಂಬರೆಲು	ಪಾಟು	ಯೆಳದಿಯಂಡು	ಉಳ್ಳೆ.
	nánu	*kómbarelu*	*páṭu*	*yeḷadiyanḍu*	*uḷḷe.*
	I	in the room	song	writing	am.
Tel.	*nénu*	*koṭṭaḍiló*	*kírtana*	*rasukoni*	*unṭi.*
Sans.	,,	,,	,,	,,	,,
Can.	*nánu*	*koṭṭaḍioḷage*	*kírtané*	*bariutá*	*iddhéne.*
Tamil.	*nán*	*húṭuhuḷḷe*	*páṭu*	*yélúdikonḍu*	*irunde.*
Mala.	,,	,,	,,	,,	,,

---

* Anantanàd being a proper noun is the same in all languages. The word nàd in Telugu, Tamil, Canarese, and also in Malayalum means a country or region as we have in Mysore Malnàd, the Wynàd, and the numerous nàds in Coorg.

5. The word "Mangalam" in Sanscrit means a wedding and auspiciousness and a wedding is considered by all the Hindus to be an auspicious event in a man's life. Vide note in the other paper.

6. Indu is used in Telugu not in the sense of to day but here.

7. Kuppiya means the long coat worn by the Coorgs

8. Hittulu means in Canarese the back yard.

9. & 10. As explained in note 1. we observe clearly the change of *p* in Coorg language into *h* in Canarese.

6. THE SERVANTS HAVE DONE THE WORK OF THE CATTLE SHED NICELY.

Coorg.	ಆಳ್ಳುಅ	ಕೊಟ್ಟುಡ	ಪಣಿ	ಚಾಯಿಲೆ	ಕೆಜ್ಜಿಯತ್ತು.
	áḷua	*koṭṭuḍa*	*paṇi*	*cháyile*	*kejjiyattu.*
	Servants	of the Cattle shed	work	nicely	have worked or done.
Tel.	*sévakalu*	*koṭṭayeyokká* 11	*pani*	*suchiga*	*kájéyu.*
Sans.	,,	,,	,,	,,	,,
Can.	*áḷugalu*	*kotigiya*	*kelasa*	*channági*	*máḍi iddáre.*
Tamil.	*áḷugal*	*kottayé nodayo* 11	*véle*	*nalladáyi*	*séyindu áchi.*
Mala.	,,	,,	,,	,,	,,

---

7. YOU ARE GOING TO THE BACK-YARD TO PLUCK A CUCUMBER.

Coorg.	ನೀನು	ತೊಡಿಯಕು	ಚಉತೆ	ಕೊಯಿವಕು	ಪೋಪಿಯಾ.
	nínu	*toḍiyaku*	*chaute*	*koyivaku*	*pópiyá.*
	You	to the back yard	cucumber	to pluck	are going.
Tel.	*nívu*	*inṭianaku*	*dósakáyi*	*koyuṭaku*	*póthava.*
Sans.	,,	,,	,,	,,	,,
Can.	*nínu*	*hittalige*	*santekáyi*	*kuyuvadakká*	*póguthiyá* or *hóguthiyá.*
Tamil.	*ni*	*polikaḍe*	*velrikáyi*	*arakurataku*	*pogirai.*
Mala.	,,	,,	,,	,,	,,

---

8. THE WALL BUILDER HAS PUT UP THE WALL OF THE BATHING HOUSE WELL.

Coorg.	ಕೋಲೆಯು	ಗುಡ್ಡತುರ	ಕೆವತುನ	ನಲ್ಲಾಣ್ಣೆ	ಬೆಚ್ಚಿಯತು.
	kóleyu	*guḍḍatura*	*kevatuna*	*nallánṇe*	*bechchiyatu*
	builder of the wall	bathing house	wall	well	has put.
Tel.	*góḍapanivádu*	*stanamusése illu*	*góḍa*	*bága*	*peṭṭenu.*
Sans.	*kudya kara* 12	,,	*kudya*	,,	,,
Can.	*góḍe kaṭṭuvavanu*	*stánada mane*	*góḍe*	*channági*	*kaṭṭiddare.*
Tamil.	*sivaru kaṭṭuvavan*	*taṇṇi úḍu*	*sevarú* 13	*andrayi*	,,
Mala.	,,	,,	,,	,,	,,

---

11. & 11. Kottayae also means a pent roof or a temporary shed put up in front of a temple to celebrate a religious procession.

12. Kudya means in Sanscrit wall and Kudya Kara, builder of a wall. Kuleya and Kudya or Kudeya have nearly the same sound but I do not know how to account for the change of *d* in Sanscrit into *l* in Coorg.

13. Sevaru is the word in Tamil for a wall.

9. THE CARPENTER FINISHED THE DOOR FRAME AND WENT TO THE NAD THIS YEAR.

Coorg.	ಆಯಿರಿ	ಕಟ್ಟಳೆಪಣಿ	ತೀತಿತ್ತ್	ಯಿಯಾಂಡು	ನಾಡಕು	ಪೋಚಿ.
	áyiri	*kaṭṭaḷepaṇi*	*tititt* *u*	*yiyáṇḍu*	*náḍaku*	*póchi.*
	Carpenter	work of the door frame	having finished	this year	to the nad	went.
Tel.	*mánipanivádu*	*vákilapani* 14	*tírchi*	*í* 15 *yáḍḍdi*	*náḍuku*	*póyanu or póyináḍu.*
Sans.	,,	,,	,,	,,		,,
Can.	*marakelasaduvanu*	*bágala kelasa*	*tírisi*	*í* 15 *varuṣha*	*nádige*	*pódanu or hódanu.* 16
Tamil.	*tachchen*	*kuttulu* 17	*teerti*	*inda* 15 *varuṣham*	*nattikku*	*pónán.*
Mala.	,,	,,	,,	,,		,,

---

10. THE CATTLE ARE GOING FROM THE HILLS TO GRAZE ON THE GRASS LANDS.

Coorg.	ಅತ್ತ್	ಕುಂದಲಿಂಜಿ	ಬಾಣೆಕು	ಮೇವಕು	ಪೋಪಳ. *
	atta	*kundalinji*	*báṇeku*	*mévaku*	*pópaḷa.*
	Cattle	from the hills	to the grass lands	to graze	are going.
Tel.	*ávulu*	*konḍanunchi*	*kasavu nyálaku*	*meyuṭaku*	*póvuchunávi.*
Sans.	,,	,,	,,	,,	,,
Can.	*danagaḷu*	*beṭṭadinda* 18	*málakka* 19	*méyuvadakke*	*póguttave or hóguttave.*
Tamil.	*pasugaḷ*	*koondragalilirindu*	,,	*mayuvadarkku*	*pogindrana.*
Mala.	,,	,,	,,	,,	,,

---

14. Pani in Telugu means work.
15. 15. 15. *i* in Telugu and in Canarese means this and inda in Tamil.
16. See note 1.
* The ಳ may be left out when speaking and is understood.
18. Gutta or betta is the word for hill in Canarese.
19. Màla means pasture land but the people generally say hullu mala.

CARDINAL NUMBERS.

ಒಂದು *wondu,*	೧	1
ದೆಂಡು *dandu,*	೨	2
ಮೂಂದು *múndu,*	೩	3
ನಾಲು *nálu,*	೪	4
ಅಂಜಿ *anji,*	೫	5
ಆರು *áru,*	೬	6
ಏಳು *éḷu,*	೭	7
ಎಟ್ಟು *eṭṭu,*	೮	8
ಒಯಿಂಬದು *oyimbadu,*	೯	9
ಪತ್ತು *pattu,*	೧೦	10
ಪಂನೊಂದು *pannondu,*	೧೧	11
ಪಂನೆರಂಡು *pannerandu,*	೧೨	12
ಪದುಮೂಂದು *padumúndu,*	೧೩	13
ಪದುನಾಲು *padunálu,*	೧೪	14
ಪದುನಂಜಿ *padunanji,*	೧೫	15
ಪದುನಾರು *padunáru,*	೧೬	16
ಪದುನೇಳು *padunéḷu,*	೧೭	17
ಪದುನೆಟ್ಟು *paduneṭṭu,*	೧೮	18
ಪತ್ತೊಯಿಂಬದು *pattoyimbadu,*	೧೯	19
ಇರುವದು *iruvadu,*	೨೦	20
ಇರುವತ್ತೊಂದು *iruvattondu,*	೨೧	21
ಇರುವತ್ತೆರಂಡು *iruvatterandu,*	೨೨	22
ಇರುವತ್ತಮೂಂದು *iruvattamúndu,*	೨೩	23
ಇರುವತ್ತನಾಲು *iruvattanálu,*	೨೪	24
ಇರುವತ್ತಂಜಿ *iruvattanji,*	೨೫	25
ಇರುವತ್ತಾರು *iruvattáru,*	೨೬	26
ಇರುವತ್ತೇಳು *iruvattéḷu,*	೨೭	27
ಇರುವತ್ತೆಟ್ಟು *iruvatteṭṭu,*	೨೮	28
ಇರುವತ್ತೊಯಿಂಬದು *iruvattoyimbadu,*	೨೯	29
ನುಪ್ಪದು *nuppadu,*	೩೦	30
ನಾಪದು *nápadu,*	೪೦	40
ಐಂಬದು *eimbadu,*	೫೦	50

ಅರುವದು *aruvadu,*	೬೦	**60**
ಎಳ್ಳುವದು *eḷuvadu,*	೭೦	**70**
ಎಂಬದು *embadu,*	೮೦	**80**
ತ್ತೊನೂರು *ttonúru,*	೯೦	**90**
ನೂರು *núru,*	೧೦೦	**100**
ನೂಯಿತ್ತೊಂದು *núyittondu,*	೧೦೧	**101**
ನೂಯಿತಪತ್ತು *núyitapattu,*	೧೧೦	**110**
ಇಂನೂರು *innúru,*	೨೦೦	**200**
ಇಂನೂಯಿತ್ತೊಂದು *innúyittondu,*	೨೦೧	**201**
ಇಂನೂಯಿತ್ತುಪತ್ತು *innúyittupattu,*	೨೧೦	**210**
ಮುಂನೂರು *munnúru,*	೩೦೦	**300**
ಮುನ್ನೂಯಿತ್ತೊಂದು *munnúyittondu,*	೩೦೧	**301**
ಮುನ್ನೂಯಿತುಪತ್ತು *munnúyitupattu,*	೩೧೦	**310**
ನಾನೂರು *nánúru,*	೪೦೦	**400**
ನಾನೂಯಿತ್ತೊಂದು *nánúyittondu,*	೪೦೧	**401**
ನಾನೂಯಿತಪತ್ತು *nánúyitapattu,*	೪೧೦	**410**
ಐನೂರು, *einúru,*	೫೦೦	**500**
ಐನೂಯಿತ್ತೊಂದು *einúyittondu,*	೫೦೧	**501**
ಆರುನೂರು *árunúru,*	೬೦೦	**600**
ಆರುನೂಯಿತ್ತೊಂದು *árunúyittondu,*	೬೦೧	**601**
ಎಳನೂರು *eḷanúru,*	೭೦೦	**700**
ಎಳನೂಯಿತ್ತೊಂದು *eḷanúyittondu,*	೭೦೧	**701**
ಎಟ್ಟುನೂರು *eṭṭunúru,*	೮೦೦	**800**
ಒಂಬೈನೂರು *wombeinúru,*	೯೦೦	**900**
ಆಯಿರ *áyira,*	೧,೦೦೦	**1,000**
ಆಯಿರತ್ತೊಂದು *áyirattondu,*	೧,೦೦೧	**1,001**
ಆಯಿರತಪತ್ತು *áyiratapattu,*	೧,೦೧೦	**1,010**
ಆಯಿರತನೂರು *áyiratanúru,*	೧,೧೦೦	**1,100**
ದಂಡಾಯಿರ *danḍáyira,*	೨,೦೦೦	**2,000**
ಮೂಂಡಾಯಿರ *múndáyira,*	೩,೦೦೦	**3,000**
ನಾಲಾಯಿರ *náláyira,*	೪,೦೦೦	**4,000**
ಅಂಜಿಆಯಿರ *ánjiáyira,*	೫,೦೦೦	**5,000**
ಪತ್ತಾಯಿರ *pattáyira,*	೧೦,೦೦೦	**10,000**
ಲಕ್ಷ *lakṣha,*	೧,೦೦,೦೦೦	**1,00,000**

ORDINAL NUMBERS.

The ordinal numbers are formed by adding the affixes ಅನೆ *ane* to the Cardinal numbers.

ಒಂದನೆ	*wondane,*	1st.
ದಂಡನೆ	*danḍane,*	2nd.
ಮೂಂದನೆ	*múndane,*	3rd.
ನಾಲನೆ	*nálane,*	4th.
ಅಂಜನೆ	*anjane,*	5th.
&c.	&c.	&c.

MONTHS.

ಯೆಡಮ್ಯಾರು *yaḍamyáru,* April—May.
ಕಾದ್ಯಾರು *kádyáru,* May—June.
ಆದ್ರೆ *ádre,* June—July.
ಕಕ್ಕಡ *kakkaḍa,* July—August.
ಚಿಂಙ್ಯಾರು *chingyndru,* August—September.
ಕಂನ್ಯಾರು *kannyáru,* September—October.
ತೊಲೆಯಾರು *toleyáru,* October—November.
ಬ್ರಿಚ್ಚಿಯಾರು *brichchiyáru,* November—December.
ದರುಮೆಯಾರು *darumeyáru,* December—January.
ಮಾಲ್ಯಾರು *málíyáru,* January—February.
ಕುಂಬ್ಯಾರು *kumbyáru,* February—March.
ಮೀನ್ಯಾರು *mínyáru,* March—April.

The Coorgs always commence to plough their fields on the first day of ಯೆಡಮ್ಯಾರು *yaḍamyáru,* whether rain has fallen or not. If the seasons be propitious and rain has fallen, the ploughing is continued ; otherwise the ploughing is not continued till a sufficiency of rain has fallen. The following legend is assigned as the reason for the Coorgs thus punctually commencing to plough every year. It is said that Coorg formerly belonged to the descendants of the Pándus, one of the Lunar races mentioned in the

Puránas. These Pándus were carried off by force to heaven, and ever afterwards prayed for their lands to be restored to them. The deity promised to restore their lands on the first day of the new year, and to prevent such restoration the Coorgs punctually commence to plough their fields early in the morning of the first day of each year.

On the first of the ತೊಲೆಯಾರು *toleyáru* the Káveri feast commences and the goddess Káveri is worshipped in each house. A great annual festival is also held at Thula káveri, the source of the river.

The Huttri, or Harvest Festival is held during the month of ಬ್ರಿಚ್ಛಿಯಾರು *brichchhiyáru*. The Coorgs call it the Puttri Feast. The word Puttri is compounded of ಪುತು *putu,* new, and ಅರಿ *ari,* a sheaf of corn.

DAYS.

ನಾರಾಚೆ *nárúche,* Sunday.
ತಿಂಗಳಾಚೆ *tingaḷáche,* Monday.
ಚೊವುಅಚೆ *chovuáche,* Tuesday.
ಪೊದನಾಚೆ *podanáche,* Wednesday.
ಬೇಳಾಚೆ *béḷáche,* Thursday.
ಬೊಳ್ಳಿಅಚೆ *boḷḷiáche,* Friday.
ಚನಿಅಚೆ *chaniáche,* Saturday.

As regards the origin of the names assigned to the different days of the week, I have only been able to ascertain that ನಾರಾಚೆ *náráche,* is compounded of ನಾರಾಯಣ *náráyaṇa,* a name of the deity used also for the sun, and ಅಚೆ *áche,* a day; and ತಿಂಗಳಾಚೆ *tingaḷáche,* of ತಿಂಗಳು *tingaḷu,* the moon, and ಅಚೆ *áche,* a day.